BERLIT

DISCOVER
EGYPT

Edited and designed by
D & N Publishing,
Ramsbury, Wiltshire.

All cartography by Hardlines, Charlbury, Oxfordshire, except for the maps on pages 152 and 186-7 by Visual Image, Street, Somerset.

Although we have made every effort to ensure the accuracy of all the information in this book, changes do occur. We cannot therefore take responsibility for facts, addresses and circumstances in general that are constantly subject to alteration.

If you have any new information, suggestions or corrections to contribute to this guide, we would like to hear from you. Please write to Berlitz Publishing at one of the above addresses.

Phototypeset, originated and printed by C.S. Graphics, Singapore.

Acknowledgements

Our thanks are due to the Egyptian Tourism Authority for its help with the preparation of this book, in particular to Amin Atwa and Naheed Rizk in Paris, and Yousreya Ismail in Cairo; to Ragaa Younes and Mohammed Salem of Misr Travel; and to Sylvie Alric of Hilton International.

Photographic Acknowledgements

All photographs by Pete Bennett © Berlitz Publishing Company Ltd except for those taken by the author on the following pages: 59, 130, 164, 207, 219, 226, 229, 232/33, 234, 236 and 251.

Front cover: Sphinxes at the Great Temple, Luxor © Berlitz Publishing Company Ltd

Back cover: View through arch of Elephantine Island © Berlitz Publishing Company Ltd

Photograph previous page: a riot of taste and colour to suit every kind of palette.

 The Berlitz tick is used to indicate places or events of particular interest.

BERLITZ®

DISCOVER
EGYPT

Jack Altman

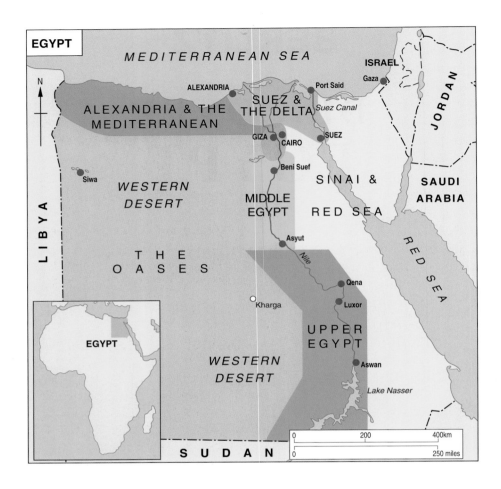

EGYPT

MEDITERRANEAN SEA

N

ISRAEL

ALEXANDRIA

Port Said

Gaza

JORDAN

ALEXANDRIA & THE
MEDITERRANEAN

SUEZ &
THE DELTA

Suez Canal

GIZA

CAIRO

SUEZ

Siwa

WESTERN
DESERT

MIDDLE
EGYPT

Beni Suef

SINAI &

RED SEA

SAUDI
ARABIA

LIBYA

THE
OASES

Asyut

Nile

RED SEA

Kharga

Qena

Luxor

UPPER
EGYPT

EGYPT

WESTERN
DESERT

Aswan

Lake Nasser

SUDAN

| 0 | 200 | 400km |

| 0 | | 250 miles |

Contents

MAPS: Egypt 4, 8; Cairo and the Pyramids 144; Pyramids at Giza 152; Middle Egypt 156; Upper Egypt 168; Luxor, Theban Necropolis and the Valley of the Kings 186/187; Oasis 228; Alexandria and the Mediterranean 251; Sinai and the Red Sea 258; Suez and the Delta 275.

Town Plans: Alexandria 242; Aswan 205; Cairo 114; Luxor 169.

Rules of Thumb for Exploring a Noble Past and Present

However much you like to improvise, some careful planning pays off if you are to enjoy to the full both Egypt's ancient splendours and its colourful modern life. In a land of warm emotion that often triumphantly defies rhyme and reason, there is no clearly defined 'instruction book'. Here we offer some guidelines to what you might normally expect as you travel around the Nile Valley, the deserts, the Red Sea and the Mediterranean.

Egypt, like any exciting country, is an adventure, but you don't have to be Indiana Jones to handle it or any other kind of archaeologist to appreciate it all. The gigantic Pharaonic monuments are wonderful for any remotely curious human being, but they're only the tip of the pyramid. There are also seaside resorts and lush green oases out in a bewitching desert; and a cruise along the Nile past fields of sugar cane and Nubian villages can be one of the most soothing experiences on earth. Decide first when you're going and how long you can stay.

No, these are not circus-wagons, they are Nile Valley taxis. What they lack in speed, they make up for in colour and the ride is breezy rather than air-conditioned.

When to Go

If you are not restricted in your choice by school holidays, and feel happiest in a temperate climate, the months of October and November are the most enjoyable time to visit Egypt. April and May are also pleasantly mild but the weather is more unpredictable.

The mid-winter break around Christmas attracts heavy tourist traffic despite the fact that December, January and February are, for Egypt, quite chilly. The climate remains comfortably dry (except for occasional rain in Alexandria and along the north coast).

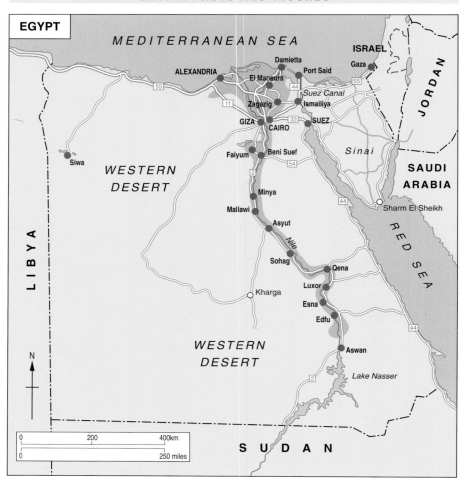

AVERAGE MONTHLY TEMPERATURES

		Ja	Fe	Ma	Ap	My	Jn	Jl	Au	Se	Oc	No	De
Cairo	C°	14	15	18	21	23	27	29	28	26	24	20	15
	F°	57	59	64	70	73	81	84	82	79	75	68	59
Luxor	C°	14	16	20	25	30	31	32	32	30	26	21	16
	F°	57	61	68	77	86	88	90	90	86	79	70	61
Alexandria	C°	14	15	16	19	22	24	26	27	25	23	20	16
	F°	57	59	61	66	72	75	79	81	77	73	68	61
Hurghada	C°	15	15	18	21	25	27	29	29	27	24	21	17
	F°	59	59	64	70	77	81	84	84	81	75	70	63

Even in the sweltering summer from June to September, the dry heat can be perfectly manageable. In Lower (northern) Egypt, Cairo and the Delta are more humid than Luxor and Aswan in Upper (southern) Egypt, but just observe the old adage that there is no such thing as bad weather, only bad clothing. Major hotels, cruise-ships and tourist buses are air-conditioned. This is the season to round off your trip along the Nile Valley with a spell at the breezy Mediterranean or Red Sea.

How Long to Stay

As you will see from the riches we describe in this book, discovering Egypt takes time. To help decide how long you want to go for and what to see in the time available, our ON THE SHORTLIST chapter (see page 94) makes a first choice of the main attractions.

One week would be frustratingly short, scarcely enough for a glimpse of Cairo and the pyramids and a whirl around the temples at Luxor and the monumental tombs of Thebes, but at least it would whet your appetite for another trip.

Two weeks would allow you to get a better sense of the capital, add a sound-and-light show to your visit of the pyramids, and make a more leisurely tour of Luxor and the surrounding sights as part of a cruise on the Nile, taking in the splendours of Aswan and Abu Simbel, too. You might even manage a couple of days' relaxation at a beach resort on the Red Sea or the Mediterranean.

*T*he clue to enjoying a holiday in Egypt is to combine your tour of the ancient monuments with some relaxation at a beach resort, like this on the Red Sea. Try also the Sinai peninsula or the Mediterranean.

WHAT ABOUT THE KIDS?

If you keep the sightseeing to small doses, Egypt can be marvellous fun for youngsters, though the climate may be tough on the under-tens. Ancient monuments become much more palatable when visited on the back of a camel or mule. In Cairo, visit a papyrus factory to see how hieroglyphs are painted. On the way to the pyramids at Giza, children can see some of the wildlife of Egypt and the Sudan at the Zoological Gardens across the University (El Gamaa) Bridge. The recently reopened Mummy Room and Tutankhamun's treasure should get them into the Egyptian Museum.

In Luxor and Aswan, half the fun comes with a ride in a horse-drawn carriage (*calèche*) or a river trip in a tall-sailed *felucca*. The alabaster-carvers near Luxor's Theban Necropolis, the botanical gardens and Philae Temples on Aswan's islands and the Aswan High Dam itself are all of great interest to children. Finish it all off with a visit to a Red Sea, Sinai or Mediterranean resort and the game is won.

Three weeks would be ideal: time to wander around Cairo, visit its Islamic and Coptic quarters, and enjoy its café life. You could avoid peak traffic at the pyramids, take a longer Nile cruise (eight rather than five days), consider a side-trip to the Sinai or the oases in the Western Desert, and still have time to unwind at a beach resort before heading for home.

How to Get There

By Air

Egypt Air and British airlines operate direct flights from London to Cairo out of both Heathrow and Gatwick airports. Irish and provincial flights make the connection in London for the four-hour non-stop journey. For people starting their visit in the Sinai, Egypt Air offers connecting flights to Sharm El Sheikh through its domestic subsidiary, Air Sinai.

Daily direct flights link New York and Cairo, with connecting services available from major cities in North America. Egypt Air operates from New York and Los Angeles and has an office in Toronto to advise on convenient flights out of Canada.

Charter Flights and Package Tours
United Kingdom: There is a wide range of package tours to Egypt, the more expensive ones including a cruise on the

Life for these Barbary sheep at Cairo Zoo is pretty lazy compared with the days when they used to leap from crag to crag on some escarpment in the Sahara Desert.

Nile with accommodation, meals and sightseeing. Check with your travel agent on the growing number of charter flights (and cheaper options) available to Luxor and Sharm El Sheikh, as well as to Cairo.

North America: There are currently available dozens of Group Inclusive Tours (GITs) of Egypt for periods of 7 to 22 days, with Cairo as the starting point. Tour features include round-trip air transportation, hotel accommodation, some or all meals, transfers and porterage, sightseeing, the services of an English-speaking guide, taxes, and all service charges. Optional features include a Nile river cruise, lasting from four to eight days, or an air tour to Abu Simbel.

By Land and Sea

Buses and tourist coaches come into Egypt from Israel via the Sinai, making

After sunset, Cairo's skyscrapers begin to light up on the Corniche promenade along the Nile River. Somebody is working late.

daily trips from Tel Aviv to Cairo. Those thinking of taking the same route in their own cars should remember that they will need four-wheel-drive if they intend to venture off the main highways in the Sinai or into the oases outside the Nile Valley.

You can also ferry in your car from Italy (via Venice or Ancona) and Greece (from the port of Piraeus) to Alexandria or Port Said, but it can be quite complicated getting the right papers and reservations. Book well in advance.

Some Mediterranean cruise-ships also call at Alexandria or Port Said, giving passengers the opportunity for at least a quick trip to Cairo and the pyramids.

Getting Ready

Visas
Besides a valid passport, you need either a transit visa for a stay not exceeding seven days or a tourist visa for a period of one month (renewable for up to six months). Tour-operators usually take care of visa formalities as part of the package, but if they do not or if you are travelling independently, be sure to make early arrangements for your visa from the Egyptian consulate. Passport authorities at the point of entry do issue tourist visas for those who did not get them back home but, as with all bureaucracy everywhere, this can be time-consuming and frustrating.

(Once in Egypt, you must register with the Interior Ministry at the 'Mugamaa' in Tahrir Square, Cairo, or at one of the similar immigration offices in Luxor or Alexandria, within seven days of arrival. This may be done by the hotel, tour agent, host or in person. But it *must* be done. You can prolong your visa through the same offices.)

Health Matters
Check before leaving home that your travel insurance policy covers medical treatment in Egypt. Combined change of climate and diet can cause intestinal upsets for which your doctor probably has a simple preventive or curative remedy. Good bottled mineral water is easily available all over Egypt. Drink it both for your stomach's sake and to prevent dehydration – even when you don't feel particularly thirsty.

The sun is a constant threat. Take a hat (a floppy is best – easily packed), sunglasses, and protective lotions or creams for both before and after exposure. Take insect repellent for use against flies and mosquitoes, but you may prefer to get one of the local or imported sprays available in Egypt; local brands tend to have more effect on local insect life. Malaria is not generally a problem in the main tourist areas, but this volatile disease does occasionally crop up in the Delta or in the remote south, so check with a qualified doctor for the appropriate precautions.

(The waters of the Nile are inhabited by a dangerous parasitic flatworm called bilharzia. Don't swim in the river and don't walk barefoot near it.)

An address to note that we hope you won't need:

Anglo-American Hospital
behind Cairo Tower
Zohorreya
Zamalek
Tel. 340 6162.

Disabled Travellers
Although the desert terrain surrounding most of the ancient monuments does not always make it easy for travellers to get around in wheelchairs, Egypt is by no means 'off limits' for the disabled. Special bus and taxi tours are organized by ETAMS Tours, the Egyptian Company for Tourism and Medical Services, 99 Ramses Street, Cairo; tel. 754 721. First-class amenities are available at major hotels in the Red Sea and Sinai resorts.

Public Toilets
Levels of hygiene are variable and it is often easier for men to find adequate toilets. There are generally usable male facilities in cafés, restaurants, and even mosques.

DRINKING THE WATER

Egyptians have a saying that if a visitor drinks even a little water from the Nile, he will return to Egypt for sure. Foreigners have a saying that he won't even leave. Tap water in Aswan, Luxor and Cairo comes from the Nile by way of a purification plant, and the authorities insist it is safe to drink, though not very pleasant. Whatever you do, don't drink *directly* from the Nile.

You're safest of all with the local bottled mineral water. Produced as a joint venture with Vittel of France, the most popular brand is *Baraka*, an Arabic word meaning appropriately 'blessing' or 'good luck'. It is perfectly acceptable to take the unfinished bottle away with you from a restaurant or hotel dining-room.

Women will find acceptable amenities almost only in hotels and rest houses.

What to Pack

Take as little as possible. Bear in mind that from hotel to bus and bus to cruise-boat and back again, you will very often be lugging your own bags.

Clothes

From May to September, you will need only the lightest things, preferably cotton, plus a broad-brimmed sun hat and sunglasses. Since Egyptian cotton is of superb quality, you may want to buy T-shirts, for instance, on the spot. In winter (November to March) it can be surprisingly chilly at night, so take warm pullovers or a wrap. Warm clothing is necessary for evenings in the desert at any time of year. Don't expect to dress up too much, though some first-class hotel dining-rooms or top-rated restaurants require men to wear jackets.

When visiting mosques, shorts are taboo for men and women alike: women should wear modest, longish dresses with sleeves, while men should wear trousers and sports shirts. For the town, take flat shoes, moccasins or sandals that are easy to kick off at the entrance to a mosque. High heels are a mistake anywhere. Comfortable walking shoes are *essential,* both for the sand and rough stone terrain of archaeological sites, and for the city centre where roadworks are constantly in progress. If you're planning a trip to Mount Sinai, take more sturdy shoes – and *very* warm clothing.

Electric Appliances

Practically all of Egypt has 220-volt, 50-cycle electric current. Sockets are of the European type with two cylindrical prongs. Anybody planning to keep his travel diary on a computer-notebook should beware that the current may not be constantly at full voltage strength.

A pocket torch (flashlight) with plenty of extra batteries is a precious companion, for exploring underground tombs and other darkened monuments by day, a walk in the desert at night or a (very rare) power-failure in the hotel.

Maps

Unless you plan to drive yourself, you will probably not need any more detailed maps than those you will find in this book. Otherwise, be sure to obtain the most recently published maps, as roads have changed in the past few years, particularly in the Sinai and along the Suez Canal, since the peace treaty with Israel. The best are by Kümmerly & Frey (published under licence in Cairo by Landrock & Lehnert).

What to Read

Egypt is one of those countries for which it is truly rewarding to do some reading before you go – or on the trip itself, just before the siesta. The material for history or archaeology buffs is endless, but there are also plenty of colourful novels about the ancient and modern eras. Here are just a few suggestions:

Ancient Egypt

Aldred, C., *Egyptian Art* (Thames & Hudson, 1990).

Aldred, C., *The Egyptians* (Thames & Hudson, 1988).

Edwards, I.E.S., *The Pyramids of Egypt* (Penguin, 1986).

James, T.G.H., *Pharaoh's People* (London, 1984).

Quirke, S. and Spencer, J., *British Museum Book of Ancient Egypt* (British Museum Press, 1992).

Modern Egypt

Afaf Lufi Al Sayyid Marsot, *Short History of Modern Egypt* (Cambridge, 1990).

Moorehead, Alan, *The White Nile; The Blue Nile* (Penguin, 1983).

Vatikiotis, P.J., *History of Egypt* (Weidenfeld & Nicholson, 1991).

Novels

Christie, Agatha, *Death on the Nile* (Fontana, 1987).

Durrell, Lawrence, *The Alexandria Quartet* (Faber & Faber, 1957-1993).

Mahfouz, Naguib, *Cairo Trilogy (Palace Walk, Palace of Desire, Sugar Street)* (Doubleday, 1991).

Photography

Although you can find plenty of film for still-photography or video in Egypt, it is best to stock up before you go to be sure of getting exactly what you need. When choosing film speed, remember that the light in Egypt is dazzling, particularly around the sand and limestone of the ancient monuments.

At high season, the cruise-boats have to 'double park' when docking, and the gangplank takes you from one boat to another before you reach dry land.

Getting Around

Whenever you have the time, it's a good idea to vary your forms of transport. Use planes to cover long distances, from Cairo to Luxor, for instance, but go from Aswan to Abu Simbel by road, at dawn if possible, to get an unforgettable close-up look at the desert. For a more leisurely view of town, take a horse-drawn carriage rather than a taxi. And time disappears altogether when you glide across the Nile on a tall-sailed *felucca* rather than a diesel-motored ferry-boat.

Flying

Air travel *everywhere* is surreptitiously time-consuming when you include delays at the airport, so be patient. Advance reservations and reconfirmation of tickets are essential. Not all services are daily, so plan your itinerary carefully. Overbooking is a frequent phenomenon and the only defence is prompt reconfirmation and early check-in. For most flights inside the country, operated by Egypt Air, you have to start out from or backtrack through Cairo.

PHOTOGRAPHIC RESTRICTIONS

You must accept that most of Egypt's important museums do not allow photographs without a special permit – charging a quite hefty fee for video. You will often be asked to leave your camera before entering. Photography is also forbidden in most of the ancient tombs. The bans should be respected as automatic-flash cameras pose a great threat to the fragile colour on the Pharaonic monuments.

Do not take pictures of bridges, public buildings, airports, or other 'strategically sensitive' places. Ask permission before taking photos of people or of the interiors of mosques or churches.

Flights in the Nile Valley link **Luxor, Aswan** and **Abu Simbel**. For the oases, **New Valley** airport is located just outside Kharga. On the Mediterranean, you can fly out to **Alexandria** and **Mersa Matruh**. On the Red Sea, **Hurghada** has its own airport, while **Sharm El Sheikh** serves the Sinai.

Airport Transfers

Normal taxis, Misr Limousines and air-conditioned buses operate between Cairo airport and downtown hotels. In the occasional scramble for cars, it's accepted practice in Egypt to share a cab. On the day of your departure, allow *plenty* of time – at least two hours – both for Cairo's traffic snarls and airport bedlam.

Nile Cruises

Taking a cruise on the Nile is quite unlike any other travel experience you are likely to have. It is not to be compared to an ocean cruise, when for long periods of time you have nothing to see but the sea. On the Nile, at every moment, a whole civilization is unfolding in front of your eyes: a farmer pushing a plough no different from that his ancestors might have worked with in Pharaonic times; towering above the river bank, a grandiose temple dedicated to the ancient gods; women busily preparing breakfast in a Nubian village – as you take yours on the upper deck of your boat.

The most common itinerary starts out from Luxor or Aswan, cruising between the two points for five to eight days and stopping at major temples and sights on the way – coordinated with bus or air transport for side trips. There are also longer trips between Cairo and Aswan in either direction, usually at the beginning and end of the season.

The ultimate river adventure is to sail in a *felucca* all the way between Cairo and Aswan, a three- to four-week journey – shorter from Luxor. With typical authentic cuisine prepared by the boatsman, amenities for groups of four or six people are naturally less luxurious than they are on a cruise-ship, but not less comfortable than, say, a barge-holiday in Europe. Best organized through a specialized travel agency back home, the journey allows you to improvise an *à la carte* itinerary as you sail up or down the valley.

Public Transport

Buses
Intercity buses are usually air-conditioned and comfortable but not luxurious. Seats can be booked two days in advance – check the local Tourist Information Office for

*N*egotiating the fare for a felucca *ride on the Nile is all part of the fun, but the boatsmen rarely try to charge too much. They are just out to make a living like the rest of us.*

Feluccas
The lofty triangular sails of the *feluccas* have graced the Nile since earliest antiquity. These romantic vessels are as practical as they are picturesque. They will give you a more flexible timetable for your visits from Luxor to the Valley of the Kings or from Aswan to the river islands. You can arrange to hire a boat and helmsman in any Nile town or village, or at many of Cairo's riverfront hotels. Fix the price and itinerary, especially if there's a return trip, before getting aboard. The local tourist office can advise you on appropriate – and approximate – prices.

ever-changing details. Inside Cairo, the city buses are just too crammed full and hectic for all but those seeking a truly stressful experience. For trips from the centre of town to the Coptic sights of Old Cairo, head instead for the river and take the **Nile Bus** from the jetty near the Television Building upriver to the terminus at Old Cairo. (The Coptic quarter is a 5-minute walk from the terminus.) The quiet 40-minute journey, stopping four or five times *en route*, is a perfect antidote to the downtown jangle.

Metro

The modern metropolitan partly underground train system through Cairo is expanding. Rapid, clean and efficient, the Metro is a good alternative way of getting out to the Coptic Museum and Old Cairo from Tahrir Square to the Mar Girgis Station and south to Maadi.

Trains

The Egyptian State Railway links all of the country's major cities. Overnight trains from Cairo Station are equipped with air-conditioned sleeping and restaurant cars for the Nile Valley route via Minya and Assyut to Luxor and Aswan, and back. First-class compartments are comfortable, second-class adequate; advance reservations are advisable. There is also a special faster luxury tourist train between Cairo and Aswan, with an all-in price that includes meals and sleeping-berths.

Railway platforms are not always this deserted when you choose to travel by train, but it is always less stressful than the hustle at the airport.

Taxis

Some city taxis have meters, but drivers cannot always be persuaded to use them – giving the (often valid) excuse that the machine is out of order. With or without meters, most cities have official rates – available from the Tourist Information Office – but these are usually overridden by the law of supply and demand. To avoid unpleasant surprises, agree on fares in advance, with the tip included. It is useful to know how to tell the driver your destination in Arabic, as many do not know a foreign language (ask your hotel receptionist to write the address in Arabic).

Taxi ranks are situated near the larger hotels and tourist attractions, and at the airport. Nearby, a Tourist Police officer will often be laboriously recording the number of each cab, its time of departure and its destination (which is useful if you subsequently have a complaint or leave something in the cab).

Shared Taxis

This grand institution operates for intercity travel. Fares are fixed, cheap and remarkably well regulated. Tips are not expected. Cars move out once full – usually with seven passengers. Generally they will not operate on a lengthy run after 8pm. Cairo has several ranks: one for Alexandria, one for the canal cities, and so on. The ranks are found close to the main railway station or bus station serving a particular destination, as the taxis absorb all the surplus traffic. Fares are slightly more than the bus fare, usually less than the train fare. If the overall price for all seven places is reasonable, a group of four in a great hurry can often buy up the three remaining seats so as to leave at once.

(Besides the official shared-taxi system, it's increasingly common around metropolitan Cairo to share an ordinary taxi with a passenger going more or less in the same direction. The practice is not strictly legal but very convenient.)

Limousines

Most of the major hotels have a fleet of chauffeur-driven limousines at the main entrance. They are the most comfortable and reliable means of transport, usually with set rates, but once again be sure to agree on the fare beforehand.

Horse-Drawn Carriages

Commonly known as *calèches,* these romantic cabs from a bygone era operate in Luxor, Aswan and throughout the Nile Valley, and are governed by an official price list. Consult the list in the Tourist Office before you ride – and then haggle around the going price. There are even a few *calèches* still in Cairo, if you can bear the traffic fumes!

Car Rental

With the possible exception of relatively uncomplicated resort areas like Sharm El Sheikh in the Sinai and Hurghada on the Red Sea, it is usually too much of a

---

HANDLING TRAFFIC

The authorities have not made it illegal for foreigners to drive inside the Cairo city-limits. This is an oversight. Only local residents have even the remotest idea of how to cope with traffic jams on the main roads, side-streets, downtown squares and roundabouts. Combat for parking spaces makes the average Arab-Israeli war seem like croquet. Outside the capital, roads are serviceable but beset by Pharaonic farm-vehicles and unhurried pedestrians and cattle quite properly claiming right of way. Road-signs are rare and not generally intelligible.

hassle to drive a rented car in Egypt. Local and international rental companies provide chauffeur-driven cars for longer tours, which are best reserved in advance as part of your travel package. Rental is by credit card or advance cash payment. Otherwise it's cheaper and simpler to stick to taxis.

You trot off into another age when taking a horse-drawn calèche *along the riverfront at Luxor, with the hectic rush of city life back home barely a faint memory.*

*M*irages are common in the Western Desert. Stare long enough and you will see Omar Sharif or Peter O'Toole coming up on the crest of that dune.

Driving

Unless you already know the country well, or your spirit of adventure defies hazards rarely encountered on even the most hair-raising roads of Europe, we would advise against bringing your own car to Egypt. However, if you do, you will need:
- International driving licence
- Car registration papers
- *Carnet de passage*

The above documents exempt you from paying tax or having to pass an Egyptian driving test. You will have to purchase third-party liability insurance in Egypt. For information on driving laws and help with any automobile matter, contact:
Automobile Club of Egypt
10 Sharia Kasr el-Nil
Cairo
Tel. 74 33 55.

Desert Safaris

Day-dreamers travelling around the Western Desert or the Sinai can imagine themselves to be reincarnations of Lawrence of Arabia, Rommel, Montgomery or Moshe Dayan. For longer tours

off the highways into the desert, **jeeps** need to be reserved in advance, but you can usually hire a **camel**, **horse** or **mule** on the spot. In the Western Desert, local contractors organize **camel safaris** from one oasis to the other over several days, camping and cooking amid the dunes. If time is no obstacle, these sturdy beasts of burden offer a delightful way to visit the pyramids at Giza or Saqqara, the tombs in Thebes' Valley of the Kings, or even to climb the first stretch of Mount Sinai.

Bicycles

The beach resorts at the Red Sea, Sinai and Mediterranean all rent out bicycles, often through the major hotels. They are also available at Luxor and Aswan.

Where to Stay

Hotels

At the top end of the scale, from 3-star up to luxury class, Egypt's hotels meet the best of international standards. There has been a building spree at the top end, but many more moderately priced hotels have also opened up in Cairo and Luxor, with particularly rapid expansion at the Red Sea and Sinai resorts. We offer you a comprehensive selection ranging from moderately priced to expensive in our list of hotels *(see* page 302).

Since group tour-operators usually have priority in room allotment, have an agent make the arrangements to guarantee reserved accommodation. If you're travelling alone, make reservations well in advance and even then come armed with written confirmations – overbooking is a constant problem.

Competition for rooms is most intense during the prime winter months from December to April. Alexandria and the Mediterranean resorts are busiest in the hot summer months but virtually deserted from November to April.

Hotel rates are usually quoted in US dollars, and bills can be settled by credit card, with foreign currency or with Egyptian pounds.

Cruise-Boats

Cruise-boat cabins are of course smaller than hotel rooms, but amenities are otherwise comparable, with special attention being paid to cuisine. Luxury-class and other more modest but comfortable cruise-boats are operated by hotel chains and major travel companies. Because demand often exceeds that of land-based hotel rooms, advance reservations are best made back home through your travel agency. However, last-minute space is sometimes available on the spot through local agents. We include a selection in our list of hotels *(see* page 302).

Youth Hostels

Hostels in Egypt's main cities offer students and hostellers low-price accommodation, though standards of comfort vary. The best hostels are often full, so advance reservations by mail are advised. For full information contact:

The Egyptian Youth Hostel Association
7 Doctor Abdel Hamid Said Street
Marrouf
Cairo
Tel. 758 099.

There are hostels in Cairo, Alexandria, Luxor and Aswan; their addresses are listed in the hotels section *(see* page 302).

Camping

Camping facilities are improving in the Nile Valley, the oases and at the Mediterranean, Red Sea and Sinai resorts. Contact the Tourist Information Office for details of sites and amenities.

Money Matters

Currency

The Egyptian *pound* (LE) is divided into 100 *piastres* (pt.). You may see prices written several ways: LE 1.50, LE 1.500 or 150 pt., which all mean the same amount of money, one pound and a half. 'LE' is the most common usage in Egypt itself, at banks, hotels, etc.

Banknotes range from 25 and 50 pt. to LE 1, 5, 10, 20 and 100. Coins come in 5, 10 and 20 pt. pieces.

Currency Restrictions

Not more than LE 20 can be imported or exported, but there is no restriction on the amount of foreign currency you may bring into or take out of Egypt, provided it is declared to customs on arrival. The law requires visitors to list *all* funds in their possession on an official currency declaration form. Demand the form if it is not offered to you and have it stamped at customs: it must be shown along with currency exchange receipts when you leave the country. It is very important to have the currency declaration form available and in order, as customs officials may confiscate currency not entered on the form when you leave the country.

Banking Hours

Banks are open from 8.30am to 2pm, Sunday to Thursday. All city banks are closed on Fridays and Saturdays, but banking desks at the airports, in the larger hotels and aboard most cruise-boats have special hours for the convenience of tourists.

Changing Money

It is illegal to exchange foreign currency except at a bank or at other authorized establishments. Obtain official receipts for any expenditures, to prove you have not changed money on the black market, so you can reconvert Egyptian money to foreign currency at the end of your stay.

At Cairo airport, there are bank desks before the check-in counters and passport control.

Credit Cards and Traveller's Cheques

More and more establishments accept and even prefer credit cards, but be sure the 'Total' amount you're signing for is filled in *below* the 'Tips' entry and not *above* it!

Traveller's cheques are best cashed at banks or hotel bank desks.

Baksheesh

The time-honoured Middle Eastern custom of informal tipping for services rendered has expanded in direct proportion to the phenomenal growth of the tourist industry. It becomes tiresome only where tourists gather *en masse* – at pyramids, museums, temples, bazaars, and similar spots. Seasoned travellers suspect it is only the exotic flavour of the word *baksheesh* that makes it seem more prevalent in Egypt than in Manhattan, Montmartre or the Piazza San Marco.

Tour-group leaders usually organize *baksheesh* for guides around the monuments and museums, but have a wad of 50-piastre or one-Egyptian-pound notes available anyway for when you're on your own, for the guardian that shows you an off-limits tomb in the Valley of the Kings or a hidden treasure behind a closed door in the mosque. It is often their only source of income. All foreign currency is welcome, but single dollar-bills work wonders far beyond their face value.

Though a service charge is included in hotel and restaurant bills, you should leave an additional tip. You are also expected to give something extra to porters, bellboys, cinema and theatre ushers, and so on.

Prices

To give you a general idea of what to expect, here's a list of average prices in Egyptian pounds (LE) and piastres (pt.) and, where applicable, US dollars. Bear in mind the variables of inflation and *baksheesh*.

Airport: Porter 50 pt. per bag. Hire of baggage trolley LE 1. Taxi to centre of Cairo LE 27, by limousine LE 18.

Boat services: *Felucca* (per hour for entire boat) LE 20-25 in Cairo, LE 20-25 in Aswan and Luxor. Nile bus LE 1.50 to Old Cairo, LE 2 to Nile Barrages.

Car hire (with unlimited mileage): Fiat 128, $50-56 per day; Fiat Nova Regat (air-conditioned), $72-83 per day; Peugeot 505 (air-conditioned estate), $86-117 per day. Add $1.25 personal insurance per day and 5 percent local tax.

Cigarettes: Egyptian filter brands LE 2 for 20, foreign brands LE 3.50.

Entertainment: Cinemas LE 2.50-5.50, discotheque LE 15-20, nightclub (including dinner but not drinks) LE 40-60.

Guides: LE 10-15 per hour depending on language and place.

Hotels (double room with bath per night): Luxury class $120-160, first class $90-120, second class $40-75, third class $25-35. Add 12 percent service, 14 percent municipal tax. Breakfast is extra, LE 12-18 per day.

TIPPING SUGGESTIONS

Porter, per bag	LE 1
Maid, per week	LE 10
Waiter	10 percent
Table attendant	3-5 percent
Lavatory attendant	50 pt.
Taxi-driver	LE 1
Tour-guide	10 percent
Cruise-guide, per week	LE 20
Hairdresser	10 percent
Felucca boatman	LE 1 per passenger

23

Meals and drinks (depending on hotel category): Continental breakfast LE 8-20, lunch/dinner in fairly good establishment LE 10-40, *ful* and *taamia* LE 1.50, bottled soft drinks LE 1, coffee LE 1-1.50, local beer LE 4, imported beer (small can) LE 10, Egyptian wine (bottle) LE 18, cocktail LE 33, mineral water LE 2.50 per litre.

Museums: LE 5-10.

Nile Cruises: four to seven nights $344-800 per person, double occupancy.

Transport: *Train:* Cairo to Alexandria LE 25-42, special tourist train (overnight sleeper) Cairo to Luxor/Aswan, LE 216 per person including meals. *Air:* Cairo to Luxor $75, Aswan $103, Abu Simbel $164, Hurghada $80, Sharm El Sheikh $85, Alexandria $42.

Public Services

Egyptian public officials will most often bend over backwards in their efforts to help tourists, sometimes even falling over in the process, it's true, but their good will is sincere and abundant and requires only patience on your part for things to function pretty well.

Tourist Information Offices
The Egyptian Ministry of Tourism has information offices in all the larger Egyptian cities, and in many foreign countries as well. They are eager to help and provide brochures, maps and detailed advice on itineraries. Inside Egypt, they can also provide information about local accommodation and other practical problems. A few addresses are listed below:

*B*e generous to the guardian at the royal tomb. He has a large family, but also a fair-sized tummy of his own to feed if he is to fill out that handsome gallabiya he is wearing.

Cairo:
Ministry of Tourism
5 Adly Street
Tel. 390 3000/390 1835.
(Other offices are at Cairo airport and at the pyramids.)

Alexandria:
Tourist Office Information
Saad Zaghloul Square
Tel. 482 0258.

Luxor:
Tourist Market
Just south of Luxor Temple
Luxor
Tel. 82215.

Aswan:
North of old part of town
Just off Corniche
Aswan
Tel. 23297.

Egyptian Tourist Offices Abroad

Canada:
Egyptian Tourist Authority
Place Bonaventure 40
Frontenac
P.O. Box 304
Montreal
P.Q. H5A 1V4
Tel. (514) 861 4420.

Ready Reference

To the uninitiated, Egyptian gods are as plentiful and mystifying as, say, Hebrew prophets and Christian saints. More than in most countries, the traveller in Egypt needs a dictionary to understand some of the intricacies of its complex layers of culture. For easy reference, in addition to the briefer explanations given in the text, here is a necessarily incomplete but, we hope, useful list of architectural, artistic, religious and political names and terms, that crop up in the text and as you travel through the country. They cover ancient Pharaonic Egypt, but also the Coptic church and the world of Islamic Egypt. Spelling of names varies greatly in different texts, but we stick to popularly accepted rather than scholarly recondite usage. (Terms available for cross-reference are *italicized*.)

Abbasids: The Arab empire's second ruling dynasty (750-1258) based in Baghdad.

Agora: The market and main square in Greco-Roman towns.

Aïn: (Arabic) A water-spring as part of place name.

Akbar: (Arabic) 'Great' or 'greatest' as in '*Allahu Akbar*.' 'God is great'.

Ali: The cousin and son-in-law of Mohammed, regarded by *Shi'ites* as the prophet's only legitimate heir.

Amulet: A talisman in blue faïence, lapis lazuli or sometimes gold, worn by ancient Egyptians to ensure health or good fortune, both for the living and the dead. Most common were the *Ankh* life-symbol and the *Scarab*.

Amun: The primeval creator-god whose name means 'hidden'; at Thebes personal deity of Pharaohs with great temple at Karnak. His headdress has two tall plumes; his sacred creatures are the goose and the ram.

Ankh: A looped hieroglyphic symbol for life in form of sandal-strap, often presented in a tomb by a deity to the deceased; worn as amulet and assimilated to the cross by early Copts.

Anubis: The jackal-headed god of the dead seen embalming the dead.

Apis: A sacred bull with cult at Memphis, herald and soul of *Ptah*.

Aten: A radiating solar disk deity, with hands at the end of its rays, worshipped by Akhenaten at Tell El Amarna.

Atum: A god who by self-generation achieved creation from the chaos of the primeval mound.

Ayyubid: An Islamic dynasty (1171-1250) founded in Egypt by Saladin.

Ba: The soul or a psychic force manifested as a human-headed bird hovering near deceased.

Bab: (Arabic) Gate.

Bahr: (Arabic) River or sea.

Barque: A sacred vessel with a god's shrine in place of cabin, borne in procession by priests, incorporated in Pharaohs' funeral.

Bastet: The cat-headed goddess of love and joy, carrying a basket on arm.

Bes: An ugly, impudent old dwarf-god, often sticking his tongue out, who warded off the evil eye, a motif on beds and mirrors.

Bey: An Ottoman Turkish title meaning 'lord' introduced to Egypt by the *Mamelukes*.

Bir: (Arabic) Water-well.

Birka: (Arabic) Lake.

Book of the Dead: A collection of religious texts and magic formulae on papyrus placed in a sarcophagus to accompany the deceased into the Afterworld.

Burg: (Arabic) Tower or cliff.

Caliph: Literally 'successor' of Mohammed, a spiritual and political ruler, though often only nominal, of the Arab empire.

Canopic jars: Four containers for the entrails of the deceased – lungs, stomach, liver and intestine – each guarded by a son of *Horus* and buried with the coffin. (Named by Egyptologists after similar vases found at Greek Delta town of Canopus.)

Capital: The crown of column in the shape of a lotus or papyrus-plant, later more elaborate in Greco-Roman Corinthian columns, with grapevine or basket motifs in Coptic architecture.

Cartouche: A small shield-like form bearing hieroglyphs of king's two principal names, its elongated rounded shape symbolizing universe encompassed by the ruler.

Cobra: See *Uraeus*.

Crowns: Distinctive head-dresses of gods and kings, variations include the White Crown of Upper Egypt, the Red Crown of Lower Egypt (merged into one when the two realms were united) and the double-plume crown of *Amun*, as well as symbols like cow's horns, a solar disk, arrows, palm fronds, a lotus or a scorpion.

Dar: (Arabic) Mansion.

Deïr: (Arabic) Walled monastery.

Demotic: Popular or commonly used script in hieroglyphics, as opposed to hieratic (sacred) scripts of religious texts.

Dervish: (Persian: 'poor') A Moslem mystic in trance, whirling or otherwise.

Dikka: The platform in a mosque for the reciter of prayers.

Duamutef: The jackal-headed son of *Horus*, the guardian of the stomach in a *canopic jar*.

False beard: The Egyptian aristocracy was clean-shaven but tied false beards to the chin on ceremonial occasions as symbols of virility, those of gods, kings (and Queen Hatshepsut) being elaborate, long, plaited and turned up at the end.

False door: A niche in a tomb-chapel simulating an open doorway to the Afterworld permitting the deceased to partake of offerings left there by living visitors.

Fatima: The favourite daughter of Mohammed, wife of *Ali*, rare female cult-figure in Islam.

Fatimids: rulers of Egypt (969-1171) claiming heritage from Fatima and *Ali* as *Shi'ites*.

Geb: human-shaped god of the earth, wearing Red Crown of Lower Egypt; like St Peter, welcomes deceased at gates of Afterworld; father of *Osiris*, *Seth*, *Isis* and *Nephthys*.

Gebal: (Arabic) mountain as in Gebal Musa, Mount Moses in the Sinai.

Gezira: (Arabic) island.

Haikal: sanctuary of Coptic church.

Hammam: Turkish bath.

Hapi: baboon-headed guardian of lungs in *Canopic jar*, son of *Horus*.

Hapy: god of Nile in flood, represented as long-haired man with pendulous breasts, wearing papyrus-plant head-dress.

Haramlik: women's quarters in Moslem household.

Hathor: sky goddess, often depicted as cow – sky-symbol in Delta – or with head-dress of cow horns and solar disk; major cults at Denderah and Thebes.

Head-dress: see *Crowns*.

Heb-Sed: royal jubilee festival after 30 years' reign with rejuvenating rites.

Heket: frog-goddess of midwives, participates in royal births.

Hieroglyphics: *see* page 221.

Horus: falcon-headed national sun-god (symbol of Egypt's airline), child of Osiris and Isis incarnated on earth as Pharaoh (often shown protected by falcon's wings).

Hypostyle hall: temple's large columned hall assembling congregation of worshippers and priests.

Iconostasis: in Coptic (and Greek Orthodox) church, icon-screen between nave and sanctuary.

Imam: in absence of priesthood in Islam, learned guide of the faithful.

Imhotep: Djoser's pyramid-architect (*see* page 60) deified by later generations as god of medicine and healing, portrayed in bronze figurines as seated scribe.

Imsety: guardian of the deceased's liver, portrayed by human head on *Canopic jar*, son of *Horus*.

Isis: most popular of Egypt's divine maternal figures; sister, wife and saviour of *Osiris*, mother of *Horus* ; head-dress initially throne, later horns and solar disk of Hathor.

Ithyphallic: of male figure in state of erection, sometimes the case of gods like *Amun.*

Jihad: originally meaning 'effort' to combat infidelity to the Islamic faith, struggle is interpreted either as militant proselytism or violent holy war, depending on degree of pugnacity.

Ka: intellectual and spiritual power, symbolized by two upraised arms.

Kaaba: Islam's holiest cubic stone shrine at Mecca.

Kafr: (Arabic) village.

Khamsin: hot desert wind causing sand-storms.

Khedive: high Ottoman Turkish title in 19th-century Egypt to replace viceroy.

Khepri: primeval god representing sun and resurrection, in form of *scarab*.

Khnum: ram-headed god of creation, protector of Nile's source.

Khons: 'traveller' moon god with head-dress of crescent or full moon.

Kiosk: open temple-shrine.

Kom: (Arabic) mound.

Kufic: early angular Arabic script, gradually elongated.

Kush: African kingdom to the south of Egypt, part Sudan, part Ethiopia.

Lotus: emerging from water of chaos and re-emerging each dawn to face sun, symbol of birth and rebirth, amulet of eternal youth.

Maat: goddess of law, truth and order; on Judgment Day, the deceased's heart is weighed against Maat's feather, the symbol of truth that adorns her head-dress.

Madrasa: Islamic theology school attached to mosque.

Mamelukes: Ottoman troops of slave origin ruling Egypt 1250-1517.

Mammisi: chapel attached to temple in later dynasties to celebrate birth deity's birth.

Masgid: small neighbourhood mosque.

Mashrabiya: intricately carved screen of wood or occasionally stone most commonly used to allow women in harem to watch men without being seen.

Mastaba: bench-shaped tomb, usually for nobles or lesser members of royal family.

Medina: (Arabic) town.

Mihrab: decorative niche in mosque wall facing Mecca.

Mina: (Arabic) harbour.

Minaret: tower from which *muezzin* calls faithful to prayer, idea adapted from Damascus church towers of St John's seized in Arab invasion.

Minbar: mosque's pulpit from which *imam* leads Friday prayer.

Mit: (Arabic) village.

Muezzin: Moslem delegated to call faithful to prayer from top of minaret – voice now usually tape-recorded and amplified electronically.

Mummy: corpse preserved from decay by embalming; comes from Arabic word of Persian origin for bitumen, which Arabs thought explained mummy's blackened state, but used only late in Pharaonic era.

Mut: vulture- or lion-goddess, wife of Amun, eye of the sun.

Nag: (Arabic) village

Naos: temple's inner sanctuary housing gods' statues.

Narthex: in Coptic church, vestibule to the nave.

Naskhi: from 12th century, Arabic script both for handwriting and print.

Necropolis: 'City of the Dead' referring both to ancient Egyptian tombs and Islamic cemeteries.

Nefertum: lotus-flower deity, 'perfect beauty', god of fragrance.

Nemes: Pharaoh's headcloth, commonly draping his shoulders as in golden effigy of Tutankhamun.

Nephthys: head-dress hieroglyph for name, 'mistress of the house'; goddess of the dead, protector of coffins with her sister, *Isis*.

Nilometer: sunken shaft with interior stairway down past height-markers for measuring level of Nile during annual inundation.

Nùt: sky-goddess, wife of *Geb*, shown as slender star-studded body bending over to touch western and eastern horizons with hands and feet; or as sun's mother, swallowing it at night, giving birth to it next morning.

Obelisk: elongated version of primeval sun-cult monolith catching on its originally gilded tip (pyramidion) the sun's first rays at dawn and last in the evening; later set in pairs in front of temple *pylon* as at Luxor.

Osiris: god of fertility and the netherworld, represented in mummified form; dismembered by brother *Seth*, restored to life by sister *Isis*; offering mankind hope of resurrection.

Palette: used for preparing powdered cosmetics or as tray for scribe's implements, but also as carved votive tablets commemorating king's exploits, notably Narmer's at Egyptian Museum.

Papyrus: tall reed-plant growing in Delta marshes used bunched for rafts or other construction or sliced thin for making precursor to paper; emblematic plant of Lower Egypt.

Pasha: Ottoman Turkish title originally for governor of Egypt; by 19th century, a senior rank in civil or military service.

Peristyle court: open court surrounded by a columned arcade (originally roofed).

Pharaoh: from Greek version of ancient Egyptian 'pr-o' meaning 'great house' applied to its residing monarch.

Pronaos: temple-chamber immediately leading to gods' inner sanctuary.

Ptah: great creator-god of Memphis, skull-capped human head with mummified body; created with heart and tongue, i.e. power of the word; probably in origin Egypt's name - 'hi-ka-Ptah': 'house of Ptah's spirit'.

Punt: Egypt's trading neighbour, probably Somali coast.

Pylon: temple's monumental twin-towered entrance, e.g. Luxor, Karnak.

Pyramidion: see *obelisk*.

Qaah: (Arabic) main hall in mansion.

Qasr: (Arabic) palace.

Qibla: (Arabic) direction of Mecca.

Ramadan: Moslems' fasting-month, ninth lunar month in year.

Re or **Ra**: sun god of Heliopolis crossing heavens in solar *barque*, portraits shared falcon's head with *Horus* with whom he was often combined in name as Re-Herakhty; Pharaohs were proclaimed his son.

Sabil: (Arabic) public drinking fountain.

Sacred Lake: adjoining temple, artificial pond for ritual ablutions and re-enactment of Creation with sacred *barque* on primeval waters.

Sahn: (Arabic) mosque's central courtyard.

Salamlik: (Turkish) reception rooms for men.

Sarcophagus: stone coffin containing inner wooden mummiform coffin.

Scarab: sacred dung-beetle, symbol of rising sun pushed across heavens by scarab-god *Khepri* just as beetle rolls along its ball of dung; popular *amulet*.

Sekhmet: terrifying lion-headed goddess of war, wife of *Ptah* embodying evil aspect of sun; her hot breath produces *khamsin* desert wind.

Serapis: Ptolemies' deity combining *Osiris* and *Apis*.

Seth: god of the desert, of foreign invaders, murderer of brother Osiris; head-dress of unidentified snout-nosed beast; other sacred animals include hippopotamus, crocodile, pig and ass; Pharaohs eager to assimilate his great strength, notably dynasty of Ramses II.

Shaduf: ponderous leverage mechanism to hoist water for irrigation in continuous use since Pharaonic era.

Shahada: Moslem's daily affirmation that 'There is no god but Allah, and Mohammed is His Prophet.'

Sharia: Islamic law, not presently enforced in Egypt.

Sheikh: (Arabic) an 'elder', as village chief or religious leader.

Shi'ites: sectarian followers of *Ali* as Mohammed's heir, active in Egypt only under *Fatimids*.

Sobek: crocodile-god important in the Faiyum and Kom Ombo.

Sphinx: human-headed lion statue accorded prophetic powers.

Squinch: to hoist a mosque's round or octagonal dome on to a square hall, structural element filling the hall's four upper angles, Mameluke architecture favouring decorative corbelled stalactites.

Stela: stone slab or tablet bearing inscriptions and relief carving, often to commemorate ruler's exploits or as boundary marker.

Sultan: Islamic title of prince, from Arabic for 'power', used in Egypt by *Ayyubids* and *Mamelukes*.

Sunnite: orthodox Moslems in opposition to *Shi'ites*.

Suq: (Arabic) bazaar.

Taweret: hippopotamus goddess standing upright, protective of women in childbirth.

Tell: (Arabic) mound or hill.

Thoth: ibis-headed god of scribes and intellectuals in general, also identified with baboon.

Triad: trio of deities, notably *Ptah*, *Sekhmet* and *Nefertum* at Memphis, *Amun*, *Mut* and *Khons* at Thebes, and on a national scale without specific shrine *Osiris*, *Isis* and *Horus*. Also emblematic statues of Pharaoh flanked by deity and symbolic figure of Egyptian province.

Umayyads: Arab empire's first dynasty (661-750) ruling from Damascus.

Uraeus: sacred cobra, symbol of kingship, worn by royal gods *Horus* and *Seth* and by Pharaoh on forehead.

Ushabti: mummiform figurines placed in tomb to perform deceased's tasks in afterlife; name believed to signify 'answerer' as one who, when deity called on deceased to work, answered 'Here am I'; usually 365, one for each day of year, but 414 found with Tutankhamun.

Vizier: senior Ottoman counsellor, used by analogy in Pharaonic Egypt.

Wadi: (Arabic) valley.

Waha: (Arabic) oasis.

TOUR-GUIDES

Holding up their flags or coloured umbrellas and having to shout to be heard in the museums, tour-guides for big groups are often an object of fun. But on an individual basis, they can be invaluable in helping you find your way around the tombs at Luxor's Valley of the Kings, the mosques in the back streets of Islamic Cairo or the labyrinth of the Khan El Khalili bazaar. Only those licensed by the Ministry of Tourism in Egypt are allowed into historical sites. You can arrange for a licensed guide through any hotel or travel agency (for current fees, *see* prices page 23). Make sure *beforehand* that everyone understands your personal requirements – fluency in foreign languages and real knowledge of history and antiquities – and what you're prepared to pay.

United Kingdom:
Egyptian State Tourist Office
168 Piccadilly
London W1
Tel. (071) 493 5282.

USA:
Egyptian Tourist Office
630 Fifth Avenue
New York
NY 10111
Tel. (212) 246 6960.
323 Geary Street
Suite 608
San Francisco
CA 94102
Tel. (415) 781 7676.

Police

Metropolitan policemen in Cairo and Alexandria wear white uniforms in summer, black in winter. Khaki is the preferred uniform in the provinces. **Tourist Police** officers, some of whom speak English or other foreign languages, have normal police uniforms with an added green and white armband bearing the words 'Tourist Police' written in English and Arabic. They are a discreet presence around the main tourist sites and bazaars. You can contact the Tourist Police via any official Tourist Information Office.

In Cairo, the Tourist Police Public Service telephone number is 126. Their headquarters is at 5 Adly Street, tel. 247 2584. Telephone numbers for Tourist Police in the provinces are:

Alexandria	863 804
Luxor	82120
Aswan	23163

*T*his Cairo traffic cop can afford to smile. He is enjoying a rare moment of respite from the daily bumper-to-bumper and bumper-on-bumper insanity.

Crime

Egyptians are generally law-abiding people, but petty theft and pickpocketing do occur. Without undue paranoia, which somehow uncannily attracts rather than repels criminals, take normal precautions: watch your wallet or purse in crowded bazaars and on trains and buses, lock your luggage before handing it over to railway or airline porters, and don't leave valuables on open display in your hotel room. If you have been robbed, contact the Tourist Police.

Lost Property

Save time and energy by appealing only to senior staff at hotels or museums. For items lost on the train, talk to the conductor or, when you get off, to the stationmaster. If you've left something in a taxi taken from or to your hotel, the Tourist Police may be able to help from the records they keep at the taxi ranks.

Emergencies

If your hotel receptionist or a Tourist Police officer is not at hand, you can telephone these numbers:

Police emergency 122
Ambulance 121
Fire service 125

Embassies and Consulates

Remember: your diplomatic representatives are there only for the direst emergencies, not to help out with cash or lost plane tickets.

Australia:
Australian Embassy
Cairo Plaza
Corniche el-Nil
Cairo
Tel. 777 273.

Canada:
Canadian Embassy
8 Mohammed Fahmy el-Sayed Street
Garden City
Cairo
Tel. 354 3110.

Eire:
Irish Embassy
3 Abou el-Feda Street
Zamalek
Cairo
Tel. 340 8264.

United Kingdom:
Embassy of the United Kingdom
7 Ahmed Ragheb Street
Garden City
Cairo
Tel. 354 0890.

British Consulate
3 Mena Street
Roushdy
Alexandria
Tel. 546 7001.

USA:
American Embassy
8 Kamel el-Dih Street
Garden City
Cairo
Tel. 355 7571.

Opening Hours

The times we give are constantly subject to change and whim. To avoid crowds, it is worth noting certain 'tricks of the trade' like visiting museums at midday, when most of the tourists have gone to lunch, and have your own meal later, as the Egyptians do. Alternatively, shop in the morning, when others are at the museums or pyramids.

Shops: In Cairo, shops open from 10am to 7pm in winter, from 10am to 8pm in summer, and close one hour later on Mondays and Thursdays all year round. Interrupting these times is the sacred afternoon siesta. Government shops close between 2 and 5pm every day. Although there is no consistency in closing for private shops, generally the 2-5pm time-slot is observed there, too. Cairo's Khan El Khalili bazaar closes at 8pm. There are no fixed closing hours for shops during the month of Ramadan. A few close on Fridays, most on Sundays and some stay open until the early hours of the morning. Pharmacies stay open late.

Museums (in Cairo): Most of these are open every day of the week. Major establishments open from 9am to 5pm, with a break from 11.30am to 1.30pm on Fridays. The smaller museums open daily from 9am to 1pm, and on Fridays to 11.30am. (These are the winter hours; in summer, some Cairo museums close at 2.30pm.)

Public Holidays

Moslem religious holidays are national holidays in Egypt. If a Moslem feast lasts more than a day, shops and offices will close on the first day and open with shorter hours on the other days. During the Holy Month of Ramadan, when Moslems fast during daylight hours, shorter working hours apply almost everywhere in offices; shops are open late into the night. Coptic (Christian) holidays are not celebrated as national holidays, though Coptic-run shops and businesses may close. The Coptic calendar differs from the western Christian Gregorian calendar: Coptic Christmas is celebrated, for instance, on 7 January.

LEARNING TO SAY HELLO

With such outgoing, friendly people as the Egyptians, you can work wonders if you try a couple of words of Arabic before launching into your mother tongue. Nobody will expect you to be a fluent Arabic-speaker, but people are delighted with the mere gesture of your saying 'Ahlan' (pronounced like a soft version of the German *Ach* plus *-lan*) in place of 'Hello'.

In our **Eating Out** section (*see* page 296) we provide you with some special words and phrases to help you read the menu and order a meal in a restaurant. For fuller treatment of useful everyday expressions, we recommend our phrase book, BERLITZ ARABIC FOR TRAVELLERS. Meanwhile, practise with these:

Hello	**Ahlan**
Goodbye	**Ma'as-salaam**
Good morning	**Sabah al-kher**
Good night	**Tisbah al-kher**
Please	**Min fadlak (Fadlik if addressing a female)**
Thank you	**Shokran**

And most important of all, when you're not certain what's going to happen next, which is very frequently:

God Willing!	**Inch'Allah!**

Religious Holidays

The Islamic calendar is lunar and so its religious holidays vary greatly from year to year on the standard Gregorian calendar. According to Islamic reckoning, a day starts at sundown. This means that if you're told a particular day is a religious holiday, you can expect the celebrations to begin at sundown on the day before. Businesses will close on the eve of a holiday and those restaurants that stay open may not serve alcohol.

Communications

Post Office

The postal service in Egypt, as in much of the rest of the world these days, is unpredictable. For important messages, as opposed to simple holiday greetings, stick to fax, telex or the telephone. If you expect to receive mail, have it sent to a hotel address rather than the less reliable poste restante.

Public post-boxes come in such a bewildering variety of colours and markings according to their express, air mail or ordinary mail function that you are better off using your hotel's facilities to get it right. **Hours**: Cairo's main post office in Ataba Square is open from 8am to 3pm and 5pm to 7pm daily except Friday. Other offices are open from 8.30am to 3pm daily except Friday.

Telephone, Fax and Telex

Egypt's telephone system is undergoing extensive modernization, and service, especially in Cairo, has improved considerably. In the process, however, there are constant changes of numbers, so check

SECULAR HOLIDAYS	
January 1	New Year's Day (banks only)
First Monday after Coptic Easter	Sham En Nessim (National Spring Festival)
April 25	Sinai Day
May 1	Labour Day
July 23	Revolution Day
October 6	Armed Forces Day

them carefully. Ask your hotel operator or dial 140 or 141 for directory information.

Public telephones are most commonly found in cigarette shops; very often they are just a normal desk set with a coin box attached. Shops or restaurants will let you use their phones to make local calls if you pay in advance.

Remember that phone calls, telex and fax messages from your hotel are charged at much higher than the normal rate, but the convenience may make it worth while. Using the public telephone at the post office avoids surcharges, but you may have to book an overseas call up to 24 hours in advance.

The Nile and its Deserts Give Peasants and Pharaohs a Notion of Eternity

Egypt is the original, the ultimate oasis, a fertile spot in the midst of a desert: fertile in its lush, green Nile Valley and Delta; fertile in its civilization both in the unique creation of the Pharaohs and as the acknowledged heart and mind of the modern Arab world; and fertile in a population bursting the cities at their seams. The good-natured people make Egypt a most inviting oasis for the curious traveller.

This is a place to prompt lofty thoughts in the most blasé of travellers. In the desert, the Pharaohs, their nobles and their great artisans lie buried in awesome monuments, and we modern visitors wander out to contemplate eternity. Egypt's everyday reality begins with its mighty river. Allah is great and Mohammed is his Prophet, and for Egypt the waters of the Nile are clearly his gift of life.

Behind the peasant and his donkey, the modest stepped pyramids of the ancient pharaohs' family maintain their vigil in the eternal sands of Giza.

The Nile

It was in the rich soil brought to the valley by the Nile that Egyptian civilization began 5,000 years ago. Today, some 95 percent of the population, fast approaching a total of 60 million, cluster along the river's banks and in the Delta. For most of its length, the cultivated portion of the Nile Valley traces a narrow strip 8-16km (5-10 miles) wide. At one point south of Cairo, opposite the broad Faiyum oasis, the inhabited and farmed area opens out to 24km (15 miles), but south of Luxor towards Aswan it narrows in places to a couple of hundred metres.

Dating back to the days before the Aswan High Dam regulated the Nile's floodwaters, the villages are often built up on mounds or dykes, with houses of

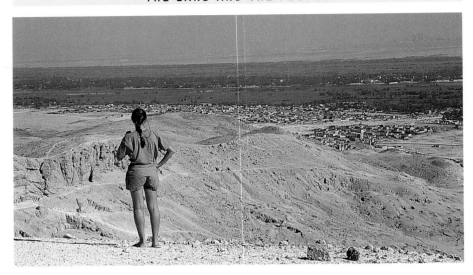

*I*n the distance the green band of the fertile Nile Valley reminds the desert wanderer of the river's miraculous survival through the greatest wasteland on the planet (above).

*T*he valley's farmland carefully husbands its resources, with fields left fallow, green with fresh corn, or shaded by groves of date palms (below).

THE MIRACLE OF THE NILE

The first miracle is that the Nile is there at all. How did it manage to flow through the middle of the world's biggest desert without just drying up? With little or no rainfall in the valley and only 100-200 mm each year in the Delta, it bears witness to the vast amounts of water pouring in from the river's sources in Equatorial Africa.

One of the striking features of the Nile Valley is the way the arable soil ends so abruptly in the desert sand. The greenery does not gradually peter out, it just stops like the edge of a carpet, so that you can literally stand with one foot in the valley and one in the desert. This is because millions of years ago, when a geological convulsion sank the Mediterranean much, much lower than it is today, the Nile rushed down to it from the Ethiopian Highlands to form a steep canyon rather than a more gently sloping valley.

Arguments about the actual source of the Nile go on as long as the river itself. Traced to its remotest headstream, the Luvironza River east of Lake Tanganyika in Rwanda-Burundi, it flows 6,720km (4,200 miles) down to the Mediterranean. This would make it the longest river in the world. If we take Lake Victoria as its more visible start, the Nile is 'only' 5,600km (3,500 miles) long.

Even more impressive than its length, is the natural wonder of the nourishment it brings to millions of people on its way. The eastern branch, the Blue Nile, is fed by the Ethiopian Highlands' monsoon waters from May to September. Beginning as a mountain torrent, it grinds the rocks of its river-bed into a fine russet silt which it sweeps thousands of kilometres downstream. At Khartoum in the Sudan, the river meets the White Nile, flowing from the great lakes of Central Africa, to advance in one narrow valley through the Nubian desert into Egypt.

Some of the river's rocks, too mighty to be ground down, form cataracts or craggy islands such as those you will see at Aswan. They stand at the northern end of Lake Nasser, the 24km (15-mile) long reservoir created by the Aswan High Dam. As it progresses, the river silt spilled across the valley leaves an increasingly rich alluvium. Before Aswan's modern technology arrived in the 20th century, Egyptians waited patiently each year for the Nile in its fertile flood to reach Aswan around mid-June, continue rising until early September, *Inch'Allah*, and then sink back down again by the following spring.

Today, Allah gets a helping hand from man in regulating and motorizing irrigation, but the marvel of the Nile's age-old benevolence in the middle of that desert aridity can still force the most hardened atheist to think twice about divine miracles.

mud-brick in the north, stone in the south. Around the green fields of sugar cane, corn or cotton and rice paddies, peasants find shade in an occasional grove of casuarina trees or a few sycamore, eucalyptus and date palms.

The peasants share the river with the Pharaohs and their gods. All along its banks, the Nile receives the silent homage of the great royal temples. From the gigantic shrine of Abu Simbel in the south – high and dry now on the western shore

*T*he temples of Philae stand high and dry now. Modern technology has rescued these island monuments from total submersion by the Aswan High Dam. In earlier centuries, they bathed constantly in the erratically rising and receding waters of the Nile (following pages).

At Aswan, sandstone and granite rocks form the most northerly half-a-dozen cataracts which break up the flow of the Nile from Ethiopia and Sudan through Egypt to the Mediterranean.

of the lake formed by the Aswan Dam – and the island temples of Philae at Aswan itself, the Nile flows by the monuments of Kom Ombo and Edfu, Luxor and Karnak, and north past the cave tombs of the court of Akhenaten and Nefertiti at Tell El Amarna.

Cairo

Though the sphinxes and pyramids of Giza and Saqqara are right there in the suburbs, the great capital on the Nile does not figure in ancient history. There was a fortress named Kheri Aha at the southern tip of the Delta in late Pharaonic times, but it was the Arabs in AD 641 who first established their capital here, calling it El Fustat. Today, as *Al Qahira* or more popularly sharing the Arabic name of Egypt itself, *Misr*, Cairo is a bewildering mass of gleaming or crumbling skyscrapers, highways and fly-overs fanning out from medieval Arabic quarters around the Khan El Khalili bazaar. There, lofty mosques tower above cramped

*G*leaming brassware is a major feature of the goods on sale at Cairo's Khan El Khalili bazaar. Much of it is still crafted in the bazaar's workshops above and behind the stalls.

houses, shops and stately mansions of Turkish or Mameluke origin.

The teeming modern megalopolis has a population of anywhere between 10 and 14 million – no one knows exactly how many – and the devastating earthquake of 1992 did not improve the housing situation. Traffic is impossible, but the new Metro subway helps out and the city persists, carrying on Egypt's special relationship with eternity. The Egyptian Museum can proudly claim one of the greatest archaeological collections in the world, and

In the Sinai, after enjoying a satisfying dinner of barbecued goat, a Bedouin lady may well invite you to relax and join her in smoking a narguileh *waterpipe.*

outside the main railway station is a statue not of some ephemeral modern politician but of Ramses himself. Its universities, publishing houses, cinema industry, Islamic architecture and collections of Islamic art maintain Cairo's position as the uncontested cultural capital of the Arab world.

The Deserts

Geographically, the Sahara Desert sweeps right across to the Red Sea, but in Egypt it divides into three deserts of quite distinct character. The Western Desert lies between the Libyan border and the Nile. Inspiring in the Pharaohs their intimations of immortality, its vastness was a natural setting for their tombs in the Valley of Kings. Apart from oases sprouting where the water table comes to the surface, the desert

*T*he wonder of the Sinai is the contrast of the parched yellow lowlands against the backdrop of the purple mountains through which Moses led his people to Israel.

is totally arid and largely flat, except for a plateau rising in its south-west corner. But those oases – Kharga, Dakhla, Farafra, Bahariya and Siwa – offer refreshing greenery amid gardens and orchards as a delightful base from which to explore the desert solitude.

From the Nile to the Red Sea, the limestone plateau of the Eastern Desert is dissected by seasonal rivers known as *wadis*. Their usually dry beds are filled in the winter by rainstorms in the Red Sea Hills. Whereas the Western Desert is inhabited by sedentary village- and even town-size populations at the oases, the Eastern Desert interior is the home of only small groups of nomadic herders of camels,

*T*his tank stopped dead in its tracks is only one of many battle-scars left from the Arab-Israeli wars fought in the Sinai. What kind of victory did the graffiti-writer mean by that V on the gun turret?

goats and sheep. You may spot them if you take an overland route from the Nile Valley to the beach resorts of Hurghada and Safaga on the Red Sea coast.

The smallest but most illustrious of the three deserts is the Sinai. Spectacular rugged mountains form the southern wedge of the triangle bounded by the Mediterranean and the Gulfs of Suez and Aqaba. In the middle is Mount Sinai where Moses met with his God and where Orthodox Christians keep the monastery of St Catherine. Resorts offer superb deep-sea diving and other water sports from

*T*he people of Alexandria are as proud and defiant as this minaret that thrusts itself up above one of the town's main thoroughfares.

47

Sharm El Sheikh in the south up to Taba on the Israeli border. The northern half of the Sinai evokes the more familiar desert images of sand-dunes, but these are scarred by the scattered vestiges of tanks, cannons and aircraft from the Arab-Israeli wars of the past. On the north coast is the fishing port of El Arish.

Alexandria and the Mediterranean

The old cosmopolitan charms of Alexandria, sung by writers like Lawrence Durrell, vanished with the last Armenians, Greeks, Italians and Jews in the turmoil of war and revolution since 1948. Like many another 'second city' around the world, however, the town affirms a strong spirit independent of the government capital. The Mediterranean also has its own attraction, attested by the many fine seafood restaurants and beach resorts along the coast from Montazah and Agami west towards the Libyan border. Resort facilities are mushrooming at Mersa Matruh and Sidi Abdel Rahman, while El Alamein has an added importance for World War II buffs visiting the battlefield museum and the military cemeteries.

The Delta

From Upper (southern) Egypt, the Nile passes through Cairo to branch out into Lower (northern) Egypt's vast expanse of the Delta. Covering an area of 3,725km^2

The propeller on the boat may be a modern innovation, but the carpenter's skills in shaping the hull can be seen already at work in many a frieze from Pharaonic Egypt.

*S*tone utensils like this one at the Coptic Museum form a vital
link between ancient and modern traditions, of which the Copts feel
themselves to be the faithful guardians.

EGYPT IN NUMBERS

Geography: Area 1,002,000km² (386,900 square miles), roughly the same as Britain, France and Italy combined or Texas and New Mexico. Only 3.5 percent of that land surface – 35,580km² (13,737 square miles) – is cultivated and inhabited: in the Nile Valley, the Delta, the oases and along the sea coasts. The rest is desert, the eastern terminus of the Sahara. The country is bounded by the Mediterranean to the north, Israel and the Red Sea to the east, Sudan to the south and Libya to the west.

- Lower Egypt covers the northern portion from Cairo through the Delta to the Mediterranean; Middle Egypt (a recent administrative term) runs from the large Faiyum oasis south to Tell El Amarna; Upper Egypt from Asyut south to Aswan and Abu Simbel.
- The Nile runs 1,520km (950 miles) through Egypt, with a total length from its remotest source in East Africa of 6,720km (4,200 miles).
- Of its mountains along the Red Sea coast and in the southern Sinai, the tallest is Mount Catherine, 2,637m (7,763ft).

Population: 58,000,000, of which 95 percent live in the Nile Valley and the Delta.

Capital: Cairo (greater metropolitan population 13,000,000).

Major Cities: Alexandria (3,170,000), Port Said (461,000), Mahalla El Kubra (Delta, 385,300), Suez City (392,000).

Government: The Constitution of 1971 proclaimed an Arab Republic with a democratic socialist system. Elected by plebiscite for a 6-year term, the president governs with a prime minister, council of ministers and 448-member People's Assembly. At the local level, the country is divided into 26 governorates.

Economy: Principal industrial resources from the deserts are oil, gas, phosphate, iron and manganese. Chief agricultural products are cotton, rice, maize, sugar cane, sorghum, wheat and beans. The major vegetables and fruit are tomatoes, potatoes and oranges.

Religion: Islam is the state religion, accounting for 90 percent of the population, which is mostly of the moderate Sunni sect. Coptic Christians number 8 percent, the rest being Roman Catholic, Greek Orthodox, Protestant and a tiny number of Jews.

Many boatmen plying the waters of the Nile can trace their ancestry to the heart of tropical Africa, often from the Ethiopian Highlands where the river has its source.

(9,650 square miles), it has enjoyed intensive agriculture since the dawn of history, when it attracted from Palestine in time of famine the clans of Abraham and Jacob. Modern irrigation permits two and three crops a year instead of one. Where once there were seven and more branches of the river fanning out towards the Mediterranean, today only two remain, the Rosetta to the west (near Alexandria) and

THE LAND AND THE PEOPLE

In a place where the temples for Luxor have stood the test of time for several thousand years, is a late-arriving bus that much of a calamity?

the Damietta to the east, linked by an intricate network of canals.

Between the Delta and the Sinai is the country's strategic linch-pin, the Suez Canal, linking the Mediterranean, the Red Sea and the Indian Ocean. Three main cities border the Canal: Port Said, port-of-call for Mediterranean cruises; the old colonial town of Ismailiya; and Suez City,

which has been attractively rebuilt since the peace with Israel.

The People

Egyptians are not by nature arrogant, but they do tend to feel a cut above or at least set apart from the rest of the Arab world. Perhaps with a history and culture like theirs, it is understandable. You will hear the statement: 'The Arabs are our brothers, but we are Egyptians.' Certainly, there is often an uncanny resemblance to the ancient ancestry in a modern Egyptian's proud profile and keen stare. The Pharaohs and princesses, warriors and scribes, artisans and peasants seem to have stepped down from the friezes and sculptures of ancient monuments to the modern streets, bazaars and fields of the Nile Valley – where many of the same hoes, ploughs and water-pumps still seem to be operating, too.

Closest kinship with the ancient Egyptians is claimed by the Copts, converted to Christianity since St Mark came to preach in Alexandria in the 1st century AD. The Copts' importance in national affairs, especially in business and industry, is out of all proportion to their mere 8 percent of the population – a frequent source of friction with Moslem fundamentalists. Their most illustrious son in modern times is Boutros Ghali, Secretary General of the United Nations.

Of course, the Moslem majority has an equal claim to direct descendancy from the ancient Egyptians, but successive waves of invaders have also left their mark. Over the centuries, Libyans, Persians and black Africans from Nubia enriched the genetic pool, followed by Greeks and Romans. The Arabs brought their language and religion in the 7th century. The Mamelukes added their fighting spirit, and the Turks their taste for the good life and fine cuisine.

South around Aswan and Abu Simbel, black Nubians today acknowledge their Egyptian nationality but insist on the distinctiveness of their ethnic identity, expressed not least of all in their stunning physical beauty. Equally proud are the Bedouins of the Sinai.

Whatever the origins, hospitality and friendliness are major national characteristics. From their rich past, most people here seem to have derived a wonderful sense of balance and moderation. The country has its share of hot-heads and fanatics – a worldwide phenomenon these days – but a temple in Luxor presents no more of a risk than a London department store or a Manhattan skyscraper. In general, you will find Egyptians among the most easy-going people on earth, whether café waiters or tourist police, taxi-drivers or shopkeepers. The vast majority practise a truly moderate form of Islam, respectful of others, asking only that you be respectful of them. It is not difficult to get to know the people and it is well worth making the effort.

A key to enjoying your stay in Egypt is patience. In a civilization that has been around for so many thousands of years, ten minutes here or there are not so important. When wondering whether some little problem can ever be solved, learn to apply the Egyptians' triple motto, a wise Arabic version of IBM – *Inch'Allah* (God willing); *Bokrah* (tomorrow); *Ma'alish!* (It doesn't matter!)

Unique Grandeur Sets this Nation on the Nile Apart from Africa and its Arab Brothers

Naturally enough for a country that was to be so dominated by its river, Egypt begins as a story of water. The ice age meltdown left the Sahara region with a humid climate and tropical vegetation. But when that dried up about 30,000 years ago into the desert we know today, wild animals and their human hunters had to cluster around the oases or along the Nile Valley. The stage was set for one of the greatest civilizations the world would ever see.

Earliest evidence of human activity (12000 BC) is provided by a few fossilized bones of Stone Age hunters and their prey found in the valley at Qaw El Kebir near modern Asyut. Archaeologists have uncovered traces of other fishing and hunting communities further south towards Aswan, at Kom Ombo. The fertile valley offered a good life to elephant and rhinoceros and abundant grazing for antelope,

The colossal statues of Ramses II marked both the ultimate expression of the Pharaohs' absolute power and a signal that that power was overreaching itself and the empire would begin to shrink.

gazelle, barbary sheep and ibex. The river teemed with fish, hippopotamus and crocodiles, and the reedy swamps attracted flocks of resident and migrant birds.

The first farm settlements, variously dated between 8000 and 3500 BC, have been located at El Badari on the Nile's east bank, upriver from Asyut, and at the Faiyum oasis beside Lake Qarun (southwest of Cairo). They grew wheat and barley, and flax for linen, introduced from Syria or Mesopotamia along with new farm implements such as the plough. They bred sheep, goats, pigs and geese in the valley, cattle in the Delta, asses in the oases. Besides basketry and mat-lined pits for storage, early pottery appears both in relatively crude clay and more refined hollowed out stoneware. Cosmetics, in particular green malachite eye make-up, protected man and woman against the hot, dry, fly-infested summers.

From 3500 BC, the African roots of Egyptian culture were enriched by contacts with west-Asian neighbours – from Syria, Lebanon and Palestine – attracted to the towns and fertile pastures of the Delta. These newcomers introduced new farming produce and methods, and also timber and bricks for construction, more elaborate ceramics, a growing use of copper, and from Mesopotamia, the first elements of hieroglyphic writing. To the new techniques and materials, Egyptian craftsmen brought their own superior workmanship. Elegant animal, plant and human motifs made their ornaments much in demand in Mediterranean markets.

THE OLD MOUSE TRAP WILL DO

As you travel down the Nile, you may wonder why so many Egyptian peasants still use the same farm implements as their ancestors in Pharaonic times. Even the ancients were perfectly happy with the simple implements originally introduced from Syria or Mesopotamia. Historians suggest it is because, with a normally functioning Nile, food has always been so easy to come by that farmers did not feel motivated to create a bigger and better plough, harrow or whatever. Occasional famine was blamed not on the way the soil was worked, but on the Nile flooding too late or too soon or not at all. So the one area of innovation was in harnessing the river's waters – better canals, dykes, irrigation-basins and ultimately the Aswan High Dam. But even today you will see a super-modern motorized water-pump and, a few metres away, an ox patiently plodding around the same kind of water-wheel as those depicted on ancient tombs in the Valley of the Kings. The peasant knows the motor breaks down more often than the ox.

The First Pharaohs – The Archaic Period

Commerce in the Delta nurtured complex local rivalries for control of this northern region of the Nile, known as Lower Egypt. By contrast, Upper Egypt, in the more isolated south, was a quiet and stable region in which a strong ruler could emerge to lead a united force against the north's warring factions.

The conquest may have taken more than one such king, but the first we know of is Narmer, who came north from Hierakonpolis (on the Nile's west bank between what are now Luxor and Edfu) to conquer the forces of Lower Egypt in 3170 BC. On one side of the famous *Narmer Palette* in Cairo's Egyptian Museum, the king wears the White Crown of Upper Egypt and receives from his falcon-god (Horus) the captive papyrus-land of the Delta. Above the king's head are the hieroglyphs of his name, *Nar* (fish) and *mer* (chisel). He raises a mace to thwack a captive northerner – an ever-recurrent theme in Egyptian royal art depicting the triumph of order over chaos. On the palette's other side, Narmer wears the curled Red Crown of conquered Lower Egypt. Two beasts intertwining their long necks symbolize the unification of the two parts of Egypt.

The saga of the Pharaohs can begin. The word *'Pharaoh'* comes from the ancient Egyptian *pr-'o* meaning 'great house', defining the ruler by his palace in the same way as the American presidency is often known as the 'White House'. Until the invasions of the Greeks and Romans, Egyptian Pharaonic history is customarily divided into five periods, not counting a couple of ill-defined intermediate eras: Archaic Period, Old Kingdom, Middle Kingdom, New Kingdom and Late Period.

Though perhaps a legendary figure possibly identifiable with Narmer, King Menes (3168-3113 BC) is named as founder of the first of the 31 dynasties listed by Egyptian historian Manetho in the 3rd century BC. He established his royal residence in a new City of White Walls, Memphis, south of the Delta at the frontier between the kingdoms of Upper and Lower Egypt. Built on land reclaimed from the Nile by a dyke, the city embodied the Egyptians' Creation myth of a primeval mound rising from the waters of Chaos. The Creation was the work of Ptah, god of Memphis.

From the outset of Pharaonic rule in the Archaic Period (3168-2705 BC), friezes show the king wielding power over every element of the nation's destiny. At their coronation ceremonies, Menes and his successors of the 1st and 2nd Dynasties are seen leading a procession around the white walls of Memphis to take possession of the kingdom. Irrigation works and land-reclamation demonstrate the king's control of the Nile's annual flood as a religious power over fertility and drought, life and death. The Pharaoh is portrayed variously as a pastoral chief or supreme hunter of birds and beasts of prey. Champion of the people against foreign enemies, he leads expeditions to conquer Libyans in the Western Desert, Nubians in the south and Bedouins in the Sinai. In death, the Pharaoh is assimilated to the Creator Ptah himself.

Scholars continue to differ as to whether the Pharaoh's family and retinue

THE DATING GAME

Dating the Pharaohs' monuments, their reigns, battles or other events is a chancy business. For prehistoric eras, Egyptologists can use radiocarbon dating on organic matter, but for some more recent periods there is no hard information available, while for others there is too much.

Egyptian temple records and tomb-biographies are usually works of blatant propaganda, ignoring failures or appropriating the achievements of predecessors: Ramses II, for example, stuck his own name on any Pharaoh's statue he happened to fancy. For the chronology of the Pharaohs' reigns, scholars have had to rely to a large extent on the detailed but often approximate data of Manetho, historian and high priest of Heliopolis in the 3rd century BC. He listed 31 dynasties from the unification of Upper and Lower Egypt under Menes to the conquest by Alexander in 332 BC – but omitted the bothersome Queen Hatshepsut as well as other rulers of whom he disapproved.

Ancient foreign sources can be highly misleading. The Hebrews' Old Testament accounts are written, long after the events, as religious and political propaganda. Comparable lack of objectivity may be surmised in the state archives of invading Hittites from Anatolia or Assyrians from Mesopotamia. Of the classical Greeks, the historian Herodotus is honest enough to say: 'I went and saw for myself as far as Elephantine (at Assuan) but further information is from hearsay.'

Often the humblest clues are the best: in the Theban palace of Amenophis III, for instance, food-jars were found with dated labels, wine-vats with their vintages. A construction foreman at the tomb of Sethi II left behind his logbook which includes the length of the Pharaoh's reign to the exact month and day. But don't forget: all the ancient Egyptian dates you find here or in the most learned books are approximate.

RUNNING A TIGHT SHIP

To organize Ancient Egypt, Inc., you had to get your sums right. Complex mathematics were needed to survey the land, organize taxes and grain distribution, make efficient use of a vast labour force and calculate the amount of masonry needed for huge edifices. Architects mastered the geometrical properties of circles, cylinders and triangles, preparing, of course, for the pyramids and temples.

The paramount importance of anticipating seasonal changes so as to make optimum use of the Nile's annual flood (*see* MIRACLE OF THE NILE page 39) also prompted scholars to study the precise movement of the sun, stars and planets. The regular reappearance of Sirius the Dog Star in summer (after a 70-day absence) heralded the rise of the river. This was New Year's Day in the ancient Egyptian lunar calendar for the farmers. There followed four lunar months for the inundation, four for planting and growth, and four for harvest and low-water. A 30-day month had to be added every three years to complete the cycle. But already in the Archaic Period, the state administration introduced a more accurate 'civil' calendar: 12 months of three 10-day weeks, with 5 extra days at the end for the gods' birthdays, roughly like Christmas.

were killed at his death. Early in the 1st Dynasty, secondary wives, servants and pet dogs may well have been sacrificed and buried around the royal tomb to attend the king in the next world. By the 2nd Dynasty, family and courtiers were allowed to die a natural death before taking up their posthumous functions.

The centralized system administering the long Nile Valley's irrigation and cultivation, digging of canals, building of dykes and dams, and harvest collection and storage, required right from the start

an extremely talented bunch of managers. Chancellors shared responsibility for the Red (Lower Egypt) and White (Upper Egypt) Treasuries. Other officials included a controller of the granaries, an overseer of the king's bounty, an organizer of the royal household, suppliers to the temples, and courtiers.

Kingpins of the whole machine were the scribes, popping up everywhere with their writing-palettes and papyrus to calculate and record the needs of engineering, draw up inventories, take down royal decrees. By permitting communication at long distance, the development of hieroglyphic writing (*see* HIEROGLYPHICS page 221) was as vital then as fax and phone are now. The Egyptian empire's far-flung authority would have been inconceivable without having writing to transmit the Pharaoh's orders. An envoy to the Sudan, for example, could happily dispatch a quick memo back to Memphis and await the boss's instructions down in Aswan, rather than waste time on a long two-way trip in person.

The Age of the Pyramids – The Old Kingdom

By the beginning of the 3rd Dynasty (2705 BC), the scribes had exploited their specialized knowledge and talents to become the major political power behind the Pharaoh's throne. Endowed with a magical and religious significance, mathematics, astronomy and writing itself were, like the learning of clerics in the early years of the Catholic Church, inaccessible to the mere layman. Egypt's first pyramid is attributed to the 3rd-Dynasty Pharaoh

*M*odern architects regard Imhotep, designer of the Step Pyramid for King Djoser at Saqqara, as the master of them all. It was an inspired act of great daring to use stone rather than mudbrick in constructing a major monumental edifice.

for whom it was built, Djoser (2687-2667 BC), but even more illustrious is its designer. His name is inscribed with equal prominence on the king's statue and on the walls surrounding the pyramid: Imhotep – architect, high priest and scribe (*see* IMHOTEP THE GREAT page 60).

The Step Pyramid, as it is known, was a truly revolutionary edifice, the world's oldest monumental structure to be built of stone. For it, Imhotep chose a plateau in the desert which would dominate the skyline at Saqqara, west of Memphis. With its four sides set precisely four-square, north and south to midnight and noon, east and west in the path of the sun, the Pharaoh's mausoleum marked the emerging dominance of Egypt's solar cult. Its god Re-Herakhty combined Re, the sun, with Horus, falcon-deity of the two horizons (from dawn to dusk). The Pharaoh was the god's earthly representative and Imhotep his high priest. The cult's 'Vatican' was at nearby Heliopolis. In the sanctuary there, the primeval mound which arose at the Creation from the waters of Chaos took the symbolic shape of a pyramidal stone. At Saqqara, it was reproduced in monumental form with steps permitting the deceased Pharaoh to climb up to a sacred boat that would carry him with the sun across the heavens.

Snoferu (2630-2606 BC), founder of the 4th Dynasty, sought to surpass the monument at Saqqara with much bigger pyramids upriver at Maidum and Dahshur, but they survived only as roughly pyramidal mounds of rubble, one of them strangely askew and now known as the Bent Pyramid. His successor, Kheops (2606-2583 BC), was even more ambitious. He abandoned the stepped form of construction and built the Great Pyramid at Giza. With the two companion pyramids of his heirs, Khephren and Mykerinus, this grandiose monument became one of antiquity's Seven Wonders of the World. The colossal sphinx, a recumbent lion with the head of King Khephren, was erected to protect the sacred precincts with their massive mortuary temples and formidable tombs of the king's family and courtiers.

Never did architecture more faithfully reflect political reality. Kheops commanded a perfectly functioning pyramidal

---

IMHOTEP THE GREAT

In modern times, someone of Imhotep's multiple talents would be known as a Renaissance man, except that in his case he was considered responsible not for a rebirth but for the veritable birth of his country's culture. Inscriptions at Saqqara list his titles as chancellor, prince, high priest of Heliopolis and sculptor. Working around the year 2680 BC, he was in all likelihood a commoner who began his career as a scribe. It was his exceptional exploits as the Pharaoh's pyramid-builder that earned him his princely title. Also revered as a sage, astronomer and physician, over the centuries he was ultimately deified, both for his miraculous healing powers and, in the New Kingdom around the time of Ramses II, as the divine patron of all scribes. Later, in the great library of Alexandria under the Ptolemies, every self-respecting intellectual worked under the watchful eye of his own bronze statue of Imhotep seated with a papyrus unrolled on his lap.

---

political structure, and could order a workforce to haul into place over 2,000,000 blocks of limestone weighing up to 15.25 tonnes (15 tons) each for the Great Pyramid. Though controversy continues over the degree of coercion, it is clear that the operation required the people's total allegiance and faith in the Pharaoh's divine authority. The bulk of the work had to be performed in summer when the peasants could leave their land after the harvest had been gathered and the Nile was in flood.

The 4th Dynasty's pretensions were already diminishing after Kheops, perhaps in proportion to the Pharaoh's financial resources and ability to command the labour-force. The courtiers of Kheops' heirs are more modestly entombed and Mykerinus' pyramid is only a third the size of the other two. The dynasty's last king, Shepseskaf, dropped the pyramid form altogether in favour of a giant sarcophagus mounted on a podium.

Away from the power centre at Memphis, relations with southern neighbours in Nubia and Sudan were organized by colonial officers based on Aswan's Elephantine Island. They supervised trade for African ebony, ivory, gold and amethyst, and recruited skilled archers for Egypt's police force. Prized incense and myrrh (aromatic resin) for sacred rituals were imported from the realm of Punt, now identified as Somalia. To get there without a canal, boats had to be transported in pieces across the Eastern Desert, assembled for the Red Sea voyage, then dismantled again for the return trip to the Nile Valley. In the Sinai and Eastern Desert, turquoise and copper were mined by Bedouins under Egyptian supervision.

To the west, the Libyans were a constant source of trouble for the Egyptian army. In the other direction, Egyptian forces pushed all the way up to Mount Carmel to keep the Palestinians quiet. It was important to keep the trade route open to Lebanon, whose cedarwood was much in demand for boats and temples.

At the end of the Old Kingdom, the pyramids made a modest comeback as part of a cunning power play by the priests of Heliopolis. In order for them to exert control over the throne, it became the custom for the priests to loan one of their wives to the Pharaoh. She mothered the royal heir, who was then proclaimed son

Unlike the other six of the Seven Wonders of the World chosen by the sages of antiquity, these pyramids of Kheops, Khephren and Mykerinus are still standing.

of the sun-god Re and not just his earthly representative. As the sun-cult's consecrated symbol, pyramids were erected at Abusir and Saqqara, but well south of Giza to avoid being dwarfed by those of Kheops and company.

The Middle Kingdom

The dilution of the Pharaohs' power signalled a breach in Egyptian unity. While the king was effectively demoted to the status of a more remote living divinity, a feudal hierarchy of priests and provincial governors came to wield more power and own more land in their own right. The Pharaoh could no longer afford a great pyramid, and his courtiers preferred to build their tombs, the monumental bench-shaped *mastaba*, in their own southern fiefs rather than grouped

subserviently around the king's tomb in the capital. If their business did keep them closer to Memphis, they affirmed their authority with more and more opulent tombs. In the funereal depiction of the afterlife, high court officials laid claim to an immortality that had previously been the exclusive prerogative of the Pharaoh.

In the transition from the Old to the Middle Kingdom, which scholars call the First Intermediate Period (2250-2035 BC), water once again played a vital role. Ruling from the Faiyum oasis at Herakleopolis, Pharaohs followed each other in quick succession as a prolonged series of droughts showed they no longer had the divine power to deliver the annual flood of the Nile to the fields of Egypt. Following a change in the pattern of monsoon rains in the Ethiopian Highlands, 'the Nile was empty,' said one inscription, 'and man crossed over it on foot.' Hot southern winds blew sand-dunes over the cultivated fields and famine spread through the land. Friezes depicted emaciated men, women and children with prominent rib cages. The only exploit of which the Pharaohs could boast was driving Palestinian and Bedouin immigrants away from the Egyptians' suddenly meagre pastures in the Delta.

The country was reunited under Menthuhotep II (2061-2010 BC), who conquered the armies of Herakleopolis and shifted power south to Upper Egypt with his capital at Thebes (modern Luxor and Karnak). His vast mortuary temple hewn from an escarpment on the Nile's west bank was the first major monument in the Valley of the Kings. Following the years of scarcity, Menthuhotep's 11th Dynasty promoted the cult of Osiris, god of the nether world, earth and fertility, with its sanctuary at Abydos, gateway to the south. Trading expeditions to the African kingdoms were resumed and dark-skinned Nubians were much in evidence at the Theban court. Medjay tribesmen from the Eastern Desert in the Sudan furnished a much appreciated mercenary police force.

With a flare-up of old feudal rivalries, the centre of power moved back north to the Faiyum region under the 12th Dynasty (1991-1786 BC) of Amenemhet and Sesostris. The dynasty sought to refurbish the sun-cult at Heliopolis under the auspices of the Theban god of Creation, Amun. Obelisks were erected around the country and new pyramids appeared at Lahun, Lisht and Dahshur (all reduced today to mounds of rubble).

In 1785 BC, the Nile again undermined the Pharaohs' authority, this time not by drying up but with a series of excessively high and prolonged inundations that disrupted seed-sowing. Amid the ensuing hardships, discredited kings quickly came and went, and only a solid civil service of strong viziers and chancellors ensured continuity.

The Hyksos

Exploiting this era of political uncertainty (known as the Second Intermediate Period, between the Middle and New Kingdoms), foreigners made their first appearance on the Egyptian throne. There is no evidence of a military invasion, but by about 1670 BC, the Pharaohs' genealogy includes western Semitic names of a people conventionally known as Hyksos, Egyptian *heka-qasut*: 'Princes of the Desert Uplands'. Centuries later, Egyptian historian Manetho claimed, in 300 BC, that the Hyksos had burned cities, razed temples to the ground and massacred, raped and enslaved the people, but this appears to be propaganda coloured by subsequent horrors suffered at the hands of Egypt's enemies.

In actual fact, the Hyksos proved to be unusually benevolent colonial rulers. Governing Lower Egypt from Avaris in the Delta, they happily adopted the local state system and pantheon of Egyptian gods, combining the Heliopolis sun-cult to Re with the worship of Seth, the Egyptians' desert-god equivalent of the Semites' Baal. They controlled Upper Egypt through indigenous Theban princes, who paid allegiance and financial tribute while continuing their own earth-cult of Osiris. This tolerance was to prove the Hyksos' undoing when the independent-spirited Thebans later spearheaded the struggle for liberation.

The Hyksos were equally easy-going with the Delta's many non-Egyptian communities, showing particular consideration, the Bible tells us, for a brilliant young Hebrew named Joseph (see THE JEWS IN EGYPT page 262).

Egyptian civilization greatly benefited from this openness to foreign influences, enhanced by vigorous trading around the Mediterranean. It brought into the country more refined bronze and silver, a new upright loom for spinning and weaving, and new musical instruments which included the oboe, tambourine, lyre and long-necked lute. Livestock was enriched with humpbacked cattle, agriculture with olives and pomegranates. The army benefited from scale armour, new bows, daggers, swords and scimitars, but above all from horse-drawn chariots and sturdy sea-going boats made of Lebanese cedar. Even when the Hyksos were driven from the throne, the Pharaohs needed their mercenaries to drive and repair the chariots.

Days of Empire – The New Kingdom

In the 16th century BC, the Theban princes moved north to reunite the country under indigenous Egyptian rule. They were responding in large part to pressure from their womenfolk. Mother or mother-in-law, wife and/or sister, these were the first in a long line of tough Egyptian queens acting as the power behind, beside or unequivocally *on* the throne. Prince Kamose pushed downriver to occupy the Faiyum region from which to attack the Hyksos strongholds in the Delta. It was his brother Ahmose who, after a prolonged siege of the capital, Avaris, drove the Hyksos out of Egypt. Founder of the 18th Dynasty, Ahmose (1552-1524 BC) then swept on into Palestine to occupy Tell Sharuhen and head off any thoughts of counter-attack.

This reconquest and the new warfare and armaments bequeathed by the Hyksos transformed the kingdom into a military state. Egypt emerged from isolation to become aware of its vulnerability as just one among many Middle Eastern powers, in Anatolia, Cyprus, Babylon and Assyria. Its position had to be consolidated. Tuthmosis I (1504-1492 BC) sent armies up to occupy Carchemish on the Euphrates in northern Syria and south to Kurgus deeper into the Sudan. A chain of fortresses was set up throughout the Nile Valley under soldiers whose loyalties were cemented by grants of land. A new military caste was born. The Pharaoh himself became a war-hero, the incarnation of the warrior-god Seth, revered for his battlefield leadership, chariot warfare, handling of horses and athletic prowess.

The new tough image was happily softened by the women the Hyksos left behind them: delicate, with their small tilted noses and almond eyes, sensual, often bare-breasted or in brightly coloured costumes, and wearing eye-catching jewellery.

The most colourful of the New Kingdom's women was undoubtedly Queen Hatshepsut (1478-1437 BC). Daughter of Tuthmosis I, half-sister and wife of the short-lived Tuthmosis II, and stepmother and regent to Tuthmosis III, she was in effect the country's ruler for 20 years. To win over the Theban priests to the idea of a female monarch, Hatshepsut dedicated the great limestone temple carved out of an escarpment in the Valley of the Kings to their chief deity, Amun. Military expeditions did not interest her, but she did mount an elaborate trade mission to bargain for the gold, spices and other riches of Punt (today's Somalia).

In contrast to the pacific years of his stepmother, Tuthmosis III (1479-1425 BC) waged no less than 17 campaigns against enemies east of the Sinai. Up in northern Syria, the Mitanni pushed back the Egyptians, but Tuthmosis was able to form a solid alliance with the formidable Hittites pressing down from Anatolia. During a dawn attack on the Palestinian rebels of Megiddo, Tuthmosis won a reputation for personal bravery by leading his army

NO BULL

Ritually, Egypt could not be ruled by a woman, so Hatshepsut is frequently depicted in man's attire, complete with ceremonial beard. With no apparent sense of incongruity, she had herself crowned 'King of Upper and Lower Egypt' at Karnak, while playing up good relations among the Theban gods as 'Re's Daughter who Embraces Amun', and optimizing the undeniable as 'First Among Women'. But she stopped short of claiming the king's usual epithet, 'mighty bull'.

through a dangerous narrow pass in the Carmel mountain ridge. Closer to home, garrisons had trouble with marauding bands of *Apiru*, literally 'dusty people', sometimes identified with the Hebrews.

At the end of his reign, Tuthmosis III shared the throne with his 18-year-old son. Amenophis II warmed the cockles of his old father's heart by winning a battle at Qadesh in northern Syria and sending back the corpses of seven enemy princes to hang from the walls of Thebes.

Amenophis III (1402-1364 BC) profited from the spoils of empire to launch an ambitious construction programme for the capital and Nubia. He made large additions to the temples at Thebes, including a great processional avenue of sphinxes between them. On the Nile's west bank, he built what was probably the largest of all Pharaonic mortuary temples, of which only the Colossi of Memnon, gigantic seated guardians of its portal, have survived the destruction of earthquakes and jealous successors. The opulent palace at nearby Malgutta included a chariot racetrack.

The Sun King

One of the most intriguing figures of the ancient world, Amenophis IV is better known to history as Akhenaten (1356-1339 BC). Spiritually inclined scholars see him as a visionary monotheist, audaciously turning his back on the traditional pantheon of Egyptian gods to preach the natural virtues of humanism. Hard-nosed historians suggest he was more interested in grabbing power and taxes away from the priests, not unlike Henry VIII breaking with the Roman Catholic church. The truth probably lies between the two.

The avenue of sphinxes was used by priests bearing effigies of the gods between the temples of Luxor and Karnak. Today it is interrupted by a mosque and Moslem cemetery.

Thebes' main deities, among many others, had been Amun (Creation), Re (the sun) and Osiris (earth and the nether world). The new king proclaimed one state god, Aten, a version of Re as visible manifestation of the sun's radiating power, and declared himself the god's earthly representative – Akhenaten, 'beloved of Aten'. The plural form of the word for god was suppressed. To make the point that he and Aten were 'unique, without a peer', the king smashed the temples and statues of Amun and Osiris, fired the priests and confiscated all their temple-revenues. He needed the money to pay for his lavish new capital 'Akhenaten' (present-day Tell El Amarna), midway between Thebes and Memphis.

A new cult of personality had already been apparent during the reign of his father, Amenophis III, who had built colossal self-aggrandizing monuments. A new naturalism in art, which shunned formal stereotypes of beauty and showed, even emphasized, human frailty instead, had also emerged in the last days of the ageing king, himself portrayed as sick and obese.

SWEET NEFERTITI

Despite her lofty position in Akhenaten's state religion, Nefertiti was always a wife and mother, with just a hint of divinity. She served as the supreme model in the new freedom of artistic expression. Intimate scenes of royal family life introduced an unprecedented personal charm. Nefertiti is variously shown sitting on Akhenaten's lap, kissing him, putting a garland of flowers around his neck, breast-feeding her children, playing with them or organizing a family lunch. At a reception for foreign envoys, Akhenaten and Nefertiti sit on their thrones holding hands, like some latter-day President and First Lady.

Akhenaten, however, undeniably broke new ground. Instead of following the custom of marrying his oldest sister as queen among his wives, he chose a commoner whose celebrated sculpture fully justifies her name: Nefertiti, 'the beauty has come'. To the exclusion of the priesthood, she was second only to the king himself in communion with Aten.

Nefertiti's devout faith outlasted that of her husband and forced her to move to a palace on the other side of town. Political events had dampened Akhenaten's religious zeal. At home, as a reward for helping him to overthrow the old order, the military had taken over tax-collection but proved to be even more corrupt and greedy than the priests. Abroad, tribute-payments were drying up from increasingly independent-minded Syrian and Palestinian city-states. The state treasury was too depleted for Akhenaten to keep his promise of gold payments to bolster the Mitanni in north Syria as a buffer against the expansionist Hittites.

After a brief period of uncertainty following Akhenaten's death, the old order was restored. The traditional priesthood was reinstated in refurbished temples. Akhenaten's sanctuaries were destroyed, and the statues, portraits and name-inscriptions of him and Nefertiti were systematically defaced. This counter-revolution was engineered by chancellor Aya and military commander Horemheb acting as regents for the new boy Pharaoh.

Probably Akhenaten's son by a secondary marriage, Tutankhamun died aged 19. He himself was totally unremarkable, but his was the only Pharaonic tomb to preserve its treasure intact until the 20th century (*see* CAIRO page 113). The tomb was tiny compared with the one originally earmarked for him but commandeered by chancellor Aya, who married into the royal family to become Pharaoh. With the dynasty crumbling, Horemheb succeeded to the throne, placed fellow army officers in key state jobs and imposed military discipline on the judicial system.

Grandeur and Decline

Without heir, Horemheb chose his chancellor and general to succeed him as Pharaoh with the name of Ramses I. He and his son, Seti I (1291-1279 BC), were men of the Delta, of partly Semitic origin. Under their 19th Dynasty, ancient Egyptian splendour attained its zenith, but the empire began to crack.

Seti continued Horemheb's resurrection of the old religious order by making majestic additions to the temples at Thebes and Abydos. He beat back new Libyan incursions into the Western Desert and reasserted Egyptian authority against the Canaanites in Palestine, but his battles against the Hittites in northern Syria were inconclusive.

The great Ramses II (1279-1212 BC) achieved a fatal apotheosis in Pharaonic power. Nearly half the temples in Egypt date from his reign, notably the Ramesseum mortuary temple at Thebes, the grand Hypostyle Hall at Karnak and the gigantic sanctuary of Abu Simbel, not to mention the myriad monuments of his predecessors which he plundered and usurped. For his new royal residential city in the eastern Delta, Pi-Ramses, he used a Hebrew work-force, probably those whom Moses was destined to lead to the Promised Land.

For Ramses II, as for his predecessors, an empire was a means of financing the good life in Egypt, by constructing numerous monuments to his own glory, rather than of extending power far afield in the later manner of the Persians or Romans. Preferring the gentler activities of the scribes and the priesthood, the Egyptian élite left the fighting to foreign mercenaries from the conquered territories: Nubia, Sudan, Canaan and Libya. But things were getting tougher.

New threats were posed by disparate bands of warriors who were collectively known to history as the Sea Peoples. These raiders, who left their names all over the Mediterranean – Shekelesh (Sicily), Teresh (Tuscany), Shardana (Sardinia), Peleset (Palestine) – threatened Egypt's territories in the Western Desert and along the Syrian coast. They gave significant support to Egypt's arch enemy, the Hittites, in northern Syria at what was perhaps the most important battle in Pharaonic history.

Ramses II demonstrated great personal courage in extricating his forces from a massive Hittite ambush at Qadesh on the Orontes river. The Pharaoh rallied the demoralized troops in repeated charges to break out of the encirclement and regroup. Though celebrated in temple friezes at Abu Simbel, Thebes and Abydos as a great Egyptian victory, Qadesh was in fact a standoff. The peace treaty of 1258 BC, sealed by Ramses' marriage to a Hittite princess, obliged Egypt for the first time to give up all claim to northern Syria and accept limits to its sphere of influence in the eastern Mediterranean.

Egyptian prestige was durably dented. Most historians agree that this was the time when Moses pressured the Pharaoh into letting the Hebrews go. Barely 80 years after Qadesh, an inscription on Ramses III's mortuary temple said of the Sea People raiders: 'All at once, these peoples were on the move... No country could stand up to them.' The pirates were beaten back in two battles on the Palestinian frontier and off the Delta coast, but could not be prevented from settling into nearby Palestinian coastal towns. As a sign of the times, the Pharaoh's envoy to Lebanon was subjected to unprecedented humiliation when purchasing an important consignment of cedarwood. By the 11th century BC, revolts in Nubia and Sudan had forced the Egyptians back behind their old southern frontiers.

The temple complex at Karnak is a conglomeration of all the self-glorifying monuments left by the Egyptian pharaohs and their Libyan, Persian, Greek and Roman successors.

The Late Period

From 1070 BC, the country was once more split into Upper and Lower Egypt. Succeeding Pharaohs ruled Lower Egypt from various administrative capitals in the Delta, but kept their sacred capital at Memphis. The Thebans governing Upper Egypt paid only nominal homage to the king of Lower Egypt.

Religious worship reflected national disunity. Amun was state god in both Lower and Upper Egypt, identified as both sun and Creator with aggressive new phallic attributes, but he was challenged by a proliferation of local cults. Animal deities proved popular: cats, bulls, crocodiles and baboons. The earth cult of Osiris, favourite of Pharaohs, still offered salvation to all mortals, but he was gradually outshone by his faithful wife Isis, a model of traditional family values in these troubled times.

In 945 BC, a dynasty of Libyan origin seized power from its base at Bubastis. Sesonchis I invaded Palestine and resumed trade with Lebanon. From Lower Egypt, he tried to reassert authority over Thebes by installing his son as high priest and financing extensive additions to the Karnak sanctuary with treasures plundered from King Solomon's temple. Civil war ensued and the Thebans sided with whichever new ruler made them the best offer.

In the 8th century BC, it was the Nubians' turn. King Piye conquered Upper Egypt and re-established traditional religion and the old social order. His successors' incursions into Assyrian-held Palestine provoked a counter-attack in 663 BC. The powerful Assyrian king Assurbanipal sacked Thebes and drove the Nubians south beyond the border.

Rushing back to deal with trouble in Babylon, the Assyrians left Egypt reunited under the Libyan King Psammetichos I, ruling from his capital at Sais in the western Delta. As merchant princes, the 26th Dynasty (664-525 BC), brought in a period of quiet prosperity in an increasingly cosmopolitan Egypt. For defence, the princes relied on Greek and Phoenician mercenaries from Asia Minor. The garrison on Elephantine Island included Jewish soldiers from the kingdom of Judah. Greek merchants worked side by side with Jews at Memphis and established new trading counters in the Delta at Daphnae and Naukratis to export Egyptian corn and wool. Necho II sent Phoenician sailors off to explore a southern trade route around Africa. He also began digging a canal from the Nile across to the Red Sea, until a temple oracle, pointing out that its main beneficiaries would be foreign merchants, instructed him to: 'Stop working for the barbarians.'

*E*lephantine Island served as the fortress for the defence of Egypt's southern frontier and for launching attacks into Nubia and the Sudan.

Sure enough, Egypt's orderly affluence made it tempting bait for the mighty Persians in 525 BC. King Cambyses led the invasion with a sea-raid on the fortress of Pelusium in the north-east corner of the Sinai peninsula. In a foolhardy effort to annex the Sudan as well, he sent a huge army south through the Western Desert, where they disappeared without a trace. Stricken with rage and epileptic fits, Cambyses reacted with bloody massacres and plunder at Thebes and Memphis. His successor, Darius I (521-486 BC) tried to restore Egyptian goodwill by honouring the state religion and building shrines at the Kharga oasis, El Kab and Busiris. For more than a century, the Persian Pharaohs ruled efficiently with power delegated to satraps, generals and Egyptian nobles. Then, after an interlude of Greek-supported native Egyptian dynasties, the Persians' last years of rule were again characterized by massacre and the wholesale destruction of shrines, which provoked popular revolt.

There is no doubt that in 332 BC, Egypt was ripe for the plucking.

From Alexander to Cleopatra

Emerging victorious from gruelling battles against the Persians in Syria and Palestine, Alexander the Great trekked across the north Sinai desert from Gaza to the fortress of Pelusium. The Persian satrap, far from offering resistance, begged the 24-year-old Macedonian conqueror to grant him safe passage in exchange for all his personal furniture and 800 talents in cash (worth about $350,000 in modern money).

The march continued overland to Memphis, where Alexander paid homage to Apis, the bull incarnation of the sanctuary's great god of Creation. Impressed by this change of style from the sacrilegious Persians, the priests offered him the double crown of Upper and Lower Egypt. He accepted, and sailed down the Nile to the Mediterranean to make his headquarters at Rhacotis, a fortress and fishing village that was to be transformed by his successors into the city of Alexandria.

Alexander's thoughts had turned to his divine destiny. Deeply moved by his coronation at Memphis, he decided to consult the sacred oracle of Amun at the Siwa oasis in the Western Desert. As for many a modern tourist, the trek – 600km (375 miles) across the desert with a few companions – was a test of both physical endurance and mystical experience; in Alexander's case it was also a preparation for his supreme challenge, the march to India. Whatever he learned from the oracle (*see* GETTING THE GOOD WORD page 239), he took off again in 331 BC in a high state of exaltation, leaving Egypt's administration to the able Cleomenes, a Greek tax-collector from Naukratis.

In the fight for the empire after Alexander's death in 323 BC, Egypt fell to Ptolemy Soter, the great man's bodyguard and companion and a distinguished general. He promptly executed Cleomenes and fought off his Macedonian rivals' efforts to seize what was the wealthiest and most powerful of all kingdoms emerging from Alexander's conquests.

The Ptolemies' 300-year rule over Egypt had a lot in common with the British Raj in India. Both professed to respect the great local civilization but were equally determined to preserve their own cultural identity. The Macedonian Greeks underlined this by moving the capital from the Nile Valley at Memphis to the Mediterranean at Alexandria. The Ptolemies favoured pomp and circumstance but, like the British, they loved sports and incorporated gymnastics and equestrianism into a four-yearly Olympic-style ceremony.

They maintained and restored the temples, adding friezes that portrayed themselves as Pharaohs bringing offerings to the local gods in the time-honoured manner and crushing traditional Semitic or Nubian enemies. And if the atmosphere of court life was resolutely Greek, it did not

prevent intermarriage in the Greek and Egyptian aristocracy.

Royal titles often emphasized the family ties of the dynasty – Ptolemy Philadelphus (brother- or sister-loving), Ptolemy Philopator (father-loving). Borrowing customs from the Egyptians, family solidarity was reinforced by co-regency of the king with his son and heir, and brother-and-sister marriages.

Alexandria became the cultural capital of the Hellenistic world. Its famous library attracted the most illustrious of Greek scholars: the mathematicians Euclid and Archemides; the historian Callimachus; the philologist Eratosthenes; and the poet Theocritus. Thriving trade in grain, gold, silver and bronze, textiles, wine and olive oil prompted a visiting scholar of the 1st century BC, Diodorus of Sicily, to describe it as 'the first city of the civilized world, certainly far ahead of all the rest in elegance and size, riches and luxury'.

Native Egyptians outside Alexandria resented not getting their fair share of

Unlike inland Memphis or Thebes, Alexandria's position on the sea facing Anatolia and Greece determined its cosmopolitan destiny as the cultural capital of the eastern Mediterranean for centuries to come.

JUST IN ZEST

The Ptolemies may have been overzealous in following Egyptian custom with their taste for marriage between sister and brother. Egyptian kinship terms for brother and sister were very broadly extended to what we would call uncles, aunts, nephews, nieces and cousins, so that Egyptian marriages of an actual brother and sister may have been much less common than the Ptolemies imagined. Then again, those clever Greeks may have known this all along, but preferred the brother-and-sister marriage because it kept the money in the family.

SHOWDOWN IN THE DESERT

King Antiochus IV of Syria thought that Ptolemaic Egypt, economically rich but militarily soft, would be a pushover. By 168 BC, his army had swept across the Sinai to take the fortress of Pelusium. But before the final assault on the Delta, an ambassador arrived to request an audience with him. From Ptolemy? No, from Rome. There in the desert by the fortress ramparts, the envoy asked Antiochus to leave Egypt, and proceeded to draw a circle in the sand around the feet of the astonished king. 'Give me your answer before leaving the circle,' said the Roman.

A month later, Antiochus and his army were back in Syria.

the prosperity. The celebrated Rosetta Stone of 196 BC, on which the hieroglyphic 'code' was first cracked (*see* HIEROGLYPHICS page 221), speaks of 'rebel ringleaders causing unrest in the country'. Native political tracts called for 'the end of our evils when Egypt shall see these foreigners fall like leaves from the branch'. Egypt's prosperity, however, was only whetting the appetites of other foreigners.

By the 2nd century BC, Egypt had become an important source of grain for Rome, and the new Mediterranean superpower was determined to 'protect' its trading partner against any rival interests. The Ptolemies had to kowtow. Their dynasty was doomed, but they went out in style with a queen in the great tradition of Hatshepsut and Nefertiti.

The seventh of the name, Cleopatra (69-30 BC) was a woman of great charm rather than beauty; she was tough, talented and intelligent. She was the only one of the Ptolemies to include Egyptian among her several languages as she proudly assumed both her own Hellenistic and the ancient local culture. She used Roman pa-

Let Shakespeare have the last word on Cleopatra: *'Age cannot wither her, nor custom stale her infinite variety; other women cloy the appetites they feed, but she makes hungry where most she satisfies.'*

tronage to reassert her dynasty's royal grandeur. When the Roman general Pompey backed her brother Ptolemy XII in deposing her as co-regent, she found her own Roman general, Julius Caesar, to crush Pompey and put her back on the throne. This won him her gratitude, a cruise up the Nile and a son she named

Ptolemy Caesarion. Mother and child went to Rome to ride in the conquering hero's victory parade. To avoid any further rivalry back home, she had another brother quietly poisoned.

After Caesar's assassination, Cleopatra hitched her star to the wagon of Mark Antony for a share in the lands he commanded in the eastern Mediterranean. In exchange, she bore him twins and offered him the sensual pleasures of Alexandria. In their revels, Antony dressed as Bacchus, Cleopatra as Venus or Isis, but the good life ended with the disastrous battle of Actium. Octavius, soon to be Emperor Augustus, routed the Egyptian fleet off the coast of Greece and seized Alexandria a few months later, in 30 BC. Cleopatra and Antony had both committed suicide.

For Julius Caesar, his trip to Egypt was a fund-raiser to finance his assault on the central power in Rome. For Cleopatra, it was a chance to give birth to a little Caesar of her own.

A Roman Province

Ancient Egypt had lost the last vestige of autonomy, but it remained the Roman Empire's 'jewel in the crown'. Unlike other provinces, it was governed by a prefect or viceroy answerable directly to Augustus. And like the Ptolemies, it tickled the emperors' vanity to be portrayed in the temples as Pharaohs smiting Egypt's foes. If Augustus was straitlaced in his tastes, his successors and the Roman aristocracy in general coveted Egypt's luxury goods – jewellery, glass for windows, papyrus and Aswan red granite for their monuments including the Rome Pantheon. It was Rome's dependence on Egyptian grain to feed its people that made Alexandria a pre-eminent political base from which to make a bid for the imperial crown. In AD 69, Vespasian had only to hold up the grain-ships in Alexandria to nail down the nomination in Rome.

Egyptian prestige had become the thinnest of veneers. The country was now just another colony exploited for Rome's material benefit. From AD 115 to 117, a massive revolt of the Jewish merchant community in neighbouring Libya spilled over into Egypt and was crushed with brutal massacres.

CLUMSY AND SQUEAMISH

Octavius did not have a happy memory of Egypt. The man who was to lead the world's mightiest empire was taken to view the corpse of his great predecessor, Alexander. It had been brought to Egypt to be mummified as a Pharaoh (and has since vanished). When Octavius touched it, Alexander's nose fell off. Declining an invitation to look at the mummies of the Ptolemies, too, he cut short his visit and went back to Rome.

*H*adrian fancied himself
*as something of a Greek scholar
and chose to show off his
knowledge to Greek philosophers
based in Alexandria, the centre of
all Hellenistic wisdom at the time.*

The highly sophisticated Hadrian was one of the few Roman emperors to show any interest in Egypt's civilization. But even he was more fascinated by the recent culture of the Greek Ptolemies than that of the ancient Egyptians. During his prolonged state visit in AD 130, he made a dutiful tour of the Pharaonic monuments, but he was happiest debating in Greek with the scholars of Alexandria. Emperor Diocletian was less respectful. Faced with revolt in AD 297, he threatened to slaughter the population of Alexandria until blood flowed up to the knees of his horse. When he entered the city, the horse stumbled and the emperor changed his mind. The Alexandrians erected a monument to the horse.

The Rise of the Coptic Church

Diocletian returned a few years later to try to wipe out a particularly troublesome religious sect known as the Christians. The persecution (AD 301-313) was part of an abortive last-ditch effort to reassert traditional Roman religion. Since the mission to Alexandria – attributed by Church tradition to the Apostle Mark in the 1st century AD – Christians there had kept a low profile. Egypt had not been the safe haven that Joseph and Mary were believed to have found for the child Jesus when fleeing from Herod.

The Church profited enormously from the tolerance of Emperor Constantine, especially after he moved his capital from Rome to Byzantium in AD 330. While Alexandria lost its supremacy in the Greek-speaking world to the new metropolis of Constantinople, the wealth of Church property made the Patriarch of Alexandria the most powerful figure in Egypt.

The Byzantine empire wanted a share of that wealth but the Patriarch was much too independent-minded. Once more, Egypt's grain-resources made Alexandria a key factor in the imperial power-game. The Patriarch controlled the grain-shipments. At the Alexandria docks, his own private army was given the word as to whether or not to let the Nile river-boat captains release their grain cargo for shipment to Constantinople.

Grain and theology. When Athanasius, greatest of the Alexandria Patriarchs (AD 297-373), contested the Constantinople Church elders' interpretation of whether Jesus was only a man, a half-god, both at once, or something else altogether, this, too, was seen as a direct threat to imperial authority. Athanasius was exiled five times, accused of sacrilege, practising magic, illegal grain-dealing and even murder. Each time he returned, the Alexandrians greeted him with hysterical joy.

The Coptic Church, as it became known, continued to resist all attempts to incorporate it into the Eastern Orthodox Church. National pride was at stake. 'Copt' means quite simply Egyptian, derived from the Greek *Aigyptios* which in turn came from the Egyptian *hi-ka-ptah*, 'house of the spirit of Ptah'. Imbued with the new spirit of Christ, the ancient Pharaonic tradition lived on. Indeed, pockets of the old 'pagan' religion survived, especially the popular cult of Isis, until well into the 6th century AD.

The Christians again suffered violent persecution from a Persian invasion in AD 618. Byzantine forces drove the Persians out ten years later, but the new 'protection' was experienced as a humiliating occupation. The Copts had to pay heavy taxes for a naval base installed at Alexandria. The Eastern Orthodox Patriarch Cyrus was appointed civil governor of Egypt and was regarded by the Copts as a more brutal oppressor than the Persians. The Egyptians were not unhappy to see the Arabs arrive in AD 641.

Egypt under Islam

The Arab conquest of Egypt began in 639, seven years after Mohammed had declared an Islamic *jihad* (holy war) against the Byzantine empire. A force of some 3,500 ragged Bedouins on camels and horses came in from Palestine across the northern Sinai. They pushed through the Delta to take the Faiyum oasis and, with reinforcements of 12,000 cavalry, won the fierce and decisive battle of Heliopolis. The hated Orthodox Patriarch Cyrus signed the surrender in 641 before fleeing with the Byzantine fleet.

Weary of Christian sectarian infighting and Byzantine oppression, many Copts converted quickly to Islam. The new governor, Arab Commander-in-Chief Amr ibn al'Asi, followed the advice of his caliph in Mecca to stop plundering the local wealth and start collecting taxes. 'Tribute is better than booty,' said the caliph, 'it lasts longer.'

Feeling unable to defend Alexandria against the seafaring Byzantines, the Arabs moved the national capital back to the southern tip of the Delta, where they built the town of Fustat, just south of present-day Cairo. As a conciliatory gesture to the local Coptic community, Governor Amr brought their patriarch back from his desert refuge where he had been in hiding for 12 years from Byzantine persecution. Amr was aware of the sharp differences between his Arab desert nomads and the sedentary Egyptians of the Nile valley, and admonished his Moslem officers to treat the Copts with respect.

Amr revived the Nile's long-neglected irrigation system, repairing dams and canals. Most important was the de-silting of an ancient canal of the Ptolemies between the Nile and the Red Sea. After Rome and Constantinople, the grain-shipments headed now for Arabia. There, the new caliph demanded higher taxes: 'The camel can yield more milk.' 'Yes,' said Amr, 'but its young will suffer.' This subversive play with words cost Amr his job in favour of his half-brother Abdullah. Sure enough, the harsher tax-policies caused a revolt. The caliph was assassinated and his successor, Muawiya, founder of the Umayyad Dynasty (661-750), brought Amr back as governor. The camel yielded quite enough milk to keep the caliph happy and bring Amr a huge personal fortune that included 400 pounds of gold.

Gradually the Copts lost ground. Umayyad rulers were oppressive tax-collectors, brutally crushing Coptic resistance. To avoid extra taxes imposed on 'infidels' and other discriminations, conversions to Islam increased. Arabic became the official administrative language. (Today, the Coptic language, rooted in ancient Pharaonic Egypt, persists only in the church liturgy and Copts constitute at most 8 percent of the population.)

Governors appointed by the new Abbasid Dynasty (750-1258) proved even tougher and more unscrupulous. Against their illegal extortion, the only recourse of the population, Moslem or not, was a local *qadi* (religious judge) applying the *sharia* law of the Koran.

From the 9th century, the caliphate was under the control of a Turkish military oligarchy. They appointed one of their own, the great Ibn Tulun (868-905), as governor of Egypt. Scornful of his masters' stupid vulgarity but popular with his fellow Turkish mercenaries, this son of a slave was a talented and highly cultivated man. He ran the country as a *de facto* independent state, paying lip service to the caliph in Friday prayers and only a modest sum as tribute.

He needed all the money he could get to pay for Nile irrigation works, aqueducts and an opulent new capital. West of Fus-

According to tradition, the sycamore wood used in building the Mosque of Ibn Tulun came originally from Noah's Ark, brought from the mountains of Ararat, now part of Armenia.

tat, he built a grand palace with an extensive harem, hippodrome, stables and a menagerie for exotic wild animals. His handsome new mosque, still standing, was designed – by a Coptic architect in 876 – to house his whole army.

Ibn Tulun was a cruel despot towards his entourage, imposing discipline by summary execution, but fair taxation and sharing-out of the wealth made him popular among merchants and rural *fellahin*. He proceeded to carve out a mini-empire to secure Egypt's trade routes north east through Syria, west to Libya and even south towards Mecca until rebuffed by the caliphate. He died of diarrhoea caused by an overdose of buffalo milk.

Incompetent and profligate, his heirs squandered the family fortune and provoked an invasion of the caliph's army in 905. The capital was sacked and over the next 30 years the country's wealth was despoiled by a corrupt administration.

The Al-Ikhshik Dynasty coming in from Syria (935-968) brought only a semblance of order. The court led a life of luxury, but the country at large was beset by catastrophes: earthquake, drought and famine.

Rise and Fall of the Fatimids

In 969, Egypt passed into the hands of Al-Muizz li Din al-Fatimi, caliph of the North African portion of the Arab empire. He dispatched an invasion force of disciplined, well-paid Berbers under Jawhar al-Siqili to take over a country in utter disarray from famine and plague. Grain was shipped in for the starving population until the level of the Nile in flood returned to normal in 972.

Under the efficient governorship of General Jawhar, the people were put to work on public projects that included palace buildings and the Al-Azhar mosque for the Fatimid capital, Cairo *(see* FOR WHOM THE BELL TOLLS page 117). It was designed as a residential compound for the caliph, his family and entourage – 18,000 in all. Two lavish palaces were separated by a hippodrome on which 10,000 troops could parade. It was out of bounds to civilian commoners, whose residential quarters were to the south at Fustat; equally Fustat was off limits to the caliph's army.

The Fatimids governed in the style that the Middle East has always liked in its rulers: tough and generous. Adopting the title of caliph, Al-Muizz claimed direct descent from Mohammed's daughter, Fatima. When he finally arrived in Egypt in 973, he was questioned on his genealogy by the *ulema* (Moslem elders), many of whom were themselves genuine descendants of the Prophet. Brandishing his sword, Al-Muizz said: 'There is my genealogy and,' scattering gold coins over the carpet in front of the *ulema,* 'that is my lineage.'

His Shi'ite Fatimids were tolerant of the Egyptian Sunni majority. Tax-collection was cleaned up, the bureaucracy reformed and citizens' complaints treated with respect. Over the next 200 years, vicious and equitable rulers balanced each other out. Even when the Fatimid Empire shrank with revolts in North Africa, Syria and Sicily, Egyptian trade continued to prosper. Famine and plenty followed the vagaries of the Nile flood.

In the 12th century, power struggles weakened the Fatimid caliphate. The Crusaders invaded and were finally rebuffed only by a strongman from the caliph's

Syrian forces, Salah al-Din Al-Ayyubi. Known to posterity as Saladin (1138-1193), he forced the Fatimids out and founded his own dynasty. In Cairo, incorporating Fustat into one city, he abandoned the opulent Fatimid palaces to build his citadel on strategically safer high ground. With three new theological seminaries, this visionary leader brought Sunni Egypt back into the Moslem mainstream (*see* ISLAM IN EGYPT page 124). He pursued the Crusaders into Syria and Palestine, leaving the government of Egypt to an efficient triumvirate formed by his brother Safadin, vizier Al-Fadil and public works supervisor Qaraqush. The latter, a eunuch known for his rigid discipline, streamlined the country's irrigation system, redigging canals in Upper Egypt that had been abandoned since the time of the Pharaohs.

From 1210, Saladin's Ayyubid successors took the title of Sultan. To counter a potential power challenge in his army, Al-Salih Ayyub brought in a fierce military élite of Mamelukes, originally slaves of Turkish stock (their name derives from the Arabic *mamluk:* meaning 'owned'). But after destroying the 1249 Crusade mounted by Louis IX of France, they assassinated the contemptuous new Sultan Turanshah and took over the reins of power.

The Mamelukes (1250-1517)

Egypt's new rulers, at first as regents behind the throne and then as fully fledged sultans, introduced an era of military-style efficiency and vicious palace infighting. These mercenaries were used to being handsomely – and instantly – rewarded for their prowess as warriors and never hesitated to remove ungrateful masters.

Al-Zahir Baibars had distinguished himself: in battle, as a crossbowman against the Crusaders; in commanding forces that headed off in Syria a Mongol invasion by Hulagu, grandson of Genghis Khan; and then in assassinating various Mameluke generals who did not give him an appropriate share of the spoils. In 1260, he took the sultanate for himself and over the next 17 years created a government structure that lasted for three centuries. He reformed the administration, lowered taxes, organized land-distribution for his Mameluke officers, and streamlined the army. A chain of forts and garrisons protected territory all the way north to the

OL' BLUE EYES

The Mamelukes, the toughest of Egypt's warriors, were bought as slaves from the Russian Urals, central Asian steppes or the Caucasus mountains. Separated from their families as boys, they showed personal loyalty only to their Mameluke 'brothers'. The head of the household became their father, teaching them the military arts of horseback riding and combat. As adults, they were given land and their own households in which they in turn trained new Mamelukes. The growth of the system encouraged new conquests, to meet the need for more land.

Sultan Baibars was the archetypal Mameluke hero, whose exploits were retold well into the 20th century. All the more ferocious for a cataract in one of his piercing blue eyes, this giant Kipchak from the Urals was renowned for his amazing strength and courage. When the fast-rising flood of the Nile threatened to engulf his men, Baibars plunged into the torrent to swim across, dragging a raftload of Mameluke troops to safety behind him.

Turkish Taurus mountains. Not being a sailor, he dismantled the ports rather than let them fall into enemy hands. A new road network provided travellers with hotels, shops, water wells and food markets. It enabled Baibars' twice weekly postal system to take a letter from Cairo to Damascus in four days, express rate two days – today, only fax is faster.

Having clambered to the throne over the corpses of Ayyubid and Mameluke rivals, Baibars met an appropriate end. He died by mistake from a poisoned drink which he had prepared to knock off an uppity general. His son proved incompetent and was soon succeeded by Qalawun, who ushered in the Mamelukes' golden age. After fending off the Mongols in 1281, Qalawun brought Egypt welcome peace and prosperity. Cairo was given its first public hospital, part of a famous complex of school, medical library and the sultan's funerary mosque. It still presents a classic example of colourful Mameluke architecture and sculpture. The hospital was free, with isolation wards for contagious diseases and musicians playing soothing melodies.

Despite the natural disasters of earthquake, famine and the plague in the 14th century, ambitious building continued in the Egyptian capital, notably under Sultan Hassan. Agriculture shrank with the population, decimating the land-taxes that were the Mameluke officers' only source of income. Compensatory urban taxes were imposed, causing popular unrest which in turn added to conflicts among the exasperated Mamelukes.

In 1400, in the face of a new Mongol threat from Tamerlane, the Mamelukes had to give up their eastern empire to keep the invasion out of Egypt. Plague continued to devastate the population. From 1382 to 1517, *coups d'état* had become

the rule of the day, and of the 23 sultans, only nine were of any consequence. The outstanding ruler was Qaitbay (1468-1496), a typical mixture of brutality and intelligence. He offered rebel generals two alternatives: either he would flog them personally or he would send them off to meditate in his new *sufi* monasteries. His vast programme of building – for roads, bridges, mosques, schools and military forts – was financed by a savage 30 percent increase in land-taxes.

In 1516 came the ultimate blow to Mameluke pride: the annihilation of their vaunted military prowess by the Ottoman Turks. The valiant Mameluke cavalry, swordsmanship and brilliant use of crossbow were suddenly helpless against the Ottoman infantry's new artillery and firearms. Their outdated code of honour was rendered irrelevant by the Turks' pragmatic use of highly efficient force. Routed in Syria, the Mameluke leader Tuman Bey was offered viceroy status under Ottoman suzerainty. His reply was to kill the messenger who brought the offer. The Turks responded by invading Egypt in 1517 and crushing the last Mameluke resistance. The Ottoman Sultan Selim entered Cairo. He invited Tuman Bey to provide a briefing on details of Egyptian government and then hanged him – alongside that week's batch of common criminals – from the city's southern gate, Bab Zuweila.

Ottoman Rule (1517-1805)

The Ottomans controlled Egypt with a fragile balance of power between Turks and Mamelukes in local government. The Turks began with a submissive viceroy in the person of Khair Bey, nicknamed *Khain Bey* ('traitor') by fellow Mamelukes. The latter were held in check by the Ottomans' crack infantry of janissaries, originally war-captives or Christians converted to Islam.

In the reforms of Sultan Suleiman the Magnificent after 1525, Egypt was divided into 14 provinces administered by a Turkish *pasha* or a Mameluke *bey* (governor). The territory was parcelled out to tax-collectors who became virtual private landowners. Valued for their intimate knowledge of the country, the Mamelukes were appointed to high office and given their own regiments. After 60 years of peace, the influx of silver from the Americas caused inflation, devaluing the soldiers' fixed salaries, and prompted a series of revolts from 1586 to 1609.

The Mamelukes, who led the revolts, were strong enough to force out any unpopular *pasha,* but their factional rivalries could in turn be manipulated by the *pashas.* In the 18th century, life in town and country was at the mercy of the soldiery. The Ottoman janissaries operated a protection racket to defend city guilds of merchants and artisans against government tax-collectors in exchange for a 10 percent 'death-duty' from guild-members' testaments. The Mamelukes' more widely spread control of the countryside through land-taxes gave them national supremacy. But they had a surprise coming.

On 1 July 1798, the French forces of Napoleon Bonaparte sailed into Aboukir Bay and the next day captured the neighbouring port of Alexandria. With the aim of blocking British trade and access to India, he had slipped past Admiral Nelson's Mediterranean fleet to make Egypt his base. In a declaration in Arabic, Napoleon proclaimed himself a friend of Islam and the Ottoman sultan, who had come to punish the Mameluke usurpers and liberate the Egyptian people. At the Battle of the Pyramids, he defeated the Mamelukes, who fled east to Gaza and south to Upper Egypt. There, they controlled the grain resources, limiting French authority to Cairo and the Delta.

One month after landing in Egypt, this restriction became an entrapment when Nelson destroyed the French fleet at Aboukir. Deprived of supplies and pay, the French troops had to start living off the land. The enraged people of Cairo rose in a revolt which ended in bloody repression. Plague, malaria and dysentery only added to the misery of the French forces.

Ultimately more important than his troops, Napoleon had brought along an army of 187 scientists and scholars to help Egypt retrieve the grandeur of its Pharaonic past. These intrepid geographers, geologists, botanists, zoologists, archaeologists and linguists were to be followed 30 years later by Jean-François Champollion, the first man to decipher hiero-

MENOU'S FOLLY

France's last colonial administrator in Egypt was a wild visionary who might have stepped from the pages of a Joseph Conrad novel. Baron Jacques-François de Menou defied his class by championing the French Revolution but ended pathetically, a subject of ridicule. In Egypt, he went native. Converting to Islam with the name Abd Allah, he thought he was marrying into the Egyptian aristocracy when told his wife was a descendant of Mohammed. He was determined to make a *grande dame* of her, much to the amusement both of his Egyptian in-laws and his fellow French officers. She turned out to be the daughter of a bathhouse keeper from Rosetta on the Delta coast.

Mohammed Ali's 19th-century mosque is a monumental pastiche inspired by Istanbul. It is filled with bronze, marble and stained-glass ornament reflecting his admiration for things European.

Jacques Menou. This ambitious officer wanted to reorganize Egypt along the lines of a French province, but his experiment was stopped by an Anglo-Turkish force which drove the French out of the country in 1801. Among the archaeological treasures confiscated by the British was the Rosetta Stone which revealed the secret of hieroglyphics (now in London's British Museum).

glyphics for the modern world *(see* Hieroglyphics page 221). An Institute of Egypt was founded for the arts and sciences, on the model of the *Institut de France*. Besides digging out the old canals, French engineers prepared the way for the most important of them all, from the Gulf of Suez to the Mediterranean.

Napoleon tried to fight his way out of the Egyptian trap through Palestine but had to retreat after an abortive siege of Acre. Leaving Egypt in the hands of General Kléber, he sneaked back to his greater destiny in France. Kléber was assassinated in another uprising and was succeeded by

Mohammed Ali

The Mamelukes expected to be reinstated, but the Ottomans were reluctant to deal with leaders who in the past had failed to make the appropriate tribute-payments to Istanbul. They preferred their own Turkish viceroy supported by a predominantly Albanian occupying force. The Egyptian people had been encouraged by the short-lived French reforms to put their faith in a council of *ulema* Moslem elders. With the *ulema's* support, the Albanian troops mutinied against the Ottomans' *pasha* in

1803 and their leader, Mohammed Ali, emerged as the new strongman.

Sultan Selim III had no alternative but to confirm him as Egypt's governor. As a soldier born in what is now Greek Macedonia, Mohammed Ali (1805-1846) was simple only in his origins. He had earned a tough reputation fighting Napoleon's army in 1799, but was more successful in beating back a British invasion in 1807. This did not stop him a year later selling Egyptian grain to British troops, who were fighting the French in Spain. He revealed another facet of his diplomacy in dealing with rival leaders. In 1811, he invited 24 Mameluke beys to a sumptuous banquet at the Citadel in Cairo. At the end, belching happily on their way to the gate, they were all shot dead.

Mohammed Ali ran the country almost completely independently from the Ottoman Empire to which it nominally belonged. After centuries of lethargy, the dynamic new ruler was determined to have Egypt play its full part in the modern world. He wanted it exporting its own manufactured goods, not just subsisting as an entrepôt for east–west trade. In agriculture, the grain-sales to the British paid for a large-scale new irrigation system, permitting two or three annual harvests where previously there had been only one. Textile factories were built for locally grown linen, cotton and flax. Silk was developed with silkworms; mulberry trees were imported from Syria and Lebanon, and cashmere goats for wool from India. Cash crops of cotton, sugar cane and indigo were expanded to compensate for periodic slumps in coffee and manufactured goods.

To gain markets for the new industries, Mohammed Ali embarked on an ambitious programme of military expansion. In 1818, he exploited the Ottoman request to crush a revolt in Hijaz (modern Saudi Arabia) by making his own son governor of the region around Mecca and Medina. In the Sudan, he had to do without Ottoman support. This prompted him to create for the first time since the Pharaonic era a native-born Egyptian army. Guided by veteran French officers he had fought against in the Delta, Mohammed Ali modelled it on Napoleon's *Grande Armée*. He wanted to imbue in the 100,000-strong force of Egyptian *fellahin* the same spirit that had developed among the French peasantry. Admittedly, for the time being, Egyptians could not rise above captain, since generals were exclusively Ottoman.

The army was modernized with up-to-date weaponry, staff colleges, an engineering corps, medical surgeons, and veterinary surgeons for the cavalry. This training led to all-round development of national education as students learned new technology abroad and brought their learning back to Egyptian schools. European books were translated, reviving Arabic as a literary language. Mohammed Ali, himself illiterate until the age of 47, was obsessed by education. He doted over his 30 children, but terrorized them if they were slack at school.

His habitual brutality hurt the Egyptianization of the army. *Fellahin* were ruthlessly press-ganged right off the land into the infantry, but many maimed themselves to evade conscription into Mohammed Ali's wars. After Hijaz and the Sudan, more campaigns followed in Crete, Cyprus and the Peloponnese in the 1820s, and in Syria in the 1830s. This uppity expansionism clashed with the imperial interests of the British, French and Austrians in the Greek territories and the Turks in Syria.

Most of all, Britain resented Egyptian competition in the textile trade. By 1840, Mohammed Ali's foreign advances had all been repelled. The Treaty of London which pushed Egypt back inside its old borders, also ended its protectionist trade and tariffs system. This halted Egyptian industrialization for the next century, effectively reducing the country to the status of a colony providing raw materials for European industry.

Mohammed Ali's heirs suffered variously from disease and indolence, too often preoccupied with personal profit. Their great patriarch had resisted French pressure to dig the Suez Canal, dismissing it as an over-costly project serving European rather than Egyptian interests. Despite opposition from the Turks and British (who were building an overland railway), Saïd Pasha (1854-1863) caved in to the French and left his nephew Ismail to complete the construction under an enormous burden of debt.

The unmistakably imperialist character of the Suez Canal was evident at its inauguration in 1869. It was attended by French Emperor Napoleon III's wife Eugénie, the Crown Prince of Prussia and a host of other European royals. The

---

SUEZ SAGA

The struggle to build the Suez Canal was a classic story in colonial heroism. Saïd Pasha loved spaghetti. He would give anything for a plate of pasta. As a young man, he was mercilessly persecuted by his father, Mohammed Ali, for being obese. Wily French consul Ferdinand de Lesseps won Saïd's eternal friendship with secret spaghetti feasts. French savvy in affairs of the stomach paid off when the fat fellow came to power and gave de Lesseps the concession to build the Suez Canal.

Egyptians installed Western-style street lamps in the cities built along the canal – Port Said and Ismailiya – to show off the new architecture, which was strictly European neoclassical. Giuseppe Verdi wrote the opera *Aïda* to open Cairo's new opera house, but the costumes were not ready, so the romantic epic of Pharaonic Egypt was replaced by *Rigoletto,* the story of a court fool betrayed.

Under British Protection

The Suez Canal sounded the death knell for the autonomy that Mohammed Ali had fought to win for Egypt. Close to bankruptcy, Ismail was forced to abdicate in favour of his son Tawfiq (1879-1892), who became completely dependent on the European consuls. Britain took over Egypt's shares in the company running the Suez Canal. Foreign residents exploited their immunity to Egyptian law and taxes to engage in widespread smuggling and racketeering.

Tawfiq's membership of a progressive lodge of Freemasons had misled liberals and nationalists into expecting political reforms towards Egyptian independence. In 1882, Egyptian colonels, blocked for promotion under Ottoman generals, led an angry group of soldiers crying 'Egypt for Egyptians!' outside Tawfiq's palace. Fearing a full-scale military revolt, Tawfiq asked for British armed intervention. British troops landed at Alexandria and Ismailiya and joined forces to defeat the Egyptian colonels' army east of the Delta at Tell El Kebir. The leaders surrendered in Cairo and were exiled to the British colony of Seychelles in the Indian Ocean. To control the Suez link with

THAT WASN'T MY WIFE, EITHER

Preparing for battle at Tell El Kebir, an elated Egyptian scouting patrol reported to the rebel colonels that the British had brought their wives with them. It was immediately decided to strike a blow at enemy morale by sending in a crack group of Egyptian commandos to stage a night-time kidnapping raid. Faced with an astonishingly violent reaction, the commandos were forced to beat a hasty retreat. They had woken up an enraged platoon of kilted Gordon Highlanders.

India, Britain installed a military and political presence that was to last until 1954.

Egypt never formally became a colony, but the British ran the country by placing an 'adviser' in each ministry, topped by a consul general serving as agent to the Egyptian government. The Egyptian officer corps was disbanded and the army placed under British military command. The man who installed the system, known as the 'veiled protectorate', was Sir Evelyn Baring (later Lord Cromer), previously the viceroy's deputy in India, with the

THE DINSHWAI MARTYRS

Whether in India or Egypt, as a colony or a 'veiled protectorate', the imperial experience is uncomfortably familiar. Unrest boiled over in 1906 when British officers on a pigeon-shoot at Dinshwai in the Delta were forced to flee by angry villagers who depended on pigeon-hunting as their means of livelihood. One officer died of heat-stroke before he could make it back to the British camp. In retaliation, 52 Egyptians were arrested, four hanged, six imprisoned and others publicly flogged. The martyrs became heroes of revolutionary folk-poetry throughout the 20th century.

nickname Over-Baring. He kept landowners happy with guaranteed profits under peaceful British rule, and this restored financial solvency and fed the people.

Egypt's economic activity was reduced to growing raw cotton for Britain's Lancashire mills, all other crops being blocked by prohibitive tariff restrictions. Aswan's first dam was built in 1902, but due to inadequate drainage, it caused more problems than it solved: salination built up, and crop roots were saturated by the rise in subsoil water. Unable to adjust to the demands of the cash-crop economy, desperate *fellahin* turned to brigandry. Opposition to the British presence mounted.

With the Liberals governing in London, Egyptians could let off steam in a new national legislative assembly in 1913. World War I blocked progress to independence when Turkey sided with Germany. Still nominally part of the Ottoman Empire, Egypt became a fully fledged, 'unveiled' British protectorate under martial law. The unreliable pro-Turkish Ismail was deposed and replaced by his docile uncle, Hussein Kamil.

After the war, Egyptian politicians were encouraged by the liberationist talk of American President Woodrow Wilson. In 1918 Saad Zaghlul, head of the new nationalist *Wafd* ('delegation') party, demanded to plead the Egyptian cause at the Paris peace negotiations. In the face of street agitation supporting his demand, the British reflex was to exile Zaghlul to Malta. Violent reaction across the country forced the British to let him go to Paris.

The British continued to resist the nationalists. Even the abolition of the protectorate and martial law in 1922 installed only a semblance of parliamentary democracy. Under a constitutional monarchy, with Prince Fuad as king, free speech was

In time of peace, the Suez Canal is a great commercial blessing, but its strategic importance between the Mediterranean and the Indian Ocean make it a prime target in wartime.

restored and banned political parties reinstated. But foreign affairs, defence matters, and above all the security of communications with the British Empire through the Mediterranean and Suez Canal, remained in British hands.

King Fuad, highly intelligent but ruthless, scorned parliament and was forever at loggerheads with his first prime minister, Saad Zaghlul. The charismatic *Wafd* leader had his own share of arrogance, but combined it with a common touch, speaking the language of his peasant origins. Against the king's blithe contempt for the constitution, Zaghlul used the threat of the mob.

Arbiter in this perennial power struggle, happily applying the classical imperial technique of divide-and-conquer, was the British High Commissioner, Lord Allenby. In an atmosphere of constant intrigue, the *Wafd* Party's paramilitary group assassinated the Egyptian army's British commander-in-chief, Sir Lee Stack. Though this was done without Zaghlul's knowledge, the British blamed his inflammatory speeches. An indemnity of £500,000 was imposed and Zaghlul resigned.

Minority governments nominated by Fuad in the early 1930s were repressive and authoritarian. Subsequent popular discontent played into the hands of the Moslem Brotherhood. Founded in Ismailiya in 1928, the Brotherhood moved to Cairo to lead a religious revival amid economic depression and political disillusionment. Precursors of the fundamentalists of the 1990s, they brought traditional Moslem learning back to the schools, supported hard-pressed small businesses and helped people find jobs. They created associations for women alienated from modern urban life. All foreign influences were rejected as sinful, equated then with British imperialism. Other activists included the Young Egypt movement, green-shirted fascists inspired by Mussolini, the *Wafd*'s blue-shirted youth movement and a small Communist Party, but none had the success of the Moslem Brotherhood.

After Fuad's death in 1936, the *Wafd* returned to power at the head of an all-party coalition to negotiate the Anglo-Egyptian Treaty. Egypt was admitted to the League of Nations as an independent state, but the rumble of war again impeded total sovereignty free of British influence. If new roads were built, it was for British troop movements after Italy's invasions of neighbouring Libya and Ethiopia. British forces were concentrated in the Suez Canal Zone – off limits to Egyptians. A side-effect of the treaty was to open the military academy to sons of poor families, including the young Gamal Abdel Nasser and Anwar Sadat. A leader of a different stripe,

*T*he El Alamein
memorial at the British
Commonwealth Military Cemetery
pays tribute to the men killed in
the desert halting Rommel's
advance across North Africa.

Fuad's son Farouk became king, idolized
by the people despite, or perhaps because
of, his outrageous playboy tastes.

In World War II, on the principle that
'the enemy of my enemy is my friend,'
many Egyptians were hoping for a German victory in the Western Desert. The
British were blamed for the wartime food
shortages, provoking widespread hunger
riots. Moslem traditionalists were shocked
by the British soldiers' behaviour in the
city bars and nightclubs. Trained at a Ger-

man military academy, King Farouk's
chief military adviser, General Aziz Ali al-
Masri, openly sympathized with the German cause. Many young officers like
Anwar Sadat had pictures of Hitler in their
bedrooms.

In June 1942, pushing his Afrika Korps
towards El Alamein, just 100km (62
miles) from Alexandria, Field Marshal Er-
win Rommel had become a popular hero.
Shepheard's Hotel in Cairo had prepared
a suite for him. On the verge of evacua-
tion, the British military headquarters
burned its files. British tanks surrounded
the royal palace to counter pro-German
feeling. Out in the desert, however, Rommel paused before pressing his advantage,
giving Field Marshal Bernard Montgomery's scattered forces time to regroup,
resist and launch the counter-attack that
was to end in decisive victory for the
British in November.

A Republic in Turmoil

Peacetime brought new problems for the country. Egypt's independence was still compromised by British troops in the Suez Canal Zone and along the southern border with Sudan. Having led the formation of the Arab League five years earlier, Egypt was in the vanguard of the 1948 Arab war against the new state of Israel. Humiliating defeat exposed a country weakened by political and financial corruption. The people were no longer amused by King Farouk's scandalous life of eating and drinking orgies, heavy gambling and loose women. It was time for a radical change.

In 1951, Egyptian troops launched a series of guerrilla attacks on British soldiers in the Canal Zone. The British responded with a punitive assault on the Ismailiya police station, leaving 40 dead. This provoked an armed uprising in Cairo: mobs burned and looted targets symbolic of the British presence or the recent Arab-Israeli War – Shepheard's Hotel, Barclay's Bank, the celebrated Groppi Café, the Turf Club, cinemas and Jewish-owned department stores were all attacked.

TIPS FROM THE ENEMY

At the end of the Arab-Israeli War of 1948, the Egyptian forces occupying Gaza were besieged by the Israelis. Participating in the prolonged truce negotiations, Gamal Abdel Nasser, adjutant to the Egyptian commander, had frequent chats with his Israeli counterpart, Yeruham Cohen. He was curious about life on an Israeli kibbutz, but more interested in how the Jews had managed to get the British out of Palestine. He dropped the kibbutz idea, but the advice on the British proved very useful.

On 23 July 1952, a *coup d'état* by the 'Free Officers' of the Egyptian Army ousted King Farouk, who left the country with his family, unharmed. A year later, a revolutionary council headed by Gamal Abdel Nasser proclaimed Egypt a republic with General Mohammed Neguib as its first president, the first truly Egyptian ruler since the Pharaohs.

The mild-mannered veteran, one of the few real heroes of the Arab-Israeli War, brought an air of respectability, but his insistence on constitutional parliamentary government irritated the impatient young revolutionaries. Within a year, Nasser had replaced him as *rais* (supreme leader). Nasser's charismatic dictatorship skilfully combined army and police with well organized mass popular support – he spoke to the people in familiar Cairo dialect rather than classical Arabic. Only the Moslem Brotherhood offered serious competition to his popular appeal. An assassination attempt in 1954 provided the excuse to outlaw them – and all political parties other than his own.

At the 1955 Bandung Conference of non-aligned countries, Nasser emerged as a major Third World leader on a par with India's Nehru and Yugoslavia's Tito. At the height of Cold War paranoia, it made him immediately suspect to America's secretary of state, John Foster Dulles. Refused Western arms, Nasser got them from the Soviet bloc. Dulles promptly withdrew US financing for the projected Aswan High Dam. Intended as an alternative source of funding (until the Soviet loan of 1958), Nasser nationalized the Suez Canal. The British were enraged at this breach of their Canal treaty. In their concern for the smooth passage of vital oil supplies, they were joined by the French, who had built and managed the canal. Add to that the

Israeli fear that the arms build-up was aimed at them, and the makings of the Suez War of 1956 were all in place. With Anglo-French bombardment of Port Said and the Israelis invading the Sinai all the way to Suez, Nasser sank ships in the canal to block passage. Fighting was halted by joint Soviet-American pressure via the United Nations. The canal was duly cleared for international shipping and a UN force replaced the Israelis in the Sinai.

In the aftermath, British and French nationals were deported, along with thousands of Egyptian Jews who had been in Cairo and Alexandria for centuries. In the face of an intense wave of nationalism, and denied the traditional protection of the Egyptian government, the large Greek and Italian communities of Alexandria chose to emigrate.

In 1958, Syria joined Egypt in a United Arab Republic, but abandoned it three years later because of Nasser's autocratic style. At home, acute suspicion of colleagues made the *rais* rely more and more on the army and the dreaded *mukhabarat* secret service. Having excluded all political opposition, he was elected president with 99.9 percent of the vote. He nationalized banks, insurance and other major companies and introduced a more equitable tax-system, but widespread corruption continued as of old.

Nasser's most spectacular achievement was the Aswan High Dam, which he inaugurated in 1964 with the Soviet Union's Nikita Khrushchev. The dam was built in large part with Soviet funds and engineering. Sharing in the rewards of controlled irrigation and hydroelectric power, Sudan co-operated with Egypt in the massive shift of the Nubian population affected by the dam on either side of the border. Dozens of villages were sub-

merged under the dam's huge new Lake Nasser. In Egypt alone, 33 farming communities of 17,000 families were given new villages with their old names and arranged in the same geographical pattern as they had been on their original sites. UNESCO organized the rescue of Pharaonic temples, Coptic churches and ancient cemeteries.

Confrontation with Israel continued. Harassed by tough Israeli response to incidents over the Golan Heights, Syria pressed Egypt to make a forceful gesture of solidarity. In May 1967, Nasser ordered UN forces out of Sharm El Sheikh at the southern tip of the Sinai and blocked off the Gulf of Aqaba to shipping bound for the Israeli port of Eilat. The Israelis launched a pre-emptive strike at 5am on 5 June, destroying on the ground three-quarters of the Egyptian air force. Informed in his Heliopolis bunker six hours after the event, Nasser declared in desperation that the attack was in fact carried out by American and British aircraft. The Soviet Union ignored his call on them to retaliate. Denied air cover, 12,000 Egyptian infantry were killed in the Israeli advance across the Sinai to the Suez Canal. This humiliating Six Day War exposed Egypt's military inefficiency, with a command structure demotivated by Nasser's obsessive suspicion of possible rivals. The *rais* offered his resignation, but mass demonstrations were organized to keep him in office.

There was nobody to challenge Nasser's hold on power, but his authority looked less certain. Hostile demonstrations broke out in Alexandria. A bloody war of attrition continued in the Israeli-occupied Sinai, where Egypt had lost access to important oil resources and revenues from tourism. Nasser had to promise the Soviet

SOMETHING FOR EVERYONE

Defeat in the Six Day War provoked a wave of religious fervour. The mosques' Koranic study groups flourished and Coptic monasteries were flooded with recruits. People flocked to a small church in a Cairo suburb where the Virgin Mary had been spotted, bathed in a blue light in the sky. In a country where Mary was an atavistic figure easily identified with the ancient goddess, Isis, the phenomenon attracted thousands of Moslems and Christians alike, especially relatives of war victims. Nasser's Arab Socialist Union sold tickets for seats.

Union a naval base on the Mediterranean in exchange for ground-to-air missiles and pilots to defend Egyptian air space. With the economy buckling under the one-party system and its ponderous bureaucracy, the country depended on Saudi Arabia and Kuwait for massive loans. Yet when Nasser died of a heart attack in 1970, more than 5,000,000 grief-stricken Egyptians poured into the streets of Cairo for his funeral. The *rais* was a giant with feet of clay, but he was *their* giant, an authentic full-blooded Egyptian leader.

The new president, Anwar Sadat, was regarded as a lightweight, Nasser's yes-man. Yes and no. Like Nasser, he began by removing all potential rivals. Unlike Nasser, he decided the Americans would be more useful than the Soviets in removing the Israelis from the Sinai. In 1972, he ordered all Soviet personnel out of Egypt. The following year, on 6 October 1973, while the Israelis were observing the Jewish Holy Day of Yom Kippur, Egypt crossed the Suez Canal and invaded the Sinai. The stunned Israelis hit back and broke through Egyptian lines. Egypt's encircled 3rd Army was saved from annihilation only by American pressure on

the Israelis to desist. For the Egyptians, after so many humiliations, Sadat's bold and brilliant crossing of the Suez was in itself a victory; 6 October is now a national holiday.

As part of his pro-American stance, Sadat turned away from state socialism to win over the bourgeoisie and attract foreign investment. Loans from the International Monetary Fund were dependent on the government halting food subsidies. The people of Cairo rioted over food prices, burned nightclubs and expensive cars, symbols of the new consumer society, and chanted slogans hostile to Sadat and his high-living family.

Sadat's journey to Jerusalem in November 1977 can be seen as an act of great courage, but it was also an act of necessity. Weighed down by the country's huge population explosion (a 40 percent increase in a decade), the Egyptian economy could no longer bear the cost of the 'no-war, no-peace' with Israel. Despite the opposition of Arab nations and fundamentalists back home, the peace agreement that Sadat reached with Israel's Menahem Begin the next year was greeted by most Egyptians with great sighs of relief. The Sinai was to be retrieved and 30 years of war came to an end.

Hostility to Israel did not disappear. Israeli tourists flocked to Egypt, but few Egyptians went to Israel. The Arab League withdrew from its Cairo headquarters. Most resentful were Moslem fundamentalists. Sadat had tried to use them as a counterweight to his opponents among nostalgic Nasser supporters, but they turned against him for introducing Western materialist values and for his blind eye to high-level corruption. Peace with Israel was the last straw. In 1981, fundamentalists in the army assassinated

Sadat at a military parade. It was 6 October, anniversary of his great triumph.

His successor, Hosni Mubarak, was the air force hero of that 1973 war. After Nasser's charisma and Sadat's flamboyance, he brought to the job plain down-to-earth diligence. He remained unperturbed by aggressive Israeli attitudes until the last piece of Sinai territory was back in Egyptian hands, and quiet diplomacy won the return of the Arab League to Cairo in 1990. The next year, in exchange for committing troops to the Gulf War against Iraq, he got the USA and Gulf states to write off Egypt's debts of 13 billion dollars. He needed every cent he could get to deal with overpopulation, unemployment and declining agriculture.

Mubarak was patiently dismantling the excesses of the privileged bourgeois minority, but the Moslem fundamentalists remained his most dramatic preoccupation. People did not at first take seriously verbal attacks on Egypt's 20,000 belly-dancers for 'waging war on God and His Prophet and spreading corruption on earth'. But with their efforts to disrupt the key economic sector of tourism, the fundamentalists have shown an acute sense of political realities. In the aftermath of the 1992 Cairo earthquake, they were the first on the scene in the badly hit poor quarters, with food, medicine and blankets.

The ordinary people of Egypt have welcomed the blankets, but by nature they have always seemed to prefer moderation in their religion, coupled with hospitality towards strangers.

A s commander of the Egyptian air force, President Hosni Mubarak was a war hero in 1973 but is depicted here as a peacemaker in civilian clothes.

HISTORICAL LANDMARKS

Prehistory

30000 BC	Desertification of Sahara shrinks Egypt's fertile land to Nile Valley and oases.
12000 BC	Stone Age hunters and fishermen in Nile Valley.
3500 BC	Farmers at Faiyum oasis.

The First Pharaohs

3170 BC	Upper (southern) Egypt's King Narmer conquers Lower (northern) Egypt.
3168-3113 BC	Menes founds 1st Dynasty at Memphis.
2687-2667 BC	First pyramid built at Saqqara for Djoser, designed by Imhotep.
2606-2583 BC	Kheops (4th Dynasty) builds Great Pyramid at Giza.
2575-2550 BC	Sphinx erected for King Khephren.

Middle Kingdom

2061-2010 BC	After prolonged split, Menthuhotep II reunites Upper and Lower Egypt; capital at Thebes (Luxor).
1991-1786 BC	Power shifts back north, sun-cult reasserted at Heliopolis.
1670-1552 BC	Hyksos, cultivated Semitic warriors, rule Egypt from Delta; Biblical hero Joseph at court.

New Kingdom

1552-1524 BC	Ahmose drives out Hyksos and founds 18th Dynasty.
1504-1492 BC	Tuthmosis I extends empire north to Euphrates and south deep into Sudan.
1478-1437 BC	Queen Hatshepsut, iron lady of Thebes.
1402-1364 BC	Amenophis III, temple-builder at Thebes and Sudan.
1356-1339 BC	Akhenaten and Nefertiti create monotheistic cult at Tell El Amarna.
1339-1329 BC	Tutankhamun restores traditional cult; his the only Pharaonic treasure to survive to modern times.

Golden Age of 19th Dynasty

1291-1279 BC	Seti I, temple-builder, notably at Abydos; empire pressed by Libyans and Hittites.
1279-1212 BC	Ramses II, summit of Pharaonic power – Abu Simbel, Ramesseum, Karnak; Moses' Hebrews build royal residence in Delta.
1258 BC	Indecisive battle of Qadesh against Hittites in north Syria; Egypt forced to limit imperial power.
1240 BC	Probable date of Hebrew exodus from Delta.

The Last Pharaohs

1070 BC	Country split in two: Lower Egypt ruled from Delta, Upper Egypt from Thebes.
945 BC	Libyan dynasty in Delta.
753-663 BC	Nubians conquer Upper Egypt, driven out by Assyrians.

664-525 BC	Greek, Phoenician and Jewish merchants prosper under 26th Dynasty.
525 BC	Persian conquest led by bloodthirsty Cambyses.
521-486 BC	Penitent Darius I builds shrines at Kharga oasis and in Delta.

Greeks and Romans
332 BC	Alexander the Great conquers Egypt.
320-30 BC	Under Ptolemies, Alexandria becomes cultural capital of Mediterranean.
69-30 BC	Cleopatra seduces Julius Caesar and Mark Antony, but not Augustus.
30 BC	Egypt becomes a Roman province.
AD 1st century	Apostle Mark preaches Christianity in Alexandria.
AD 115-117	Jewish revolt ends in massacre.

Copts and Byzantines
301-313	Roman persecution of Coptic Christians.
325-373	Alexandria's patriarch, Athanasius, contests Byzantine authority.
618	Brutal Persian invasion.
628	Byzantines drive out Persians but persecute Copts.

Under Islam
639-641	Invading from Palestine, Arabs conquer Egypt.
661-750	Umayyad governors' capital at Fustat, southern edge of modern Cairo.
868-905	Ibn Tulun rules independently of Abbasid caliphs.
876	His mosque built by Coptic architect.
969-1171	Fatimid dynasty founds Cairo with Al-Azhar mosque.
1171-1193	Saladin conquers Crusaders, builds Cairo Citadel.

The Mamelukes (1250-1517)
1260-1277	After leading palace revolution, Baibars reforms administration, taxes and army.
1277-1290	Qalawun, grandest Mameluke sultan; monumental complex of mosque, hospital and school.
1400	Mamelukes give up Syria and Palestine to keep Mongols out of Egypt.
1468-1496	Qaitbay last strong ruler amid *coups d'état* and assassinations.

Ottoman Empire (1517-1805)
1517	Ottoman Turks conquer Mamelukes.
1525	Reforms of Suleiman the Magnificent.
1586-1609	Series of Mameluke revolts.
18th century	Janissary and Mameluke soldiers compete for control of Turkish *pasha*.
1798	Napoleon Bonaparte lands at Aboukir; wins Battle of Pyramids; French begin first full-scale study of ancient Egypt.
1801	Anglo-Turkish force drives out French; Rosetta Stone confiscated for British Museum.

The 19th Century

1805-1846	Mohammed Ali modernizes industry, agriculture, Egyptianizes army.
1840	Treaty of London reduces Egypt to role of supplying raw materials for European manufacturers.
1869	Suez Canal links Mediterranean and Indian Ocean.

British Protection

1882	British called in to crush 'Egypt-for-Egyptians' movement by dissident colonels.
1883-1907	Lord Evelyn 'Over-Baring' Cromer runs the show.
1902	First dam at Aswan.
1913	Parliamentary experiment of legislative assembly.
1914-1918	Declared British protectorate after Turks side with Germany in World War I.
1918-1919	*Wafd* Party's Saad Zaghlul heads independence movement.
1922-1936	Constitutional monarchy under King Fuad.
1928	Fundamentalist Moslem Brotherhood founded.
1936-1952	Reign of playboy King Farouk.
1942	Allied victory at El Alamein.

The Nasser Era

1948	Defeat in first Arab-Israeli War.
1952	Republican revolution, Nasser's 'Free Officers' make Mohammed Neguib first president.
1953	Nasser replaces Neguib.
1954	Moslem Brotherhood and other opposition parties outlawed.
1956	Suez Canal nationalized; Anglo-French-Israeli invasion curtailed by United Nations.
1958-1961	Abortive United Arab Republic with Syria.
1964	Aswan Dam opened with Soviet funds and know-how.
1967	Egyptian forces crushed by Israel in Six Day War, Sinai occupied.
1970	Nasser's death mourned by 5,000,000 in streets.

Peace and Problems

1972	Anwar Sadat expels Soviets; renounces state socialism for Western-style liberal economy.
1973	Despite defeat, October War's recapture of Suez from Israelis restores national pride.
1977-1978	Sadat's visit to Jerusalem culminates in peace treaty with Israel; Sinai retrieved.
1981	Moslem fundamentalists assassinate Sadat.
1990	Hosni Mubarak's quiet diplomacy brings Arab League back to Cairo after 12-year boycott.
1992	Devastating Cairo earthquake.
1993	Growth of fundamentalist opposition, but Mubarak re-elected.

Just the Essentials

The problem with Egypt is that it has too much to see, and you have too little time to see it all. To help you to tailor your trip to the length of your stay, we offer here our choice of the best attractions each place has to offer.

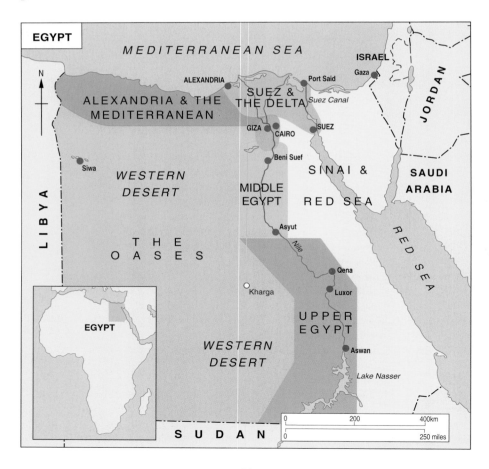

Cairo...

Egyptian Museum: the Pharaohs'
  mummies and ancient treasures
Khan El Khalili: bustling bazaar
Mosques of Sultan Hasan and Ibn Tulun:
  Islamic masterpieces
Coptic Museum and Churches: the
  Christian view

...and the Pyramids

Saqqara: the Step Pyramid, an historic
  first
Giza: Kheops' great wonder and the
  Sphinx

Middle Egypt

Beni Hasan: nobles' tombs carved from
  cliff
Tell El Amarna: Akhenaten's mystic
  capital

Upper Egypt: Luxor...

Luxor and Karnak: awesome temples
Valley of the Kings: Pharaohs' tombs in
  the desert
Abydos and Dendara: great temples of
  Seti and Hathor
Esna and Edfu: best preserved of
  Ptolemies' monuments

...and Aswan

Aswan: mighty dam and romantic island
  sanctuary of Isis
Abu Simbel: Ramses II's colossal statues
  saved from submersion

The Oases

Kharga: desert city
Dakhla: spring-watered orchards; Roman
  tombs
Farafra: cool gardens; White Desert

Alexandria...

Fort Qaitbay: on the Old Harbour
Greco-Roman Museum: memories of
  Cleopatra
Montazah: palace and beaches

...and the Mediterranean

El Alamein: Rommel's and Montgomery's tanks in desert
Sidi Abdel Rahman: relax on beach

Sinai...

Mount Sinai: Moses' mountain and St
  Catherine's monastery
Sharm El Sheikh: water sports at great
  beaches
Ras Mohammed: deep-sea diving at
  marine park

...and the Red Sea

Hurghada: resort beaches, deep-sea diving

Suez...

The Canal: strategic kingpin of Egyptian
  commerce
Ismailiya: faded charm of colonial era

...and the Delta

Tanis: poignant remains of Pharaohs'
  Delta capital
Rosetta: handsome Ottoman houses

Going Places With Something Special In Mind

All visitors to Egypt nurture their own private day-dreams about one aspect or another of this endlessly rich and various civilization, ancient and modern. We all have our own personal interests that we like to follow up wherever we go. Trace the footsteps of favourite historical characters – Ramses II, Moses, Alexander the Great, Cleopatra, Napoleon Bonaparte, even King Farouk. Alternatively, pursue hobbies, such as craftwork, birdwatching, or appreciating architecture and engineering. Even irrigation can work its fascination when we have the leisure to observe it.

Some of the routes and themes we propose here can be followed as itineraries, partially or completely. Others pinpoint on the map where the objects of interest are to be found as you travel around Egypt with these particular ideas in mind. Some spots are just chosen for the beauty of the view, a good enough reason to go there.

Besides the artistic treasures of its richly textured civilization, Egypt offers an endless source of special interests, from the simple traditional crafts of pottery to the modern engineering achievements of the Nile's hydraulic dams.

Prehistoric Origins

Tracing Egyptian settlements before the Pharaohs arrived is strictly for archaeology buffs, but they get at least a rewarding sense of the places where it all began.

1 CAIRO
Start out at the Egyptian and Geology Museums to get your bearings.

2 LAKE QARUN
Early farming and fishing communities in Faiyum oasis.

3 BADARI
Nile Stone Age settlements near Asyut.

4 KOM OMBO
Early hunting and fishing community.

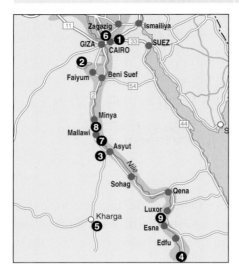

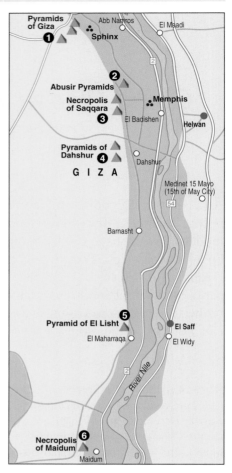

*E*gypt before the Pharaohs (1-5) and the fascinating Akhenaten, Egypt's sun king (6-9).

5 KHARGA

Prehistoric hunters at the oasis left their tools and weapons. Good for fossils.

In the Footsteps of Akhenaten

The mystic Pharaoh with his pioneering ideas on monotheism has long fascinated modern thinkers.

6 CAIRO

The Egyptian Museum is the best starting-point to study the unique artwork of the sun king.

7 TELL EL AMARNA

His capital, the town and tombs in Middle Egypt.

*T*he best of Egypt's awe-inspiring pyramids.

8 TUNA EL GEBEL

Inscribed stela on the West Bank near Ptolemaic Hermopolis, marking limits of his capital's territory.

9 LUXOR

Remains of his temple at Karnak and in the Luxor Museum from the time when he was King Amenophis IV.

The Pyramids

Getting to know more about these fantastic constructions can quickly become a hobby in itself. Archaeologists have located at least 16 sites where these gigantic tomb-complexes were built. Here are some of the best known.

1 GIZA
For the great pyramids of Kheops, Khephren and Mykerinus.

2 ABUSIR
Impressive ruins of 5th-Dynasty monuments, originally 14 in all.

3 SAQQARA
For Djoser's pioneering Step Pyramid.

4 DAHSHUR
Site of Snoferu's famous aborted Bent Pyramid.

5 EL LISHT
Two relatively late pyramid complexes from 12th Dynasty (Middle Kingdom).

6 MAIDUM
Beautiful desert setting for collapsed but still towering pyramid completed by Snoferu.

The Holy Family in Egypt

The flight to Egypt of Joseph, Mary and Jesus is traced more by tradition than chronicled history, but has created an itinerary for Christian pilgrims since the Middle Ages. The Holy Family is said to have come through the Delta via Bilbeis before shrines begin to mark their passage.

1 PELUSIUM
Their first stop: a fortified town in northwest Sinai.

2 CAIRO
The crypt in the Coptic Church of Abu Serga.

3 GEBEL EL TEIR
The monastery of the Virgin north of Minya.

4 DEIR EL MOHARRAQ
The Coptic church built over the Holy Cave near El Qusiya in Middle Egypt.

The Holy Family in flight to Egypt (1-4); travelling in grand old style (5-8); Imhotep, deified designer of the first pyramid (9-12).

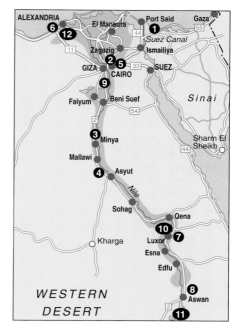

Neo-Colonial Nostalgia

Fans of Agatha Christie and old-fashioned travellers in the grand Victorian and Edwardian style can seek out their watering-holes, refurbished but still haunted by the old ghosts. Even if you cannot afford to stay at the hotels in question, it is still worth taking a drink at the bar. (For addresses *see* page 302.)

5 CAIRO
Marriott, originally a palace built to receive royalty for the opening of the Suez Canal in 1869.

6 ALEXANDRIA
Pullman Cecil, favourite haunt of Lawrence Durrell's pals from his *Alexandria Quartet*.

7 LUXOR
Winter Palace, for the old wing's splendid garden and terrace at the back or grand bar inside.

8 ASWAN
Cataract, grand dining room, wonderful garden view of the river islands.

Imhotep, the Divine Architect

The man who designed the first pyramid in Egypt, at Saqqara, was deified in following centuries for his attributed powers of healing, with shrines being constructed all around the country.

9 SAQQARA
The stage for his original triumph, Djoser's Step Pyramid.

10 THEBAN NECROPOLIS
In Queen Hatshepsut's mortuary temple near the Valley of the Kings, Imhotep was given his own shrine.

11 PHILAE
Temple for Imhotep in outer court leading to Temple of Isis.

12 ALEXANDRIA
In the Greco-Roman Museum, a seated statue of deified architect, protector of intellectuals at Alexandria's great Library.

The Exodus

Controversy continues as to exactly when Moses led the Hebrews out of Egypt and as to which route they took. This is the most commonly accepted.

1 TANIS
This vies with nearby Avaris as the site of the Pharaoh's capital Pi-Ramses from which the Hebrews departed.

2 SUEZ
Between Bitter Lakes and Suez City lies the site where the Sea of Reeds parted for Moses to lead his people to Sinai.

3 UYUN MUSA
On the Sinai coast, the spring found by Moses to quench his people's thirst.

4 WADI FARAN OASIS
The Hebrews' camp in Plain of Raha where Aaron prepared the Golden Calf.

5 MOUNT SINAI
Where Moses presented the Ten Commandments to his people. At the foot of the mountain, St Catherine's Monastery holds

the shrine of the Burning Bush where Moses had his first encounter with God.

6 TABA

The Biblical Ezion Geber across the border from Eilat, where Moses turned his people west across the Paran Wilderness (now militarily off-limits) before they entered Canaan without him.

Birdwatching by the Sea

For the birdwatching enthusiast, Egypt offers a pleasing array of feathered friends. Here are a few of the best waterside sites.

7 SUEZ BAY

Gathering spot for migrating birds of prey.

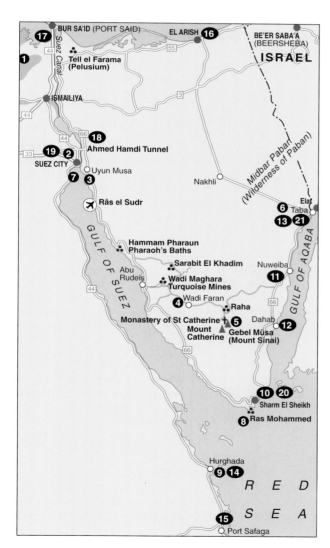

*C*atering for a variety of interests: Moses leads his people out of Egypt (1-6); seabirds to content the ornithologist (7-9); deep-sea fishing (10-15); the progress of the Arab-Israeli wars (16-21).

8 RAS MOHAMMED
Superb selection in a protected park.

9 HURGHADA
Cruise out to offshore islands for rare Red
Sea species.

Deep-sea Fishing

Deep sea fishing and lakeside angling are
both much appreciated sports by Egyptians and tourists alike.

10 SHARM EL SHEIKH
Ultramodern facilities, unique possibilities
at South Sinai confluence of gulfs of
Aqaba and Suez.

11 NUWEIBA
Quiet village resort.

12 DAHAB
Ancient fishing-port.

13 TABA
Newly developed facilities for offshore
fishing at Israeli border.

14 HURGHADA
First-rate deep-sea equipment on Red
Sea.

15 PORT SAFAGA
Fast-developing watersports Red Sea
resort.

Arab-Israeli Wars

The perennial conflicts came to an end, at
least as far as Egypt was concerned, in
1973. They left their traces throughout the
Sinai and the Suez Canal.

16 EL ARISH
Strategic Mediterranean port on route
from the Gaza Strip to Suez.

17 PORT SAID
Heavily bombarded for control of canal
zone, Military Museum gives Egyptian
version of 1973 War.

18 AHMED HAMDI TUNNEL
Monument celebrates Egypt's recapture of
Suez Canal in 1973.

19 SUEZ CITY
Canal's kingpin recovering from war ravages.

20 SHARM EL SHEIKH
Where Nasser closed Gulf of Aqaba,
motivating Israeli pre-emptive Six Day
War.

21 TABA
Last disputed piece of Sinai, returned to
Egypt in 1982.

Nubia

The proud southerners' towns and shrines
in large part reclaimed from submersion
by the Aswan High Dam.

1 KOM OMBO
Temple-town, major centre of resettled
New Nubia.

2 ASWAN
Important market for Nubian products,
Nubian shrines on Island of Philae.

3 KALABSHA
Nubian temple rescued from Lake
Nasser.

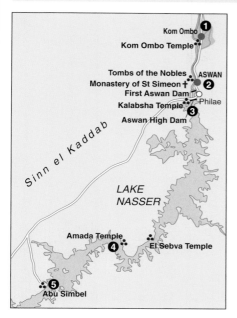

Kom Ombo ❶
Kom Ombo Temple

Tombs of the Nobles — ASWAN
Monastery of St Simeon ✝ ❷
First Aswan Dam
Kalabsha Temple — Philae
❸
Aswan High Dam

Sinn el Kaddab

LAKE
NASSER

Amada Temple
❹   El Sebva Temple

❺
Abu Simbel

*T*he reclamation of
Nubian history.

4 EL SEBUA AND AMADA
Rescued temples on the lake.

5 ABU SIMBEL
Ramses II's monument to his Nubian kingdom.

Traditional Egyptian Cuisine

They say it is an acquired taste, but a taste well worth acquiring (for addresses *see* page 307).

Cairo

ABOU SHAKRA
Downtown, popular with locals.

ARABESQUE
Chic art-gallery décor.

DAHAN
Popular with Egyptian showbiz crowd.

FALAFEL
Ramses Hilton, best among hotel restaurants.

FELAFEL GARDEN
Simple fare in oasis-like décor.

MASHRABIA
High-class Middle Eastern variety.

ZAHLE
Good nightclub fare, near Giza pyramids.

Best of the Rest

LUXOR
Khan El Khalili, at the Isis Hotel.

ASWAN
Le Club 1902, in the Cataract Hotel's grand Moorish décor.

ALEXANDRIA
El Saraya, high class cuisine; Santa Lucia, venerable institution.

ISMAILIYA
Ashur, succulent lamb, cheerful ambience.

Seafood Restaurants
One aspect of Egyptian cuisine that seems to please even the most sensitive foreign stomach is the simple grilled or pan-fried fish and seafood. Here are some of the best places to find it (for addresses *see* page 307).

CAIRO

Christo, near the Giza pyramids; Silver Fish, savoury Egyptian-style; Semiramis Grill, one of the best of the hotel fish restaurants.

LUXOR

White Corner, Isis Hotel's enjoyable riverside location.

ALEXANDRIA

Samakmak, grilled specialities; the Seagull, high-class fare; Taverna Beach, in delightful Montazah gardens.

ABOUKIR

Zephyrion, beachfront restaurant's deserved reputation for best seafood in Egypt.

HURGHADA

Sheraton Seafood restaurant.

SHARM EL SHEIKH

Fairouz Fish restaurant, Hilton's beach-front locale.

TABA

Salah El Din, great seafood facing Pharaoh's Island.

Lake Fishing

A pastime popular with Egyptians and tourists alike.

1 ISMAILIYA

Placid angling on Lake Timsah.

2 LAKE QARUN

The Pharaohs' favourite fishing grounds, excellent for angling from shore or line-fishing from boat.

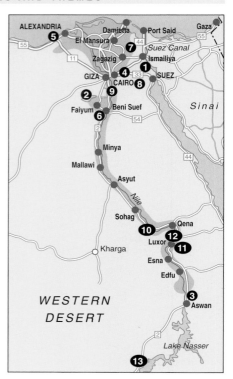

Lakeside angling (1-3); the playgrounds of King Farouk (4-6); the gall of Ramses II (7-13).

3 ASWAN

Southbound cruises for rich fisheries of Lake Nasser.

King Farouk's Egypt

The sometimes vulgar but always jolly luxury of Egyptian monarchy is on display at the fat king's favourite playgrounds.

4 CAIRO

Jewel Museum at the Citadel, and Manial Palace.

104

5 ALEXANDRIA

Montazah Palace; Jewellery Museum in Zizinia.

6 FAIYUM

Auberge du Lac, lakeside royal villa-turned-hotel.

The Colossal Pride of Ramses II

The sheer gall of the great Pharaoh is worth cataloguing as you travel around the country.

7 TANIS

Romantic desert ruins of what was probably his Delta capital, Pi-Ramses, built in part by Hebrew slaves.

8 CAIRO

Nice juxtaposition of the colossus next to Cairo Station; other oversized statues at the Egyptian Museum.

9 MEMPHIS

The giant felled, his colossus recumbent.

10 ABYDOS

Temple reliefs celebrate his would-be victory over the Hittites at Kadesh.

11 KARNAK

The great temple where the god Amun almost takes second place.

12 VALLEY OF THE KINGS

Ramesseum remains of his grand palace and temple.

13 ABU SIMBEL

The colossi rescued from watery oblivion express his ultimate self-aggrandizement.

Animal Cults

Among the fascinating aspects of ancient Egyptian religion was the spread of animal cults as decadence set in – cats, birds, baboons, crocodiles. Modern decadents can compare an impressive array of mummified animals with the royal mummies in Cairo, on display again after 15 years' away.

1 BUBASTIS

Delta shrine for the cat-goddess Bastet, with cat-cemetery.

2 MEMPHIS

Shrine for Apis bull.

*A*ncient animals (1-5) and birds to enjoy today (6-10).

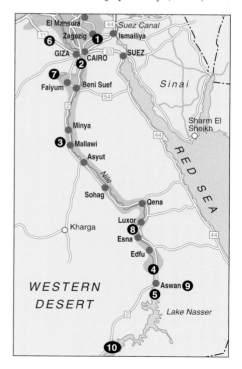

105

3 TUNA EL GEBEL

Catacombs for Toth's sacred baboons and ibis.

4 KOM OMBO

The temple houses crocodile mummies for their god Sobek.

5 ELEPHANTINE ISLAND

The temple of ram-headed Khnum, mummified rams from necropolis in museum.

Birdwatching

The variety is great: herons, storks, cranes, wild ducks, coots and terns and soaring buzzards, hawks and ospreys, and the ubiquitous Nile Valley sunbirds.

6 WADI NATRUN

Besides the monasteries, small lakes and marshes abound in birdlife.

7 LAKE QARUN

Wonderfully secluded spots in the Faiyum oasis, the Pharaohs' favourite hunting ground.

8 LUXOR

Cross to Crocodile Island to see a concentration of Nile Valley species.

9 ASWAN

Take a *felucca* out among Egypt's best heron grounds and spot vultures over the Valley of the Kings.

10 ABU SIMBEL

Southerly location ideal for African tropical birds such as pink-backed pelican and yellow-billed stork.

Islamic Cairo

Here is an itinerary to get a quick notion of Islamic culture.

1 MUSEUM OF ISLAMIC ART

For a close look at the best of the artwork.

2 IBN TULUN MOSQUE

Oldest and one of the finest.

3 SULTAN HASAN MOSQUE

A monumental masterpiece.

4 EL AZHAR

University and mosque with international prestige.

5 EASTERN CEMETERY

Fascinating City of the Dead maintaining

Islamic culture (1-5); the Ottoman Empire (6-9).

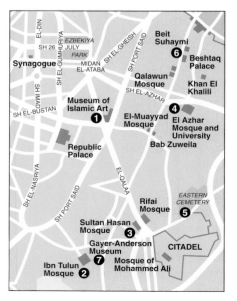

ancient rites of family visits, and houses for homeless.

The Ottoman Legacy

The Turks left most of the administration and building to their local governors, but their comfortable living style left its mark on some of the residences.

Cairo

6 BEIT SUHAYMI
Home of university dean of Turkish students.

7 GAYER-ANDERSON HOUSE
Double residence converted into a museum.

EL MAQASIS STREET (OFF MAP)
17th-century houses and Turkish bath.

And in the Delta

ROSETTA (OFF MAP)
Merchant's mansion, the Arab Keli (now a museum).

The Copts' Place in Egypt

Egypt's principal Christian church is present throughout the country, maintaining its monasteries and distinctive culture often far from the main centres of population.

1 CAIRO
The Coptic Museum and Church of Abu Serga.

2 WADI NATRUN
A grouping of four monasteries in the desert between Cairo and Alexandria.

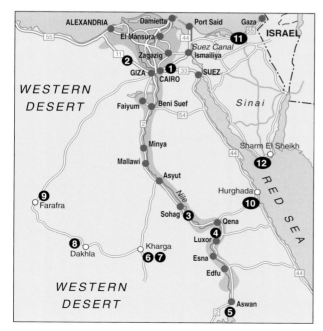

Coptic culture in Egypt (1-6); the craftwork of the Bedouin people (7-12).

3 SOHAG
Historic White and Red Monasteries.

4 THEBAN NECROPOLIS
Usurping Queen Hatshepsut's temple for their own sanctuary.

5 PHILAE
A church installed in the precincts of the Temple of Isis.

6 KHARGA
Out in the oasis at Bagawat cemetery, one of the world's earliest Christian cemeteries.

Bedouin Culture and Folk Art

The craftwork of Egypt's desert nomads still circulates, above all in Western Desert oases or the Sinai, occasionally as good copies in the towns.

7 KHARGA
Bazaar offers goods from all the oases of the New Valley region.

8 DAKHLA
Jewellery, costumes and basketware in local museum and on sale in bazaar.

9 FARAFRA
Excellent quality of rugs and basketware produced in and around oasis.

10 HURGHADA
Camel safaris to meet Bedouins of Eastern Desert.

11 EL ARISH
Sinai Heritage Museum presents superb display of Bedouin culture.

12 SHARM EL SHEIKH
Safaris organized with Bedouins in Sinai mountains.

Alexander the Great

The conquering hero stayed a short time in Egypt, but left a lasting mark. In their temples, the Ptolemies reflected his sense of the grandeur of ancient Egypt as at least the equivalent of the great Greek civilization.

ALEXANDRIA
Greco-Roman Museum, posthumous sculptures.

SIWA
Oasis Temple of Amun where Alexander consulted the oracle.

MEMPHIS
Where the priests consecrated him Egypt's divine ruler.

LUXOR
His Shrine of Sacred Barque in Temple of Amun.

World War II

With Britain's imperial stake in the Suez Canal, Egypt was a key battleground pitching Rommel's Afrika Corps against the British Eighth Army. History buffs can track down the theatre of advance and retreat.

1 SIDI BARRANI
Close to the Libyan frontier, the first domino to fall in Rommel's coastal push towards Alexandria.

The World War II battlegrounds in Egypt (1-3); the enduring appeal of a woman who can justifiably be described as Egypt's most famous queen (4-7).

2 MERSA MATRUH

Peaceful fishing port and seaside resort since Eighth Army suffered humiliating defeat before driving Rommel back here after El Alamein.

3 EL ALAMEIN

War cemeteries and museum pay eloquent tribute to brutally decisive fighting of November 1942.

Cleopatra, Queen Extraordinary

She was not *that* beautiful, as you can see from the portraits that survive of her, but she certainly fascinated her men.

4 ALEXANDRIA

Hunt down the few surviving images in the Greco-Roman Museum.

5 PELUSIUM

She made this North Sinai fortress a major defence against enemy attack, in vain.

6 MERSA MATRUH

At the foot of a cliff near the resort, Cleopatra's Baths are said to have been the queen's favourite swimming hole.

7 SIWA

Like Alexander, she consulted the oracle at the Temple of Amun, and took time off for a dip in Cleopatra's Bath, one of the oasis' famous bubbling springs.

Jews in Post-Biblical Egypt

As merchants and mercenary soldiers, Jews returned to Egypt to play a vital role under the Greeks, Romans and Moslems.

1 CAIRO

Ancient Ben Ezra Synagogue in the Coptic quarter.

2 ALEXANDRIA

Greco-Roman Museum has inscriptions and sculptural evidence of ancient Jewish Quarter at eastern edge of the old port.

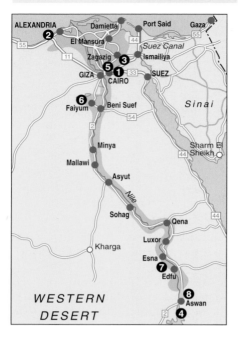

Tracing the history of the Jews in Egypt (1-4); controlling the waters of the River Nile (5-8).

3 TELL EL YAHOUDIYEH
Literally 'Mound of the Jews' with Jewish cemetery at desert's edge, a township under Ptolemies, near Bubastis.

4 ELEPHANTINE ISLAND
Evidence of 550 BC Jewish garrison under Persians, Aramaic inscriptions in island museum.

Egypt's Grand Irrigation System

Controlling the waters of its river has been an Egyptian preoccupation since the dawn of its history. The intriguing landmarks stretch the length of the Nile Valley.

5 EL QANATIR EL QAHIRYA
North of Cairo, the great barrage of Mohammed Ali at the branch of the Nile's two Rosetta and Damietta arms.

6 FAIYUM
Giant water-wheels for the irrigation of the country's largest oasis.

7 ESNA
Sandstone barrage built in 1906.

8 ASWAN
Both the old dam of 1902 and the great High Dam of 1964.

Egypt Outside Egypt

The world's fascination for the ancient Egyptian civilization has spread examples of its culture far and wide. Some of it is plundered, most of it presented in gratitude for the scholars' work of conservation. Here are some of the major museums you can consult before or after you visit Egypt itself.

Europe's Egyptian Museums

LONDON
British Museum, sculptures, mummies and the Rosetta Stone.

OXFORD
Ashmolean Museum, beautiful compact collection from its university archaeologists.

PARIS
The Louvre's splendid fruits of pioneer-

ing excavations since Napoleon Bonaparte's expedition.

TURIN
The Museo Egizio's fine sculpture, papyri and mummies.

BERLIN
Ägyptisches Museum, above all but not only for Nefertiti.

ST PETERSBURG
Hermitage has small but important collection.

Museums in the United States

NEW YORK
Metropolitan and Brooklyn Museums.

BOSTON
Museum of Fine Arts.

WASHINGTON, D.C.
Smithsonian Institute.

CLEVELAND
Museum of Art.

CHICAGO
Oriental Institute.

LOS ANGELES
County Museum of Art.

SAN FRANCISCO
M.H.De Young Memorial Museum.

Obelisks Overseas
Several obelisks have found their way around the world as landmarks of the ancient civilization.

PARIS
Surveying the crazy traffic on Place de la Concorde.

LONDON
Cleopatra's Needle watches the boats go by from the Thames Embankment.

ROME
Possibly imitation, surrounded by Bernini's Baroque fountain on Piazza Navona.

NEW YORK
Object of affection for Central Park's lovers – and others.

Boisterous Metropolis, Custodian of Ancient Treasures

It is not an easy city to visit, but to know Egypt, do not even think of sidestepping Cairo. Though a relatively late creation of the Arab conquest, all Egypt is here. The country's precious treasures are collected in Cairo's great Egyptian Museum, with the pyramids just down the road in the suburbs. Twentieth-century tumult engulfs the medieval Islamic neighbourhoods. The Nile runs through the city centre and desert sands impinge everywhere, in the air and in the buff-coloured stone of mosques and office-blocks alike.

When organizing your programme for your stay in Cairo, get your priorities clear – allocate time for shopping, for sightseeing, for just lounging around. The city's sights can conveniently be divided up according to Egypt's history: modern, ancient, Islamic and Coptic. Although for obvious geographical reasons they come at the end of the chapter, you will most probably interrupt your visit to the city to go out to the pyramids at Saqqara and

*O*verlooking Cairo from the terrace of the Citadel, this cannon never had to be fired against a foreign foe; at worst it scared away an uppity platoon of rebellious Mamelukes.

Giza, preferably *after* visiting the Egyptian Museum. Choose from the following:

The Modern City
- **Central Cairo** – around Tahrir Square
- **Gezira and Roda Islands** – Cairo-on-the-Nile
- **Heliopolis** – garden city suburb

Ancient Egypt
- **Egyptian Museum** – essential guide to Pharaonic art
- **Saqqara and Memphis** – oldest pyramids and nobles' Tombs
- **Giza** – the great pyramids and sound-and-light show

Islamic Cairo
- **The Citadel** – from Saladin to Mohammed Ali

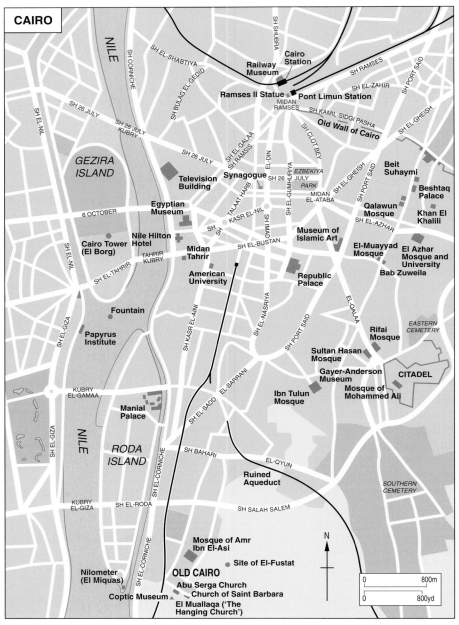

CAIRO

- **Mosques of Sultan Hasan and Ibn Tulun** – architectural masterpieces
- **Khan El Khalili bazaar** – other mosques and Ottoman houses
- **Museum of Islamic Art** – with Bab Zuweila Gate and mosques
- **Cemeteries** – Moslem tombs and shrines

Coptic Cairo
- **Coptic Museum** – and churches

We recommend the following combinations, according to how many days you have at your disposal:
- **Two days** – **1**. Central Cairo, Egyptian Museum and Saqqara Pyramids; **2**. Giza Pyramids and Khan El Khalili.
- **Three days** – add **3**. Coptic Cairo, Citadel and mosques.
- **Four days or more** – add **4**. Gezira and Roda Islands, Islamic Museum, with more time at Khan El Khalili.

Remember, if they are within your budget, personal guided tours will save time and get you more smoothly around the mosques, houses and churches. It can be easy to get lost in the narrow streets (*see* LEISURE ROUTES page 97).

T he old city's narrow streets offer welcome shade from the afternoon heat and a wonderful opportunity to get lost in the labyrinth.

Cairo

Your first view from a high floor of a hotel skyscraper or a rooftop restaurant will reveal the city's diversity. In the centre, neoclassical buildings of the colonial 19th century, crowded out by modern highrises; over in the older neighbourhoods, the domes and minarets of mosques, the cross on a belfry of a Coptic church. On the east side of town, you may see the sprawling Moslem cemeteries, vast cities of the dead whose monumental shrines now provide shelter for the unhoused poor.

When you venture out through the crowded streets, you will see clerks in light suits with short-sleeved jackets, businessmen astonishingly not perspiring in dark business suits, and corpulent merchants making stately progress in their traditional voluminous *gallabiya* robes – or sitting at a café smoking *narguileh* water pipes. Since the wine-red tarbush or fez disappeared with colonialism, the men go bare-headed or wear the Moslems' round knitted cap. Some women may be wearing long black robes from head to toe, with a veil for the more devout, but more often the married middle class wear brightly coloured, even garish dresses, with make-up to match. Younger girls wear Western fashions and, much to the disapproval of fundamentalists, favour the same T-shirts and jeans as their brothers and boyfriends.

The cacophony of the traffic is sometimes drowned out by the powerful amplifiers of heavy-beat modern Arabic music (much more popular than Western rock-and-roll) from street stalls selling cassettes. Nothing stops the stream of taxis, miraculously fixed and refixed cars, overflowing buses and trams, even an

occasional donkey and cart. Certainly not the traffic-lights, reduced to red, amber and green street-decorations. Police whistles serve more as gentle pleas to be more careful than as orders to stop or start.

And through it all flows the Nile, with its floating restaurants, cruise-boats, illuminated at night, and a few traditional tall-sailed *feluccas* to remind you of the romantic sights awaiting you in Upper Egypt. Bounded by the Eastern Desert's Moqattam Hills, the city is set in a triangle 20km (12 miles) south of the Delta with the river as its official western boundary, but in practice it is inseparable from the west-bank township of Giza.

The Town in History

In early Pharaonic times, with Memphis just to the south and the cult-city of Heliopolis to the north east, the city's east-bank site remained unsettled. The last dynasties established a fortress there, Kheri Aha, which was renamed Babylon during the invasions of the Assyrians and

Beyond the domes and minarets of the mosques and square blocks of the old houses, all in traditional buff-coloured sandstone from the Sahara, are the whitewashed offices and hotels of the modern capital.

Persians, and remained as such under the Romans. After the Arab invasion of 641, conqueror Amr ibn al-As founded the capital of Fustat, near the present-day Coptic neighbourhood of Old Cairo, but this evolved only slowly from a military garrison to a truly civilian city.

In 868, Ibn Tulun founded a city of merchant and administrative as well as military quarters. The Fatimids made it a town of royal residence, creating the nucleus of the present city in 969. Two centuries later, Saladin united all the city's quarters, to be governed from his citadel.

Islamic Cairo experienced its golden era under the Mamelukes (1250-1517), who built the city's finest mosques and palaces.

Besides a few elegant mansions, the Ottoman Turks left little architectural mark on the city. In thrall to European tastes, Mohammed Ali and his heirs gave Cairo of the 19th and early 20th century a neoclassical air. Later, Anwar Sadat encouraged American-style skyscrapers.

The population, which was 1,300,000 in 1939, had tripled by 1967 and was around 13,000,000 by 1993.

The Modern City

Before you plunge into the older neighbourhoods or make your way out to the pyramids, get your bearings around the Cairo of today. In the central downtown area, you can find the books and maps to supplement this guide, and buy the inevitable mineral water and other refreshments for your excursions.

FOR WHOM THE BELL TOLLS

For their new fortified capital, the Fatimids brought in Moroccan astrologers to calculate the most auspicious moment to begin construction. The city's square plan was marked off by a rope hung with bells, which the astrologers would ring as a signal for the builders to go to work. But a raven landed on the rope, setting off the bells and the workers before the astrologers could stop them. All the scholars could do was determine that the astral body in ascendancy at that precise moment was Mars – the warrior planet of victory, *El-Qahir*. This provided the city's name, *El-Qahira*, Cairo.

The ramparts of Saladin's Citadel were designed on the model of the great Crusader fortresses that the great sultan stormed in Palestine back in the 12th century.

Central Cairo

The bustling focus of the modern city is **Tahrir Square** with its Liberation (*Tahrir*) monument to the creation of the Republic in 1952. Surrounding the vast square are the Egyptian Museum (*see* page 119) and bus station, government ministries and the Arab League headquarters, airline offices and travel agencies on the shopping avenues fanning out to the east.

Since trips around town frequently start out from or finish up here, you should note two important landmarks as places to relax before or after a long bout of sightseeing. First of the great modern hotels to set up shop on the riverfront after World War II, the **Nile Hilton** is most convenient for museum-visitors, and has become a monument in its own right. Or at least its **terrace** facing the square has, popular with tourists and Egyptians alike for its snacks – delicious *om ali* bread pudding – and *narguileh* water pipes. South of the square, off El Qasr El Ainy Street, is the **American University** which has an excellent English-language bookshop and a pleasant quiet courtyard in which to take tea among the students.

One of the main shopping thoroughfares is the popular Tala'at Harb Street crossing Qasr El Nil, whose boutiques are a shade more chic – notice that the second language of shop- and street-signs is more often French than English. If you continue north to Adly Street, at number 17 is the 20th-century neo-Byzantine **synagogue**, one of the last in Egypt still functioning, though even on a Sabbath there are usually more police-guards outside than Jews inside.

Ezbekiya Park

Adly and Qasr El Nil both lead to the park that was until recently the town's most

*O*n Tahrir Square, the billboards of American capitalism have replaced the slogans of Soviet influence in quenching Cairo's thirst for modernity.

fashionable area – a pilgrimage for nostalgics. In the 19th century, Mohammed Ali laid out formal gardens of exotic African and oriental trees. Where once the medieval emir Ezbek had his palace, the *pashas* built their pavilions, and European and American visitors flocked to the famous Shepheard's Hotel. Erected for the opening of the Suez Canal, the park's opera house hosted the première of Verdi's *Aïda*. The Shepheard's was burned down in the anti-British riots of 1952, and an accidental fire in 1971 destroyed the opera house, which is now a car park. Today, Ezbekiya's dusty gardens are bordered by a raucous market for Islamic literature, music-cassettes, cheap jewellery and trinkets. The cosmopolitan focus has moved with the luxury hotels – including a new Shepheard's Hotel – to the banks of the Nile.

Ramses Square

Even if you are not taking a train, make the trip north to the **Central Station** to see the eloquent juxtaposition of this monument of the modern industrial age with the colossal **statue of Ramses II** created more than 3,000 years earlier. The pink granite sculpture, 9.7m (32ft) high, was brought here from Memphis in 1955. The station was founded in 1851; its first tracks, to Alexandria, were built by Robert Stephenson, the son of George Stephenson who invented the first railway steam-engine. At the north end of the station, the **Railway Museum** tells the story of Egypt's trains with models of tracks, bridges, stations and engines in their 19th-century golden age. Highlights are Saïd Pasha's maroon and gold lacquered engine, and a model of the luxury wagons and saloon cars designed for Ismail and his harem.

Egyptian Museum

On the north side of Tahrir Square, the somewhat ponderous sandstone neoclassical building was opened in 1902. Originally called the Cairo Museum it has since become recognized as one of the greatest museums in the world. In the forecourt where visitors line up for tickets, ancient statues which would be prized protected treasures elsewhere in the world

are exposed to set the tone. After all, the museum collections number upwards of 100,000 objects, only a tiny fragment of which can be exhibited at any one time.

Remember, if you can plan it that way, the best time to visit the museum is usually midday, when most people are having lunch. Beyond the souvenir and bookshops in the lobby, the exhibits are displayed on the ground floor in chronological order, to enable you to follow the evolution of Egyptian civilization. The treasures of Tutankhamun and the Mummy Room are on the upper floor.

For a two-hour visit, follow the galleries left at the main entrance in clockwise fashion, from the Old Kingdom's first dynasties (Hall 47) to the New Kingdom at the north end of the west wing. Then go upstairs to the Mummy Room, at the front, and Tutankhamun treasures in the north and east galleries. Those with the time and stamina for a longer visit can complete the ground floor circuit – the west and east wings and the central hall – before going upstairs. (To

MOVING AROUND

Our account of the collections describes their situation at the time of going to press, but you should bear in mind that the museum makes constant changes, with major ongoing reorganization. Works are lent to its sister museum in Luxor, as well as to other Egyptian collections around the world. It is planned to house the Tutankhamun treasures in a separate building. Other works may be moved to museums in the area of their original sites. After 15 years of off-limits 'hibernation' mummies of the pharaohs are back on display.

avoid confusion, our descriptions for a two-hour tour locate ground-floor exhibits by *gallery* and upstairs exhibits by *room*. Dates are all BC and approximate.)

Ground Floor

Entrance Hall: This is protected by later colossal statues of Ramses II. The **Narmer Palette** (3170) depicts the original unification of Upper and Lower Egypt by a predecessor (or perhaps founder) of the 1st Dynasty. Turn left to the west wing.

Gallery 47: The Old Kingdom stone **sarcophagi** which contained mummies were conceived as miniature palaces for the deceased, hence the motifs of buildings' façades on their sides. Three **Mykerinus Triads** (2500) portray with finely modelled detail the lithe and athletic Pharaoh and Giza pyramid-builder, flanked by the goddess Hathor and the emblematic spirit of one of 40 Egyptian provinces.

Gallery 46: A dignified enthroned statue in painted limestone, of **King Djoser**, builder of the first pyramid at Saqqara.

Gallery 42: A vivid series of statues in stone and wood show scribes, a beer-brewer, a cook roasting a goose, and a remarkably lifelike tubby priest. There is also a magnificent statue in black diorite of the enthroned **King Khephren** protected by divine falcon (2540).

Gallery 31: A carved wooden **Hesiré panel** (2700) of a court official serving as scribe, architect and dentist, shows the characteristic feature of Pharaonic art in which each part of the body is displayed to best advantage – the head in profile, the chest frontal, and so on (*see* ART AND ARCHITECTURE IN ANCIENT EGYPT page 174).

Gallery 32: Seated statues of **Rahotep** and **Nefert** (2620), the Heliopolis high priest and his wife. Their lifelike stare frightened archaeologists' diggers away when uncovering painted limestone sculpture at Maidum. Hieroglyphs on the sculptural group of **dwarf Seneb and family** (2475) show that diminutive size was no social handicap. Cross-legged to conceal deformity, this wealthy royal wardrobe master owned several thousand head of cattle. The children are typically stylized with fingers in their mouths. A mural painting of **Maidum Geese** (2620) is intricately detailed, each pair different.

Gallery 22: The mass-produced statues of **Sesostris I** (1950), from the Middle Kingdom.

Gallery 16: The Middle Kingdom grey granite **sphinx of Amenemhet III** (1800).

Gallery 11: The New Kingdom **sphinx of Queen Hatshepsut** (1450); and a green basalt sculpture of her nephew **Tuthmosis III** (1440), which clearly portrays the conqueror's prominent nose and confident smile.

Gallery 12: Amongst the items are a white marble kneeling statue of **Tuthmosis III** (1440); handsome grey granite cross-legged statues of Amenophis III's architect-scribe, **Amenhotep** (1365), which show him in youth, with folds of flesh depicting wisdom, and elderly, with a firmer belly but no less sage; the **Chapel of the Goddess Hathor** (1430) with a sandstone statue of the cow-goddess protecting Amenophis II; and a beautiful fragmentary head of **Queen Hatshepsut** (1450).

Gallery 7: A kneeling granite colossus of **Queen Hatshepsut as male** (1450) with a false beard; and her **sphinx**, destroyed by her nephew Tuthmosis III and reconstructed from 100 pieces found in the quarry.

Gallery 3 (north alcove): Exaggeratedly realistic **sculpture and friezes of Akhenaten** from Karnak and Tell El Amarna (1360-1365); also sandstone **colossi of Akhenaten** (1365), showing the human imperfections of the prophet, not a god; a brown quartzite head of **Nefertiti**; and an intimate sculpture of **Akhenaten kissing daughter**.

Upper Floor

With the aid of sophisticated technology, European, American and Egyptian scientists have collaborated in the preservation of a couple of dozen royal mummies in the museum's possession. Among the embalmed bodies on display in special climate controlled cases are those of Ramses II, Tuthmosis III, Ramses III and Merneptah.

Treasure of Tutankhamun (1347-1337)
Lord Carnarvon's man, Howard Carter, found 2,099 pieces of treasure in Tutankhamun's tomb (*see* TUT'S LUCK page 190). A few are on show at the Luxor Museum, but the most precious art-works are here in the upstairs north hall and east wing.

North Hall Rooms 7 and 8: These contain four giant wooden **burial chambers**, each functioning, one inside the other, with gilded and blue faïence scenes of the Egyptian afterlife; also royal ceremonial and hunting **chariots** of wood and gilt stucco inlaid with coloured glass.

Room 9: On a gilded wooden 'sledge' is a wooden **canopic shrine** containing a **canopic chest**, in the form of an alabaster chapel protectively embraced by four goddesses. (The chest's miniature coffins for the royal viscera are in Room 4.)

BURYING KING TUT

Nothing was more carefully packaged than a dead Pharaoh. The mummified corpse of King Tutankhamun, aged 19, was found in a grand gold coffin (in Room 4) encased by two larger gilded wooden coffins decorated with coloured glass and semi-precious stones. These three mummiform coffins were themselves placed inside a rectangular quartzite sarcophagus with a red granite lid. (The sarcophagus has been returned, with one of the gilded wooden outer coffins and the mummy, to the tomb in the Valley of the Kings.) The royal viscera – the heart, liver, kidneys, etc. – were stored separately, in four miniature ornate gold coffins placed in cavities inside an alabaster 'canopic chest', itself encased in a wooden canopic shrine. The whole glorious kit and caboodle then went into the innermost of the four gilded wooden burial chambers.

Room 4: In this room are displayed the most spectacular treasures: a mummiform **golden coffin**, weighing 204kg (450lbs), of hammered gold with incised decoration inside and out in the form of a mummified Osiris clasping the holy insignia of a hooked sceptre and flail; a **gold mask** which protected the head of the mummy, on its forehead the sacred cobra and vulture, with a superb cloisonné glass-and-gold plaited beard; **gold sandals**, **gloves**, jewelled **diadems**, **perfume boxes**, and four **miniature coffins** for Tut's guts complete the collection.

East Wing Rooms 15–45: Exhibits include the sculpted head of **Tutankhamun as a child**; and the furniture and paraphernalia of his daily life in the afterworld – **beds** in ebony and wood, carved alabaster **lamps** and **walking sticks**; copper **trumpets**; and an ivory and ebony **gaming table**, with pieces in the drawer, for the popular ancient game of *Senet*.

Gezira and Roda Islands

Escape the downtown bustle by travelling to Gezira with its sporting clubs, parks and the **Cairo Tower** (*El Borg*). Cool off with a drink in the pretty tea-garden at the tower's base and then whisk 182m (600ft) to the top for a marvellous view from the observation deck. There is a snack bar on the floor below. More chic, but more expensive, places to relax are the café terraces of the Gezira Sheraton and Marriott hotels, the latter built round an old royal palace.

At the north end of **Roda Island,** which is slightly smaller than Gezira, is **Manial Palace**, which has been a museum since the fall of the monarchy. Its pavilions and salons are filled with the luxuries and curiosities of royal daily life, from lustrous Turkish tiles and carpets to sparkling jewels and chandeliers. With its beautiful gardens, the Manial Palace complex is a pleasant refuge from the noise and dust of the city. Its ancient walls now shelter the Club Méditerranée's hotel, which serves open-air buffet meals.

*E*very metropolis these days has its landmark tower, but Cairo Tower, also known as El Borg, looks more like a minaret than the outsize radio antennae favoured in Europe.

At the island's southern tip is Cairo's **Nilometer** (*El Miqyas*), set up in the year 715 to give a clear indication of when the river would be at full flood. Now, the Aswan High Dam's control of the Nile's waters has made the Nilometer obsolete.

Heliopolis

On the north-east outskirts of Cairo, on the way to the airport, you may be curious to visit the suburb which the Belgian steel magnate Baron Edouard Empain built in 1906 on the model of British experimental garden cities. Named after the ancient cult-city (located further north), it was conceived not just as a colony for the bourgeoisie, but as a neighbourhood for the workers on the tramway the baron was constructing for the city. Instead, its villas, in neo-Moorish and every other variation of Arabic architecture, soon became a choice residential area for well-to-do Turks, Lebanese, Syrians, Jews, British and French inhabitants. A few of the finer houses survive, with pleasant gardens of eucalyptus, mimosa and magnolia. Its slightly higher altitude gives it a more comfortable climate than the city centre, and it still attracts the more prosperous Egyptians. On the south side of the El Uruba Boulevard is the bizarre and sadly neglected **Baron Empain's residence** in the style of a Hindu temple.

Islamic Cairo

To get your bearings in the mosques and other religious edifices you will visit, it is worth taking a look at our essay on ISLAM IN EGYPT (page 124). In particular, the sections on *salat* prayers and religious architecture in general explain the function and placement of various features in the mosque. The **Citadel** will provide an overview, both of the political and military past, and quite literally with its panorama of the old city. The great **Mosques** and the **Islamic Museum** present Islam's religious and artistic dimensions, while **Khan El Khalili** bazaar, the **Gayer-Anderson Museum** and other houses, and the fascinating **cemeteries** will give you a vivid insight into everyday life, past and present. **Tip**: Rather than go barefoot when you have removed your shoes for the mosque, 'borrow' a couple of the hotel's throwaway plastic shower-hats – they make ideal slippers.

The Citadel

East of the city centre, the Citadel can be reached adventurously by bus, No. 82, or more sedately by taxi. The main entrance is on the south-east side, at the car park in front of Moqattam Tower. The fortress that Saladin erected in 1176 – without ever living there himself – stands on a limestone outcropping of the Moqattam Hills. It is only 75m (250ft) above sea level, but high enough in the desert plain to command a strategic position against enemy attack. Crusader prisoners built the ramparts. It never faced foreign attack, but centuries later it was subjected to fire by Mameluke rebel artillery from the roof of the great Sultan Hasan mosque (*see* page 133). It was last used as a military base by the British in World War II.

Originally, an inner wall separated the ruler's residence in an enclosure in the south from military and civilian quarters in the north.

From the Moqattam Tower entrance, make your way left to the 14th-century **Mosque of El Nasir** with pointed-arch

Islam in Egypt

Islam in its Egyptian form is the sum of all its history, ancient, medieval and modern. It is coloured not only by the Arab conquerors who brought it in the first place in 641, then by the Mameluke, Ottoman and Egyptian nationalist rulers who followed, but even by the persistent spirit of the ancient Pharaonic civilization. Family visits to the Moslem cemetery with food and other offerings to honour the deceased trace their origin to ancient customs at Saqqara and Thebes.

In Arabic, *Islam* means 'at peace with' or 'submission to' God. *Moslem*, from the same root, is 'one who submits'

The classical Arabic as spoken at the time of the conquest is enshrined in the holy books on sale around Cairo's Esbekiya Gardens, but it has been written in its present form only since the 12th century.

totally to the rule of God – *Allah* – over every aspect of secular and religious life. Any visitor to Egypt can sense this when making an appointment, hoping to prolong a room reservation or asking whether a flight will leave on time, and getting the response: *Inch'Allah* – 'God willing'.

The religion follows the Koranic reinterpretation of the Old and New Testaments by Mohammed, God's last and thus definitive prophet. The Islamic canon recognizes the prophetic roles of Adam, Noah, Abraham (*Ibrahim*, father of the faithful, the first Moslem) and Moses (*Musa*). The patriarchs were respected for passing on the word of God – in Arabic, *Allah* – to the best of their fallible abilities, but lacking the direct revelation accorded to Mohammed. Jesus, too, is acknowledged for his teachings, but not as the Son of God. Islam (like Judaism) denies the concept of divinity to any but God alone, the idea of a Trinity being an unacceptable blasphemy.

The Prophet

Mohammed (Arabic for 'praised') was born in Mecca in AD 570, but his father died soon after his birth and he was raised in the wealthy family of his uncle, Abu Tahib. At 24, he married Khadijah, a widow 15 years his senior. Of their six children, only his daughter Fatima married to give him grandchildren. As a 40-year-old prosperous merchant, Mohammed was troubled by the immoral ways of Mecca's dominant Quraish tribe of idol-worshippers. Meditating in a mountain cave north of town, he had a vision of the Angel Gabriel teaching him the oneness of Allah and the vital need to destroy the idols of Arabia.

Over the next 12 years, prompted by more such revelations, he gathered a small band of followers, but alienated his fellow townsmen with his threat to their highly lucrative pagan cult. The danger of murder drove him from Mecca, and it is the year of his flight – *Hejira* – to found the city of Medina in 622 from which Islam dates its foundation. At Medina, he organized his theocratic state, soon strong enough in conversions among idol-worshippers to conquer the men of Mecca. By 630, he was able to take control of Mecca's sacred Kaaba shrine, destroying the 360 idols placed there by the Quraish and claiming it for the Moslems as the stone of Abraham's covenant with God, focus ever after of the holy *Hajj* pilgrimage. The way was open now, urged on by a message from the Angel Gabriel, to carry Islam beyond Arabia's borders on a universal mission.

In 632, at the age of 62, Mohammed died while planning the *Jihad* (Holy War) against the infidels. Over the next ten years, his successors (caliphs or 'followers') conquered the Persian empire to the east and the Byzantine lands of Syria, Palestine and Egypt. Among the first caliphs, Mohammed's cousin Ali was contested by the orthodox *Sunni* Moslems. As husband of Mohammed's daughter Fatima and thus father of the Prophet's only descendants, Ali was regarded by his followers as Allah's viceregent. Their extremist, schismatic position earned them the name of Shi'ites (sectarians). In Egypt, the Fatimids of the 10th century were such Shi'ites.

The Faith

Able neither to read nor write, Mohammed passed on his teachings orally. In their collected form, they were known as the *Koran*, 'recitation'. It was Caliph Umar ibn Al-Khattab (634-644) who ordered the Prophet's disciples to compile the teachings in book form. The Koran was completed under Caliph Uthman in 651 and has not been altered since. It is divided into 114 chapters or *sura*, each with a heading identifying whether it derived from a revelation in Mecca or Medina.

The Koran speaks of Allah as unique, infinite, eternal, all-knowing and all-powerful, a just god, awe-inspiring, but loving and merciful. All destiny is determined by the will of Allah and it is a sin to imagine otherwise. Life after death, whether in heaven or hell, is determined by the actions of men and women during their lives on earth.

The Moslems' place in paradise is determined by their observance of the **Five Pillars of Faith**:

● **Shahada**: The affirmation that 'There is no god but Allah, and Mohammed is His Prophet.'

● **Salat**: Prayers five times a day – at dawn, midday, late afternoon, sunset, and after dark – facing Mecca. The call to prayer is made by a *muezzin* from atop a minaret, nowadays an electronically amplified cassette. The call begins: *Allahu akbar*, 'God is great,' except

Devout Moslems will stop whatever they are doing, in the streets, at the airport or in railway stations, for their daily prayers, bowing in the direction of Mecca.

for the dawn call which begins: *Al-salatu khayrun min al-nawm*: 'Prayer is better than sleep'. In the mosque, prayers are led by an *imam*, a man versed in theology rather than a priest as such, since Islam has no formal clergy. Mecca's precisely calculated direction (*qibla*) is indicated by the mosque's *mihrab* (prayer niche), and elsewhere – in hotel rooms, for example – often by an arrow.

After ritual washing, with covered head and shoes removed, the worshipper kneels on a prayer mat to recite the brief opening chapter of the Koran. He stands for a prayer of praise to Allah, kneels again to bow down with forehead touching the floor, sits back on his heels and bows again to conclude the prayer cycle – *raka*. Depending on the time of day, the complete sequence of prayers consists of two, three or four such *raka*. Friday prayers in the mosque include a sermon by the imam. (Women pray in a separate area of the mosque.)

● **Zakat**: Alms to the poor, gifts to the mosque, calculated as a percentage of annual income.

● **Sawm**: Fasting and strict abstinence in all matters from sunrise to sunset during the month of Ramadan. The fast celebrates the anniversary of Mohammed's first revelation in the ninth month of the Islamic year. Because of the lunar calendar, the date has no fixed season, moving forward annually about 10 days through the Christian calendar year. Soldiers and the sick are exempted. Because of the fast, each evening meal during Ramadan takes on a particularly cheerful air, culminating with a veritable feast at the end.

● **Hajj**: Pilgrimage to Mecca at least once in a lifetime. This holiest of all Moslem deeds constitutes Islam's great act of unification, bringing together with the Arab world the faithful of Asia and Africa. The rites include a procession seven times around the Kaaba shrine and an assembly on the plain of Mount Arafat where Mohammed preached his last sermon.

At the Museum of Islamic Art, you can see how strict observance of Koranic law forbidding portrayal of humans or animals stimulated the decorative talent of the artists.

The Law

Without enforcing all the strict demands of *Sharia* (Islamic law) such as amputating the hands of robbers or stoning adulterers, republican Egypt from Nasser to Mubarak has attempted a delicate and sometimes fragile balance between Islamic custom and the demands of a modern secular state. In Islam, the supreme source of customary law is the Koran, which covers all aspects of religious and secular everyday life. In addition to injunctions against wine, pork, gambling, usury, fraud, slander, blasphemy and the making of images, it regulates the way to greet each other, to wash, and to eat. The Koran determines procedure in marriage, divorce, inheritance and commercial transactions, as well as laying down punishment for transgressions of civil and religious law. The second authority is *Sunna*, the recorded actions of Mohammed himself, supplemented by the authority of *Ijma*, the accumulated consensus of Moslem scholars, the *ulema*.

Islamic Art

The art and architecture of the largely nomadic Arab invaders were heavily influenced by Copts, Byzantines, Persians and Romans, with a specifically Islamic grace and sensibility.

In compensating for the images of men and beasts denied them by their religion, Islamic artists found an ornate aesthetic in floral motifs, but above all in the script of their language. Egypt was a major centre of the noble art of calligraphy. From the 8th to the 10th century, it developed the soberly elegant angular Kufic script. The black ink and gold leaf lettering was used for writing the Koran down on parchment, but also inlaid in metal, woven into textiles or inscribed on ceramics and stone walls. By the 12th century, the gentler, more cursive *Naskhi* script was introduced for commercial use, both handwritten and printed, and became the universally accepted form that we know today.

Calligraphy's florid line, consecrated in world art as 'arabesque', characterized work in wood and stone. In domestic ornament and furniture, the constraint on figurative art is occasionally breached in Fatimid carvings of animals, birds, antelopes and rabbits in the 11th and 12th centuries. The preferred motifs, particular in the decoration of mosques, remain flowers, plants and trees or abstract geometric designs. For the *minbar* pulpit in the mosque and domestic *mashrabiya* shutters, 13th-century Ayyubid woodcarvers created lattices made up of intricate polygonal panels inlaid with ivory, mother-of-pearl or ebony. Mameluke artists excelled in elaborate stone carving in Arabic lettering and floral motifs. The same ornate styles permeate the crafts of silk, gold, engraved copper, brass and glassware.

Domestic Architecture

Traditional domestic architecture, still visible around Cairo's Khan El Khalili, has developed the Syrian-style covered courtyard with a skylight and perhaps a sunken fountain at the centre, flanked by two halls, one for the men and their guests, the other for the women's harem. They might have several storeys for a living room, prayer-chapel, dining room with kitchen, bathrooms and store rooms. A common feature is an alcove with seats overlooking the courtyard. Windows have beautifully carved *mashrabiya* wooden latticed shutters to keep out the hot sun, but above all to preserve the modesty of the women. Decorative on the inner courtyard, the houses present to the street a more austere front relieved only by a balcony-like *mashrabiya* mounted on corbels. A hooded roof-ventilator facing north to catch cool breezes was a feature already present in ancient Egyptian houses.

Religious Architecture

After St John's Church in Damascus was converted to a mosque during the 7th-century invasion, the *muezzin* mounted its towers to call the faithful to prayer. This was the origin of the minaret. The characteristic layout of a mosque centres on a rectangular central courtyard, *sahn*, usually with a fountain in the centre for ritual ablutions. Open halls for prayer lead off all four sides, with a main prayer hall oriented towards Mecca. In the middle of its wall, a decorative domed or pointed-arched *mihrab* niche indicates the exact direction in which to pray. Just in front or slightly to one side is the *minbar* pulpit, often ornately carved, from which the Friday sermon is read. Beyond that is the *dikka*, a raised platform where an imam leads the congregation's prayers.

Egyptian architects took their inspiration from other centres of Islam – Persia, Iraq, Morocco or Turkey – while adding, particularly under the Mamelukes, a specifically national touch. The oldest standing mosque is that of Ibn Tulun (876), built in Baghdad style with a vast courtyard of pointed-arch arcades, baked-brick walls with wood

Up in that mashrabiya *balcony, the wives and daughters of strict Islamic families can watch the world go by without the slightest risk or opportunity of being seen.*

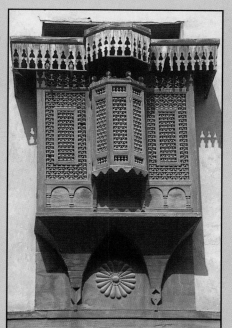

The stone and bronze ornament at the Egyptian monarchy's Manial Palace displays the intricate craftsmanship of the great Islamic tradition.

At the Islamic cemetery of Tineida, the baked-brick tombs take the form of tiny 'fortified' houses or, for the village headman, a sheikh's mosque-like shrine.

and stucco decoration. The great mosque Al-Azhar (970) is noteworthy for the prayer hall's three domes and granite pillars taken from Pharaonic temples. In the Fatimids' Moroccan-style Al-Hakim mosque (970), the monumental porch emphasizes the more generalized use of stone, as do the two minarets flanking the north-western façade.

As part of his campaign to counter the Shi'ite influence of the Fatimids, Saladin introduced *madrasa*, theological colleges which were built like enlarged versions of the domestic residence, practically twinned houses with a double courtyard. The *madrasa* was often directly adjacent to the *sahn* courtyard. In the 13th century, his Ayyubid successors added a peculiarly Egyptian feature by building their domed mausoleum adjoining the mosque. Like those of the Pharaohs, the mausoleum was an ambitious affair that had to be started during the sultan's lifetime.

Reflecting their adventurous temperament, the Mamelukes brought in a bold new style of mosque: taller, three-tiered minarets in square, octagonal and cylindrical sections. From simple ribbed brick domes, they introduced carved stone chevron patterns, evolving by the 15th century into even more intricate geometric and arabesque motifs. In the interior, these domes were supported by elaborate clusters of stalactite stone squinches. Resuming the grand tradition of the Pharaonic artisans of Saqqara, Giza and Thebes, the Mamelukes' highly skilled stone masons were snapped up by the Ottoman Turks and taken back to work in Istanbul.

Under this talent-drain and the subsequent indolence of Ottoman rule, Egyptian architecture went into decline. The 19th century was totally lacking in real creativity. Mohammed Ali's mosque is imposing in dimension but architecturally an uninspired copy from Istanbul. The mosques and palaces of his heirs showed too much deference to European baroque and *nouveau riche* bourgeois extravagance.

*W*hatever some tour-guides may tell you, Joseph's Well in the Citadel has nothing to do with the Biblical Joseph. It was dug for Saladin around 1170.

windows in its exterior walls. It has two fine Persian-style minarets. The somewhat sober interior has borrowed marble pillars and capitals from Roman and Greek temples around the *sahn* courtyard. In the main prayer-hall to the south east, Pharaonic red-granite columns support the dome of the *mihrab* niche facing Mecca.

Just south of the mosque, **Joseph's Well** (*Bir Yusuf*) refers not to the Hebrew prophet but to Saladin, one of whose first names was Yusuf. Dug in the 1170s by Crusader prisoners, and still operational in the 19th century, it runs 87m (285ft) deep through bedrock to subsoil water. Stairs spiral around the inner wall, designed for oxen or donkeys to descend and operate the water-raising mechanism.

The **Mohammed Ali Mosque** was inaugurated under his heir Saïd Pasha in 1857. The classical Turkish nest of domes and slender minarets recalls Istanbul's Yeni mosque, itself inspired by the Byzantine church of Hagia Sophia. Its interior's gigantic bombast, with the vast dome and garish stained glass, evokes the extravagant character of Mohammed Ali himself. His white marble tomb is behind a bronze grill by the prayer-hall entrance. Set in the tower above the forecourt's north-west colonnade is the **French clock** which King Louis-Philippe fobbed off on the Egyptians in exchange for the great obelisk from Luxor now in Place de la Concorde, Paris.

The **terrace** behind the mosque offers a grand panorama of the city. On the clearest days, you can see the pyramids of Giza to the south.

Egypt has been the theatre of armoured conflict throughout the 20th century, as testified by these vehicles at the Citadel's Military Museum.

Mosque of Sultan Hasan

Located at the north end of Salah El Din (Saladin) Square by the north-west corner of the Citadel, the mosque (1356-1360) incorporates the sultan's mausoleum and four *madrasas* (colleges), each devoted to a separate tradition of theology. It is an acknowledged masterpiece of Arabic architecture and one of Islam's largest mosques. A veritable fortress from which cannons on the roof could fire on the Citadel, it was seen as a threat to subsequent sultans, who dismantled some of its parts.

The mosque's majestic dome, minarets and grand portal were deliberately (and perhaps provocatively) built to be visible from the Citadel's palace, but its other façades are sober and simple. The great dome of the mausoleum is flanked by a superb **minaret**, the tallest in Cairo – 86m (282ft) high – the only survivor of four such towers originally planned. Rising

HARD TIMES FOR HASAN

You won't find Hasan buried in his mausoleum. He disappeared in one of those classic Mameluke palace intrigues. Freckle-faced and red-haired, he was only 12 when the emirs chose him as their next sultan. They kept him practically under house-arrest until he took real power six years later, in 1354. With the taste he had acquired for study, he added four *madrasa* schools to the plans for his mosque. The insecurity of those years prompted him to replace the military-minded emirs with civilians and to turn the mosque into a massive fortress. All to no avail. He was imprisoned by a rebel military emir and never heard of again, probably murdered in Damascus.

*T*he great Mosque of Sultan Hasan enjoys a prestige in Islamic architecture similar to the great Gothic cathedrals of France or the Baroque churches of Italy.

above the rectangular base, two octagonal sections each have elegant cornices with stalactite decoration, topped by an airy pavilion from which the muezzin called the faithful to prayer. The other, smaller, minaret was added during the mosque's many restorations.

Entrance to the mosque is at the north-east corner, off El Qalaa Street. Beyond the domed vestibule, a corridor leads from a second vestibule to the *sahn* courtyard. The fountain in the centre has a wood and stucco domed canopy over marble pillars. Along the wall in the main prayer-hall to the east, Koranic *surat* (verses) are inscribed in angular Kufic letters on arabesque motifs. In the pointed-arched *mihrab* niche facing Mecca, notice the fine marble marquetry. The white marble *minbar* pulpit has a remarkable bronze-plated door. To the right of the *minbar*, a door leads to **Hasan's tomb** (without the body), where two of his sons lie buried, beneath a roof with characteristic wooden stalactite squinches to carry the round dome on its square base.

Next to the Sultan Hasan mosque is the huge **Al-Rifai Mosque**, completed in 1911, of imposing size but no particular architectural distinction. It is notable as the last resting-place of kings Fuad and Farouk and the Shah of Iran.

Mosque of Ibn Tulun

Those visiting this mosque separately from the Sultan Hasan (rather than making the very pleasant 30-minute walk) should ask the driver for Sayeda Zeinab Square and walk in from there.

Built 876-879, the Ibn Tulun is the oldest mosque in Cairo to survive intact. Inspired by the Samarra mosques of the ruler's youth, but entrusted to a Coptic architect, it is also one of the city's finest. The outer walls are notable for their graceful stucco decoration and elegant pierced **crenellations** with a 'paper doll' pattern believed to fend off the evil eye. The vast open *sahn* courtyard is 92m (300ft) square and surrounded by roofed porticoes with a frieze of floral medallions and pointed arches, each enhanced by delicate arabesque tracery. A unique feature is the *ziyada* outer courtyard on three sides of the *sahn*, perhaps where Ibn Tulun's cavalry tethered their horses while praying in the mosque. Koranic inscriptions run

completely around the 2km (1.25 miles) long mosque walls, carved in sycamore wood beams, which tradition has Ibn Tulun bringing from Noah's Ark on Mount Ararat in Turkey.

A classical feature of Samarra architecture, Ibn Tulun's **minaret** was rebuilt in 1296 in its original form – an external spiral staircase up to a two-storeyed octagonal kiosk under a ribbed dome. Climb up for a grand view of Islamic Cairo from the top.

In the main prayer-hall, Mameluke Sultan Lagin (who rebuilt the minaret and the central courtyard's domed fountain house) produced a true masterpiece in the *minbar* pulpit with its ornately carved cedarwood *mashrabiya* panels, inlaid with marble and gold, and intricate stalactite canopy. The double-arched *mihrab* niche facing Mecca has handsome marble and glass mosaic work. On its marble columns, the basketware and grapevine motifs of the capitals are a personal touch of Ibn Tulun's Coptic architect.

Gayer-Anderson Museum

On Ibn Tulun Street at the east corner of the mosque, adjacent to the main prayer-hall, this museum is in fact two 16th- and 17th-century houses joined together by a bridge on the upper floor. The residence was bought in 1934 by Major Robert Gayer-Anderson, a British doctor and civil servant. He restored and refurbished it with Ottoman ornaments and furniture collected from various old Cairo houses and palaces, all with a markedly Mameluke influence. The result is a first-class introduction to the atmosphere of a typical mansion of the traditional Egyptian ruling class – with a few Moghul and Chinese treasures reflecting the Major's personal taste.

The **inner courtyard** is remarkably peaceful, with its marble stalactite decoration, carved stone windows, and arcaded upper gallery which served as a summer terrace. The iron and wooden *mashrabiya* (latticed alcove) has a Syrian-style coffered ceiling. Enter the house through the **winter living room**. Notice the mother-of-pearl tarbush hat-stand and alabaster coffee table with a Koranic inscription around the edge. As you pass into the *haramlik* (women's quarters), you get a feel for the secluded atmosphere provided by the *mashrabiya* latticed alcove, from which the women could see without being seen. A pair of **wedding thrones** has bellows on the bride's footrest to dry the ceremonial henna dye on her foot soles. In the **roof-garden**, used for summer dining, the shadow cast on the marble by the *mashrabiya* latticework spells out the *shahada* prayer: 'There is no god but Allah, and Mohammed is His Prophet.' The *salamlik* men's reception room is designed around a marble fountain in a mosaic of gold, blue, red and white. The stage for musicians and dancers has a richly ornate inlaid roofbeam ceiling. The house-guide will show you a cupboard which is in fact a **secret compartment** for a lady and her guest to observe the men's proceedings.

'*B*elieve me, my good friend, these are the best pots in the whole Khan El Khalili bazaar. You could put your mother-in-law in one of these things.'

Khan El Khalili

One of the most celebrated bazaars in the Arab world is indeed an enormous tourist attraction, but remains justly popular with Egyptians as well. They manage to get away from the purely tourist haunts and you can, too, if you want to. Besides the shopping – for fine craftwork, knick-knacks and plain junk – you will find some of the town's best cafés here, great for people-watching (or *narguileh* smoking, if you can handle it). Don't be too concerned about getting lost in the maze of criss-crossing alleys – everybody does, and everybody gets out again.

Situated north across the square from the great El Azhar mosque and university (*see* below), Khan El Khalili has been a market for Cairo's best craftsmen and craftiest merchants since 1382, when it was built over the Fatimids' royal cemetery. You can still watch gold- and silversmiths at work, as well as jewellers,

artisans in glassware, leather, wood carving, brass and other metals. For the hot and footsore, there is a modern air-conditioned café, pleasant enough but rather unimaginatively named Khan El Khalili, on El Badistan Lane. More traditional, and long popular with local writers, is the **Café Fishawi** in Atfad Ahmad Pasha Lane – everybody knows it.

West beyond Muizz li-Din Street – the quarter's main thoroughfare running north–south – is the old Ottoman neighbourhood of 17th- and 18th-century **mansions** and *hammam* **bath-houses** on and around El Maqasis Street.

Qalawun Mosque

On the west side of Muizz li-Din Street, this 13th-century mosque in fact encompasses a *madrasa*, mausoleum and public hospital. It was built by the great Mameluke sultan Qalawun, who was originally a Turkish slave bought by a Cairo emir for 1,000 dinar – his name means 'rich gift'. Of the **hospital** at the rear, where the sick were soothed by the mosque's musicians, little remains of the original structure, but it has been in continuous operation, at one time an insane asylum and now an ophthalmic clinic. The entrance windows to the **mosque** have 12th-century **Gothic grills** brought from Crusader churches in Jerusalem. With similar carefree ecumenical sense, the **mausoleum** has taken pink granite pillars from ancient Pharaonic temples. Notice, too, its beautiful mosaics and stucco work.

T he fountain in Beit Suhaymi's salamlik *reception room offered a cool accompaniment for the musicians and dancers watched by the master of the house on his throne.*

At El Azhar, religion and scholarship go hand in hand at the mosque and university of one of the most hallowed centres of Islamic culture.

Beshtaq Palace

North of the Qalawun mosque on the other side of Muizz li-Din Street, this residence was built in 1339 by the Emir Beshtaq, brother of Sultan Nasir. It was damaged in the 1992 earthquake but retains many traces of its old splendour. In the lofty reception hall is a fine coloured wooden coffered ceiling over the guests' gallery. This stands opposite the arched gallery from which the emir watched musicians performing around the central fountain. The women sat in an upper gallery, where they also had a *mashrabiya* looking out over the street.

Beit Suhaymi

Continuing north along Muizz li-Din Street, turn right on Darb El Azfar to find this equally grand mansion, 17th-century home of the Turkish dean of students at El Azhar university. Formed by two mer-

chant residences joined together, it was inhabited until the 1960s. Its **garden courtyard** is a haven of tranquillity amid grapevines, palms, shrubs, mimosa and other flowers. The wood carving in the *salamlik* reception room is of the highest quality. The marble fountain dates from 1648. Visit the **Turkish bath**, with a marble floor in the steam room, and a carved wooden divan in the massage room. The grand 18th-century **harem** has Turkish turquoise tiled walls and marble mosaic floors. The **women's garden** is at the rear, with vine-covered arbor, orange, guava and mandarin trees, along with the olive-press and flour-mill.

El Azhar Mosque and University

South of Khan El Khalili across a busy thoroughfare stands one of Islam's most prestigious seats of learning housed in one of its greatest mosques. Its director, Sheikh El Azhar, also bears the title of Sheikh El Islam, a supreme religious authority. Such is its prestige that over the centuries since its foundation, in 972, rulers have repeatedly wanted to leave their mark on it with replacements and additions right up to the present day. These and successive earthquakes and fires have

removed many of its ancient splendours, but grand features remain to be admired, notably five minarets and six massive gates.

Entrance is through the 15th-century **Barber's Gate** (where students had their hair cut before entering). The students' living quarters are grouped, according to nationality, with the *madrasas* around the *sahn* central courtyard. Thus, some of the other gates bear such names as *Bab El Shawam* – Syrians' Gate, and *Bab El Maghariba* – Gate of the Maghreb (Morocco, Algeria and Tunis). Directly beyond the main entrance is the monumental **Gate of Sultan Qaitbay** (1483) leading into the mosque's vast *sahn* **courtyard**. Its keel-arched porticoes retain the Persian style of the original Fatimid structure, with much added ornament. The main prayer-hall is on the far side to the east.

Bab Zuweila Gate and El Muayyad Mosque

South of El Azhar, the original southern entrance to the old Islamic city managed to combine the gruesome spectacle of public executions with the pious devotions of a handsome mosque. The splendid **Bab Zuweila Gate** was built in 1092. Under the Mamelukes and Ottomans, criminals were hanged from the gate or, if executed elsewhere, their heads were displayed on spikes. The towers added in 1420, octagonal with fine keel-arched niches and elegant pierced-stone balconies beneath

The gallows and the severed heads have long gone, but their ghosts still roam around Bab Zuweila Gate and the minarets of El Muayyad Mosque.

onion-domed kiosks, are in fact the minarets of the adjoining **El Muayyad Mosque**. You can reach the roof of the gate through the mosque. Beyond the mosque's black and white marble main entrance is a fine prayer-hall, notable for its marble and stucco decoration, the red, white and black chevron pattern of its *mihrab* niche, and the majestic *minbar* pulpit, its wooden doors inlaid with ebony and mother-of-pearl. The *sahn* courtyard has been transformed into a garden of shrubs and trees, popular with university students reciting their lessons.

Museum of Islamic Art

West of the old Islamic neighbourhoods, the museum stands on Ahmed Maher Square with its entrance on Bur Saïd Street. Its collections, totalling 75,000 objects, are among the richest in the Moslem world, reflecting the development of Islamic art both in Egypt and throughout the Arab and Ottoman empires. Among the 23 rooms, in a convenient circuit rather than in formal numerical order, here are some of the highlights:

Rooms 6-9: *Minbar* pulpit doors present the consummate art of wood-carving inlaid with mother-of-pearl, ivory, bronze and tortoise-shell.

Rooms 15 and 16: Arabic ceramics dating from the city's earliest foundation as Fustat.

Room 4: Rare human representations on wooden panels and frescoes, from Fatimid palaces and bath houses, of hunting, dancing, musicians, and women riding camels.

Room 5: Examples of Mameluke art, monumental bronze and silver trays, and carved wooden and bronze doors.

Room 10: The wooden coffin of Hussein, grandson of Mohammed, carved in the 12th century.

Room 21: Enamelled glassware of the Mameluke period, and 13th- and 14th-century mosque lanterns.

Islamic Cemeteries

Two great cemetery complexes stand on the city's outskirts, to the east and south east. Throughout the centuries it has been the custom for sultans, emirs and other greater or lesser notables of these cities of the dead to share their last resting places with the otherwise homeless living, who squat in and among the monumental tombs. Today, the housing shortage is such that the cemeteries have become in part veritable villages, complete with shops and little markets. The now permanent (living) residents are joined at weekends – continuing a Pharaonic custom – by families visiting the tombs of their loved ones for a picnic.

It is well worth visiting at least the **Eastern Cemetery**, for which we recommend the services of a good tour-guide if you are to find your way easily to two of its most important monuments. Much more than just a tomb, the **Mosque and Mausoleum of Sultan Barquq** (1411) is a superb complex for worship, study and meditation, quite plain in its façades, but crowned by two magnificent domes and two minarets. Not so large, the **Madrasa and Mausoleum of Sultan Qaitbay** (1474) is altogether more decorative, a true masterpiece of Islamic art, with intricately carved stone dome and elegant in

every detail of stone tracery and stalactite ornament on the octagonal three-tiered minaret.

Coptic Cairo

The neighbourhood grouping the Coptic Museum and old churches of Cairo's ancient Christian community is commonly known as Old Cairo, standing as it does over the old fortress of Babylon which the Copts occupied after the Arab conquest. To get there, take the downtown Metro to Mar Girgis (St George) station.

Two **Roman gate-towers** and remains of the walls still stand by the Metro station. A modern Greek Orthodox church has been erected on the rebuilt northern tower, attached to a monastery. East of the Greek Orthodox complex is the **Church of St Sergius** (*Abu Serga*) dedicated to a martyred Roman convert. Notice the Corinthian columns and the fine 13th-century ivory and ebony screen in front of the main sanctuary. The church stands on a site traditionally identified as a resting place for Mary, Joseph and Jesus during their flight to Egypt. Since the Middle Ages, European pilgrims have visited the crypt, reached by a stairway from the south (right-hand) sanctuary. Further east is the **Church of St Barbara**, notable for the religious scenes carved in ivory on the 13th-century wooden icon-screen.

The quarter was also a haven for Jews, whose **Ben Ezra Synagogue**, nicely restored but no longer in regular use, still stands (on the same street as St Barbara's as you make your way back to the Coptic Museum). It was converted in the 12th century from a church bought by the Jews on a site where an earlier synagogue had been destroyed by the Romans.

The Copts

Egypt's Coptic Christians are a discreet community, about 8 percent of the population. They keep to their own neighbourhoods in Cairo and Alexandria, but also have large communities in Asyut, Luxor and other towns of Upper Egypt. Many have the distinguishing mark of a cross tatooed on their wrists. Originally, there was no real ethnic distinction to make between Copts and Egyptian Moslems: both communities were of ancient Egyptian stock. However, the Copts can claim a 'purer' link to Pharaonic Egypt by the fact that they did not convert to Islam, and thus did not intermarry with the invading Arabs, Mamelukes and Ottoman Turks.

The wheels of the Baramus monastery's flour mill may have long since stopped turning, but the few remaining monks keep the faith.

The Coptic language was an ancient Egyptian dialect spoken in the early Christian era. It has since been superseded by Arabic, but remains in the church liturgy, written in an expanded form of the Greek alphabet.

In the doctrinal dispute which was the formal cause of the split with the Eastern Orthodox church, the Copts adhered to the creed of Monophytism, which holds that Jesus had a single divine nature, rather than a dual nature, human *and* divine. Many of the rites and customs are similar to those of the Eastern church – total immersion at baptism, and strict separation of men and women worshippers for example. However, circumcision and the observation of certain Mosaic dietary laws reflect their regional proximity to Islam and Judaism. The head of their church bears the official title of Pope of Alexandria, Patriarch of the See of St Mark, Bishop of Cairo, where he has his headquarters.

The Copts were the originators of the Christian monastic tradition. In 270, St

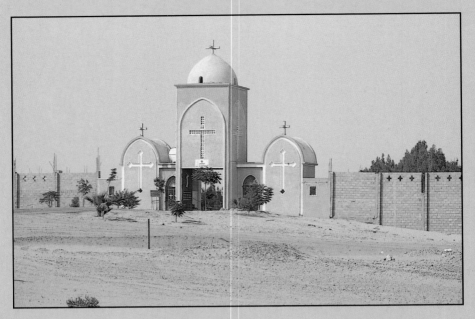

Antony abandoned his life as a wealthy property-owner for the seclusion of the desert. The ascetic life of his refuge on the Red Sea coast attracted a community of fellow hermits. Other retreats were established at places like Wadi Natrun, between Cairo and Alexandria, with Christians drawn to the desert as a magnetic force for purifying meditation. Not all Copts were of a pacific nature: some zealot monks went on the rampage through the last shrines of 'pagan' Egypt, destroying and defacing the images of the Pharaonic deities.

The Copts' own churches and monasteries often suffered a similar fate at the hands of Byzantine Christians or Arab Moslems, so that little remains of the earliest Coptic art of the 5th and 6th centuries: most of what does remain is now in the Coptic Museum. What has survived, less sophisticated than the aristocratic art of cosmopolitan Greco-Roman Alexandria, is rooted in popular peasant art of Upper Egypt's Nile Valley. Sculpture, paintings, book-

In the earliest days of Coptic Christianity, holy men set up monasteries in the desert a lot less luxurious than Amba Bishoi, less often to avoid the hurly-burly of city life than just to escape persecution.

illumination and embroidered textiles are highly stylized, with flattened forms, simple and decorative. This simplicity can be seen in the monumental tombs of Bagwat at the Kharga Oasis. After the Arab conquest, carving in wood, stone and ivory shows an Islamic influence, while icons, as with most churches, tend to be imported from Byzantium.

The typical Coptic church has its narthex (vestibule) in the west. Beyond it, a nave separated by columns from two side aisles leads beyond an icon-screen to the sanctuaries with a main altar in the centre. The side sanctuaries each have an altar and stairways leading down to the crypt.

*N*ear the Mausoleum of Sultan Qaitbay, tomb precincts have
been converted into houses for Cairo's homeless, the living and dead
coexisting in easy harmony.

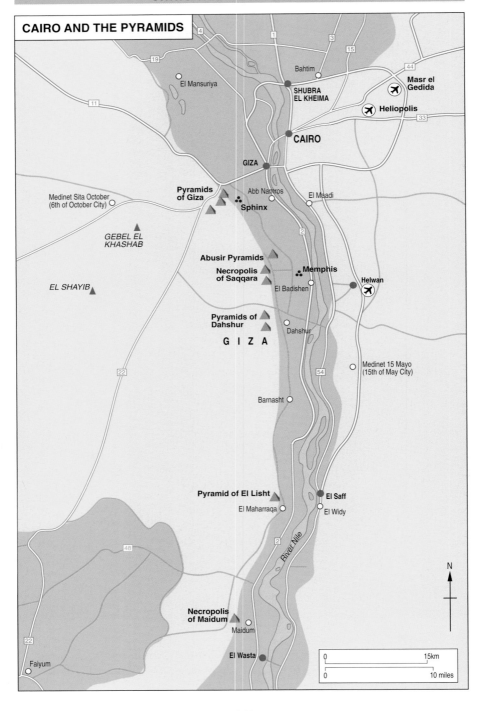

CAIRO AND THE PYRAMIDS

El Mansuriya

Bahtim

Masr el Gedida

Heliopolis

SHUBRA EL KHEIMA

CAIRO

GIZA

Medinet Sita October
(6th of October City)

Pyramids of Giza

Abb Namros

El Maadi

Sphinx

GEBEL EL KHASHAB

Abusir Pyramids

Memphis

EL SHAYIB

Necropolis of Saqqara

El Badishen

Helwan

Pyramids of Dahshur

Dahshur

G I Z A

Medinet 15 Mayo
(15th of May City)

Barnasht

Pyramid of El Lisht

El Saff

El Maharraqa

El Widy

River Nile

Necropolis of Maidum

Maidum

El Wasta

Faiyum

N

| 0 | | 15km |
| 0 | | 10 miles |

Coptic Museum

Signposted behind the southern Roman gate-tower, the museum illustrates the Coptic community's direct links with ancient Egypt, both Pharaonic and Greco-Roman. Exhibits include pre-Coptic pagan sculpture and carved capitals of Greek and Roman columns. The Early Christian art includes 5th- and 6th-century sculpture and wall-paintings from Bawit, near Asyut. From St Jeremy's Monastery at Saqqara comes some fine stucco work and a carved stone pulpit. Look out, too, for an 11th-century mural of Adam and Eve from El Faiyum. Other exhibits include manuscripts, icons, textiles and jewellery from the 16th to 18th centuries.

A stairway at the south end of the museum leads up to **El Muallaqa, 'the Hanging Church'** that derives its name from being built above the Roman Gate, where it became the seat of the Patriarch of Alexandria when he moved to Cairo. Much of the present edifice is 19th century, but it has a notable 700-year-old carved ebony icon-screen.

The Pyramids

We cannot overemphasize that, to appreciate fully the significance of these marvels, you should see the pyramids of Giza and Saqqara in conjunction with, preferably after, a visit to the Egyptian Museum. If you want to see the monuments in historical sequence, start with Saqqara, where the very first pyramid was built. Both are an hour's drive from Cairo, but the added visits to the nobles' tombs and a side-trip to Memphis make Saqqara a longer excursion. In either case, make a very early start to enjoy the light and cool of the morning since the pyramids are in the

desert. From the car park to the pyramids, a ride on a camel or in a horse-drawn carriage enhances the pleasure (remember to negotiate a round-trip fare).

Saqqara

The sanctuary of the Pharaohs' pyramids and nobles' tombs is built on a plateau on the edge of the Western Desert due west of the ancient royal capital of Memphis. For many, leaving the palm groves outside the village of Mit Rahina, this is a first and unforgettable experience of that abrupt change from rich green Nile Valley to arid, buff, desert sand where you can straddle the two totally opposite and hostile terrains. Many pharaohs built their pyramids here, but most have been reduced to at best majestic mounds of rubble. One stands out: history's first monumental structure built of stone, fashioned by the great architect Imhotep for his master King Djoser around 2670 BC.

Step Pyramid

To get there from the ticket office, take the left fork. Entrance is through a **stone gateway** at the south-east corner of the sanctuary enclosing Djoser's pyramid. The white limestone enclosure has 13 other 'gateways', but they are all false, blind entrances. As you proceed through the **colonnade**, you will see that the architect has created stone replicas of wooden doors and other architectural elements from the royal capital of Memphis, City of White Walls – 'wooden' beams and columns formed from imitation bundles of reeds. The exterior may reproduce the façade of the royal palace.

*A*ny journey to the great pyramids of Giza is like a pilgrimage. As you approach, you may feel humbled by their grandeur, but also proud that human beings could create such things *(previous page)*.

Turn right across the courtyard towards the pyramid past two B-shaped **stone altars** set in the ground, perhaps serving as markers for the king's ritual race around his realms of Upper and Lower Egypt to keep fit in the afterlife.

The **Step Pyramid** is built up in six tiers to a height of nearly 60m (196ft) on a rectangular base 121m (396ft) from east to west, and 107m (350ft) from north to south. Imhotep's original concept may have been an elaboration of the traditional *mastaba* bench-shaped tomb superstructure, piling one on top of the other to form the pyramid. Inside, a shaft $7m^2$ (22ft²) was dug to a depth of 28m (91ft) through bedrock to the burial chamber, which was sealed off by a granite block. The chamber was surrounded by corridors and galleries, some of them with blue tiling now displayed in the Egyptian Museum. Other family members were buried in chambers 4m (13ft) further down. By the time of the 19th- and 20th-century excavations, grave-robbers had taken all but a child's alabaster coffin. In the main chamber, only one mummified foot was found, probably the king's. (Only professional archaeologists now have access to these shafts.)

On the south side of the pyramid is the **mortuary temple** from which the mummified corpse was lowered to the burial chamber. Through a peep-hole, you can see a replica of the enthroned statue of Djoser – the original is in the Egyptian Museum. To the west are two more ceremonial structures, the **North Hall**, in which one of the walls has the earliest known examples of columns with papyrus-plant capitals, and a **South Hall** with finely modelled fluted columns set in one of its walls.

Nobles' Mastaba Tombs

The Old Kingdom decoration of the Saqqara tombs is among the best in the land. Scores of nobles and princesses have their bench-shaped *mastaba* tombs around Djoser's and other pyramids. Each tomb has several rooms, a shaft descending to the burial chamber, and a false door leading to the afterworld. The scenes of the finely carved bas-reliefs show the intricate symbolic preparations made for the deceased to have a good afterlife – and incidentally reveal to us their customs in the world of the living: offerings to the gods, food and drink for themselves, musical entertainment, pastimes like hunting, fishing and other sports. (Remember to tip the tomb-guardian after your visit.)

Here are four of the best tombs:

Princess Idut's tomb (2400 BC) is south of the Step Pyramid in the burial enclosure of King Unas. From here, you have a distant view of the Dahshur pyramids, including Snoferu's famous Bent Pyramid (unfortunately usually off limits to tourists). Idut's tomb is probably usurped from another 5th-Dynasty aristocrat, but she had time to decorate five of the ten funereal chambers with some beautiful bas-relief scenes of fishing and

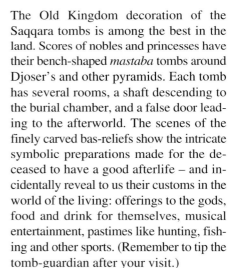

hunting. You can see her sniffing at a lotus flower as she sails along. A servant is spearing a hippopotamus. Cruel irony is displayed in a female hippopotamus giving birth to a baby which a crocodile prepares to snap up as it emerges from the womb.

Mereruka's tomb (2300 BC), north east of the Step Pyramid, is a family tomb with 32 rooms, the largest in Saqqara. Excavators found the body of Mereruka, chamberlain of the 6th-Dynasty Pharaoh Teti, and that of his wife. She had been buried at a deeper level with their son. There is a fine **statue of Mereruka** in the tomb and splendid relief friezes of boat-building, game-playing and hunting, with detailed depictions of wild goat, hyena and gazelle.

Ptah-hotep's tomb (2400 BC), north west of the Step Pyramid, is that of a high court official overseeing the pyramid's priests. Reliefs show offerings being brought to the gods, and Ptah-hotep sitting at a concert with greyhounds and a monkey beneath his seat. Servants massage his legs with oil.

Ti's tomb (2350 BC), further north west, offers an outstanding example of Old Kingdom art's meticulous attention to detail. For this steward of pyramid-builders as well as at the sun temples, the artists have carved quite wonderful fishing scenes in the marshes, portraits of birds – cranes, storks and pigeons – and an ox being prepared for sacrifice.

Memphis

On your way back to Cairo, stop off near the village of Mit Rahina to visit the remains of the Pharaohs' first capital, the City of White Walls. Only a few traces of

it remain, scattered among palm trees to the west of the main road. The town had been continuously inhabited throughout the ancient era and was abandoned only after the Arab invasion. Since then, its masonry has been carried off by other builders or fallen victim to the rising water-table and the Nile's floods. A museum-shelter houses a **Colossus of Ramses II**, originally some 12m (40ft) high before it lost its feet. Now recumbent, it had stood in front of the Temple of Ptah, the original creator-god, together with the pink granite colossus that stands today in front of Cairo's Central Station.

Damaged but nonetheless imposing is an **alabaster sphinx**, probably of Amenophis II (1400 BC). An **embalming house** has been discovered with huge alabaster tables with lion motifs, on which the sacred Apis bulls were embalmed.

Giza

Sacrilegiously, the Pyramids Road that leads from Cairo to Egypt's greatest monuments is lined with bars, nightclubs and casinos. The tawdry soon makes way for the grandiose as you approach the limestone desert plateau rising 50m (164ft) above the Nile Valley plain. Like all the world's great monuments that we think we know so well before we see them, the pyramids still manage to make a prodigious impression on the newcomer. Take time for the effect to seep in before you get up closer.

(Climbing the pyramids is dangerous and no longer permitted. You can go down inside to the burial chambers with a guide, but the excursion seems more arduous than rewarding for any but committed archaeologists, and takes one hour

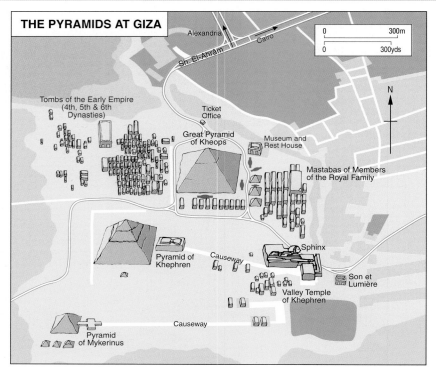

THE PYRAMIDS AT GIZA

Alexandria

Cairo

Sh. El-Ahrâm

0   300m
0   300yds

N

Tombs of the Early Empire
(4th, 5th & 6th
Dynasties)

Ticket
Office

Great Pyramid
of Kheops

Museum and
Rest House

Mastabas of Members
of the Royal Family

Pyramid of
Khephren

Causeway

Sphinx

Son et
Lumière

Valley Temple
of Khephren

Causeway

Pyramid
of Mykerinus

for Kheops' Great Pyramid and a good half hour for Khephren's.)

As at Saqqara, the Giza pyramids are part of a funereal complex, built with a valley temple to receive the king's body once transported from the river, a mortuary temple adjacent to the pyramid to prepare the body for lowering into its burial chamber, other minor pyramids for the closest family, and *mastaba* tombs for other relatives and nobles.

T ry to escape the madding crowd and spend a moment alone with the sphinx. He undoubtedly has a message for you (previous page).

Kheops' Great Pyramid

It does live up to its Greco-Roman title as one of the Wonders of the World. This despite losing some 3m (10ft) of masonry all round, smooth limestone facing stripped off by the early builders of Cairo. It is now 137m (450ft) high, with its sides each 227m (744ft) long. Its angle of elevation is 52 degrees. The structure contains an estimated 2,000,000 blocks and took all of Kheops' 23-year reign (2606-2583) to build (*see* ART AND ARCHITECTURE IN ANCIENT EGYPT page 174). That would have meant quarrying, cutting and setting in place some 240 blocks, averaging 2.54 tonnes, every day. American engineers dismiss the suggestion of Greek historian Herodotus that it needed 100,000 workers.

Their view is that just 4,000 men were working on the pyramid at any one time. This includes quarry workers for the finer limestone across the river at Tura and granite down at Aswan, barge crews to transport it and all the skilled masons and other craftsmen – but not the brute force of press-ganged slaves of popular legend.

Entry is through a passage 36m (118ft) down. (It was forced into the pyramid west of the original shaft by Caliph Mamun during his visit to Egypt in the 9th century AD.) The passage joins up with the impressive **Grand Gallery**, 8.5m (28ft) high, leading to the **burial chamber**. It was found empty except for a granite sarcophagus, which, with the later discovery of pieces of the Pharaoh's sacred barque, contradicts doubts that the Great Pyramid was truly conceived as a tomb.

Khephren's Pyramid

Standing on higher ground and with a steeper angle of elevation (54 degrees), this seems bigger than the Kheops pyramid, but is in fact fractionally shorter, on a narrower base. Some of its smooth limestone facing has been well preserved at the summit. Access via the lower of the two entrances enables you to see the **red granite sarcophagus** still set in the pavement of the burial chamber.

The remains of Khephren's **mortuary** and the **valley temples** stand to the east of his pyramid. The valley temple is a massive structure of limestone and red granite, originally housing some 20 statues of the king – one superb specimen is displayed in the Egyptian Museum (*see* page 119).

The Sphinx

Dominating the causeway between his two temples, Khephren is preserved for eternity with his head on the lion's body of the great sphinx. He has lost part of the sacred cobra headdress, his nose and ritual beard, but none of his majesty. Like the sphinx of Oedipus, Khephren's monument was attributed prophetic powers. Tuthmosis IV (1397-1384) left a stela tablet to commemorate the realization of the sphinx's promise to him in a dream that he would become Pharaoh if he cleaned up the site.

Mykerinus' Pyramid

The smallest of the three pyramids provides an attractive addition for scale and perspective. To the south are three smaller unfinished pyramids for his family.

Lakeside Refreshment and Memories of a Mystic

In all the excitement surrounding Cairo and the pyramids of Lower Egypt in the north, and the temples and tombs of Upper Egypt's Luxor and Aswan in the south, the middle is often unjustly forgotten. The Faiyum has an attractively sprawling oasis around Lake Qarun; there are splendid rock-cut tombs in the cliffs of Beni Hasan; the marriage of Greek and Egyptian art can be enjoyed at Hermopolis; and at Tell El Amarna, the capital of the poignant maverick Akhenaten can be visited.

Historically, the area known as Middle Egypt between Memphis and Asyut always provided a refuge from the pressure of events in the major centres. Provincial governors could freely flex their muscles there whenever the power of Pharaonic dynasties wavered. Akhenaten found in what is now Tell El Amarna an ideally remote spot in which to explore his new religious ideas and extricate himself from the overweening priesthood of Karnak. In the Christian era, the oasis of Faiyum was

*F*aiyum's market continues the historic role of the sprawling oasis as a major supplier of fruit and vegetables throughout the country.

remote enough from Alexandria or Cairo for the Copts to escape persecution and found 35 monasteries by the 13th century.

Today, you can see Egyptian small-town and rural life here up close, unencumbered by too many tourist buses. The Faiyum can be visited on a day-trip from Cairo with a picnic at Lake Qarun or lunch at one of its hotels. For the other destinations, plan an overnight stay at the provincial capital Minya, which has a couple of pleasant riverside hotels.

(Asyut itself is a university town and important commercial centre. It has been historically important as the Nile Valley junction for caravan routes from the Western Desert oases. The large Coptic community has aroused considerable opposition in the recent past from Islamic fundamentalists. The town's ancient monuments have disappeared and, apart from a lively bazaar, it has little to recommend to the foreign visitor, and notably few good hotel facilities.)

Since Middle Egypt is less well sign-posted than more celebrated sightseeing destinations, we especially recommend the use of an experienced guide. (Flooding in the Faiyum region regularly makes road-maps obsolete.)

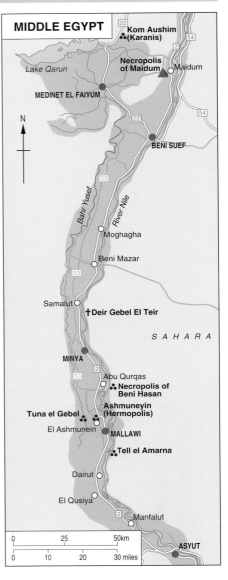

MIDDLE EGYPT

Kom Aushim
(Karanis)

Lake Qarun

Necropolis of Maidum

Maidum

MEDINET EL FAIYUM

N

Bahr Yusef

River Nile

BENI SUEF

Moghagha

Beni Mazar

Samalut

† Deir Gebel El Teir

S A H A R A

MINYA

Abu Qurqas

Necropolis of Beni Hasan

Ashmuneyin (Hermopolis)

Tuna el Gebel

El Ashmunein

MALLAWI

Tell el Amarna

Dairut

El Qusiya

Manfalut

ASYUT

0   25   50km
0   10   20   30 miles

*L*ife in Middle Egypt moves at a more leisurely pace. The burdens are heavy, no point in killing yourself or your donkeys.

Faiyum

This is the largest of the Western Desert oases, watered directly from a Nile tributary, the Yusuf river, which flows into Lake Qarun. A popular fishing and hunting ground for the Pharaohs, the lake was referred to by the Copts as a sea, *peiom*, from which the region derives its name.

The Faiyum was originally covered by lush tropical rainforest, home of mammoths, gorillas and giant crocodiles. It has been a farming centre since prehistoric times, its first human settlers dating back at least to 3500 BC. The Ptolemies experimented with new agricultural techniques and new crops, but the Romans preferred the monoculture of grain to export back home – and the Byzantines followed suit. Modern farming once again produces a great variety of crops: vegetables, fruit, flowers and cotton. Characteristic features of the Faiyum landscape are the dovecotes and especially the imposing water-wheels for irrigation.

From Cairo, take the Giza – Faiyum road to stop off at the excavated Greco-Roman town of **Karanis**, east of the highway by the village of Kom Aushim. The desert sands offer a striking setting for the mudbrick houses in which you can find kitchens with bread-ovens, the remains of a bath house and a temple to Isis up on a rise. There is a good little **museum** where you can also find information about archaeological sites on Lake Qarun.

With the Yusuf river running through the city centre, the provincial capital **Medinet El Faiyum** makes an agreeable starting point from which to embark on your explorations of the region. Its market is a good place to buy picnic supplies – first-class local farm produce – and two **giant water-wheels** provide the town's star photo-opportunity. The town was known to the Greeks as Crocodilopolis in honour of the region's deity, Sobek, but all that remains of the crocodile-god's Ptolemaic temple is a few overgrown mounds down by the railway tracks.

The cultivated fields are so extensive that it is often easy to forget that the Faiyum is still an oasis in the desert.

Lake Qarun

There are no crocodiles in the lake any more, but there are plenty of fish, quite big ones favouring the slightly salt water. The fishermen at the lakeside villages may let you try your luck. The lake measures 40km (25 miles) long and 8km (5 miles) across at its widest point. Lying some 46m (150ft) below sea level, it has a rather balmy climate which is good for sleeping if you contemplate staying overnight. If only for an after-lunch siesta, it makes a refreshing change from the city and the desert. You may also take a boat cruise across to the north shore.

Maidum

This is not part of the Faiyum, but for people returning to Cairo, the **Maidum pyramid complex** on the eastern edge of the oasis makes it a worthwhile stop on your way back. (It may also be visited if you are making the separate road trip from Cairo down to Minya.) Just 5km (3 miles) west of the main highway, the formidable mass of the pyramid (2600 BC) rises from the desert escarpment; it is perhaps the first true pyramid to be attempted after Djoser's Step Pyramid. The outer super-structure seems to have collapsed before completion – recent excavations have re-vealed bodies of workers under the rubble – leaving only the towering inner core. Scholars attribute final work on the edifice to Snoferu, who was similarly unsuc-cessful with the Bent Pyramid at Dahshur.

Lake Qarun is a popular resort area for Egyptians escaping the heat of Cairo, just as it was for the Pharaohs taking a hunting-holiday from Memphis.

Among the artwork found in nearby *mastabas* are the famous Maidum geese and the statues of Rahotep and Nefert, now both in the Egyptian Museum.

The Cairo Road to Minya

The main town, situated east of the Faiyum, is **Beni Suef**, a busy cotton- and carpet-manufacturing town with a good bazaar. It is here, 116km (72 miles) south of Cairo, that the Nile Valley reaches its widest point – 17km (10 miles) from river to desert.

The provincial capital of **Minya**, 119km (74 miles) further south, provides the best base for your excursions to Beni Hasan, Hermopolis and Tell El Amarna, by road or local river-boat. Even if you are not staying at the Nefertiti/Aton hotel, take advantage of its riverside cocktail-terrace for a moment's quiet relaxation before your next expedition begins.

Beni Hasan

The grand east-bank necropolis can be reached by ferry from Abu Qurqas, 20km (12 miles) south of Minya. The short walk from the landing-stage up to the cliff's **rock-cut tombs** is not too arduous, but donkeys are available. The 39 tombs were carved from the desert escarpment by provincial governors of the Middle Kingdom (2035-1668 BC). Twelve of the tombs have funerary chapels decorated with wall paintings, some of them with lotus-capital pillars carved from the rock as an ornament, not for any structural

It's not always this empty at the restaurants at Lake Qarun (previous page).

purpose. Shafts are sunk into the rock down to burial chambers.

Unlike in the Pharaonic tombs, the gods – principally Osiris and Anubis – are honoured only with hieroglyphic prayers, not with statues or portraits. The scenes of everyday life are more animated, if perhaps less refined, than the Old Kingdom friezes at Saqqara or those of the New Kingdom in the Valley of the Kings.

Start at the far north end of the cliff ledge and work your way back. The tombs are numbered.

Amenemhet's tomb (2) has a columned vestibule leading to the main chapel, with four pillars. Its false door to the afterworld is on the right of the entrance. Two burial shafts for the governor and his family lead from the right side of the chapel. Painted on a red plaster surface applied to the limestone rock are scenes of karate-like martial arts, wrestling, yoga, hockey and archery. You will also see here, as elsewhere, paintings depicting

---

TRUE LOVE

Some 18km (11 miles) south of Beni Hasan, the little east-bank village of Sheikh Abada covers the site of a poignant memorial of a Roman emperor's love. There is nothing left to see, but spare the place a thought as you pass by on your way to Hermopolis. On his trip to Egypt, Emperor Hadrian brought his wife Sabina along for the ribbon-cutting ceremonies, but preferred sightseeing with his Greek lover Antinoüs. Hadrian quite literally idolized the boy. When Antinoüs drowned in the Nile, the rumour arose that he had committed suicide to save the emperor from a disaster predicted by an oracle. In any case, the grief-stricken emperor immediately declared his lover a god, ordered shrines and statues to be erected all over Egypt and founded the now vanished city of Antinopolis.

hunting with a boomerang-shaped weapon, though there is no pictorial evidence that it ever returned to the sender if it missed its target. Other scenes show musicians with a seven-string harp and various craftsmen – goldsmiths, cutlers and carpenters.

Knumhotep's tomb (3), also four-columned, is smaller than Amenemhet's, but the art is more finely executed, particularly in the detail of the birds and animals. Notice the baboons trained to pick fruit in the trees. The noble and his wife are seen fishing and hunting in the marshland. Among the artisans are cabinet-makers and boat-builders. From their clothes and shoes, some of the figures are identified as Asian. The weaving loom is essentially the same as that used today for Egyptian carpet manufacture. Like too many visitors to other monuments, ancient Greeks and Copts have added their graffiti to the decor.

Baket's tomb (15) is plainer, with just two columns, but the governor seems to have brought a larger family with him, providing four burial shafts off to the left and three others to the right. He and his wife are seen hunting in the desert and watching acrobats and dancers. Other scenes to look for include a cat chasing a monstrous mouse, soldiers attacking a castle, and punishment being meted out to male and female offenders, the latter treated more gently with the official's hand placed on her head.

Kheti's tomb (17) has in its chapel six lotus columns coloured green, yellow, brown and blue and two burial shafts to the right. Among the more notable scenes are a series about marriage – three brides and three bridegrooms, and a rare instance, at least in those on public show, of love-making, on a wooden bed.

Hermopolis

On the map, the Ptolemaic sanctuary – 24km (15 miles) south of Abu Qurqas – is identified in Arabic as **Ashmuneyin**, which in turn derives from the ancient Egyptian name, *Khmun*. The sanctuary was dedicated to the local deity Thot, god of healing, wisdom and scribes, whom the Greeks assimilated to Hermes. At what was once the entrance to the sanctuary stand **two stone baboons**, emblematic creatures of Thot. A few granite columns are all that remain of the god's temple and the ancient town's market place, together with an Early Christian basilica.

Tuna El Gebel

Out in the desert, some 6km (3.5 miles) to the west, is the sanctuary's impressive necropolis – tombs for the nobles and catacombs for sacred mummified animals – a major place of pilgrimage in Greek and Roman times. Just before the archaeological site, set dramatically in a cliff on the north side of the road, is a **stela of Akhenaten**. This finely carved boundary marker (one of 14 originally set up) defined the north-west limits of the farming hinterland to the Pharaoh's breakaway capital of Akhetaten – Tell El Amarna (*see* below). A short walk across the powdery sand takes you over to the relief-carving of Akhenaten and Nefertiti with their daughters at an altar to the sacred sun-disk. The hieroglyphics describe the founding of the new capital.

The tombs' decoration attempts an intriguing synthesis of Egyptian and Greek art, combining traditional Egyptian funereal themes of the Judgment Day and the black skeleton of death with classical Greek scenes of the trials of Oedipus, the Trojan Horse and the abduction of

These few mudbrick walls and doorways are all that remain of the royal capital at Tell El Amarna, where Akhenaten practised his revolutionary monotheistic cult.

Persephone. Best preserved is the **Tomb-Chapel of Petosiris** (300 BC), resembling a miniature Egyptian temple. For the family mausoleum, the Ptolemaic high priest of Toth-Hermes placed a four-horned limestone altar in front of the entrance portico. Inside the columned funerary chapel there are scenes of farming and the wine-harvest. Distinctly Greek figures in their clothing and hairstyles are blessed by Osiris, Isis and other Egyptian gods.

Beyond this chapel is a City of the Dead, in spirit very much like the cemeteries of Cairo, where the tomb-houses provide a shrine for the deceased and quarters for the living to visit, complete with kitchen, dining-room and bedroom.

A government rest-house offers refreshments before or after you tackle the necropolis. Not far from the rest-house are the **catacombs** where Toth's sacred ibises and baboons were buried. The stone sarcophagi lie around the galleries and alcoves, some of them even containing mummified remains.

At the nearby town of **Mallawi**, stop off at the **museum** which has some of the best finds from Tuna El Gebel: sculpture, bronzes, ceramics, sarcophagi and mummifed baboons and ibises.

Tell El Amarna

The site of Akhenaten's capital, Akhetaten, takes its modern name from a local Bedouin tribe, Beni Amran. A rocky desert landscape in romantic abandon isolated from the Nile Valley's other main residential areas, it looks today much as it did before the mystic Pharaoh made it his royal residence and as it did when left by his successors after they had destroyed it. Eloquent ruins testify to the presence of Akhenaten and his wife Nefertiti – a palace, temples, houses of nobles and artisans, and rock-cut tombs in the limestone escarpment east of the town.

Six km (4 miles) south of Mallawi, the road turns east to the river for the ferry across to the east bank. There, transportation is in a not uncomfortable wagon pulled by a leisurely tractor (or on a donkey, if you prefer) over uneven terrain to the city, with an uphill walk to the necropolis in the limestone cliffs beyond. The remains are scattered in several groups over a wide area some 2.5km (1.5miles) long. For all but the most intrepid archaeology buffs, we recommend visiting just the best preserved **northern tombs** and remains of the **city**. The king and his solar-disk cult dominate the decoration of the nobles' tombs, almost to the exclusion of the deceased. Akhenaten's hostile successors have repeatedly tried to chisel away his face or hieroglyphic name, and all references to the unorthodox cult.

Huya's tomb (1) is the northernmost, carved from the cliff for the chamberlain of Tiy, the Queen Mother. At the entrance to the tomb's three chambers, the deceased can be seen praying. In the first chapel, where one of its two columns is still standing, there is a scene of Akhenaten, Nefertiti and the princesses receiving gifts from foreign envoys of Asia and Ethiopia. Another shows the royal family at dinner. Queen Tiy, wearing the sacred-cow headdress of Hathor, is seen drinking wine.

Meryré's tomb (2), similar in design to Huya's tomb, is the burial place of the royal scribe who apparently also filled the decidedly unintellectual role of chamberlain to Nefertiti's harem. We see Akhenaten presenting him with a necklace. Nefertiti is seen pouring her husband a glass of water. The king is also shown receiving gifts of gold, slaves and exotic animals from foreign delegations of red-faced Africans.

Back down in the plain, visit the fenced-off remains of **Akhetaten city** where you get an overview of mudbrick houses, the groundplan of the palace, and the temple to the north. A long-established theory that sacrifices to the new divinity were strictly vegetarian has been dispelled by the recent discovery of a butcher's slaughterhouse. Among the houses at the southern end of town is the studio of sculptor Dhutmosi, where German archaeologists found the unfinished but most beautiful sculpture of Nefertiti, now the pride and joy of Berlin's Egyptian collections.

165

Valley of Mighty Empire and Ramses II's Colossal Gall

The south is the heartland of the Pharaohs' imperial splendour. In Luxor and Karnak – ancient Thebes – they built their mightiest temples. Across the river in the Valley of the Kings, they cut their tombs deep in the rock to protect them from robbers, although all but Tutankhamun's were plundered. At Abu Simbel, Ramses II created stupendous colossi to his own glory. At Aswan, the cult of Isis survived 450 years into the Christian era. Today the High Dam harnesses the power of the Nile.

The region stretches 500km (312 miles) from Asyut to the Sudan border. It is possible to drive all the way, but the route can be arduous and the hotel accommodation is not always first class. Most visitors to the region fly or take the train from Cairo directly to Luxor. From there, visits to the monuments at Abydos and Denderah can be combined in one day-trip, with perhaps a second, for students of Coptic culture, to the monasteries at Sohag further north. For those not taking a cruise to or from Aswan, the destinations immediately to the south – Esna and Edfu – are also in easy reach of Luxor. At a stretch, Kom Ombo could also be included, but it is easier to make it a separate day-trip from Aswan, which is also the starting point for the longer excursion to Abu Simbel.

In front of the grand twin-towered ceremonial entrance to the Temple of Luxor stand colossal statues of Ramses II and one of two obelisks – the other carried off to Paris's Place de la Concorde.

Luxor

The Pharaonic temples were the gods' palaces – in Arabic, *El-Uqsor*, which gave the town its modern name. The northern part of town, Karnak, is the site of the greater of the two temple complexes. On the Nile's east bank, they form together the religious focus of the ancient

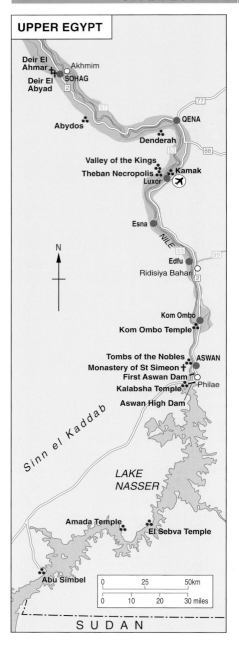

UPPER EGYPT

Deir El Ahmar
Akhmim
Deir El Abyad
SOHAG
Abydos
QENA
Denderah
Valley of the Kings
Theban Necropolis
Luxor
Karnak
Esna
NILE
Edfu
Ridisiya Bahari
Kom Ombo
Kom Ombo Temple
Tombs of the Nobles
ASWAN
Monastery of St Simeon
First Aswan Dam
Philae
Kalabsha Temple
Aswan High Dam
Sinn el Kaddab
LAKE NASSER
Amada Temple
El Sebva Temple
Abu Simbel

0   25   50km
0 10 20 30 miles

SUDAN

LIFE GOES ON

If at times you fear being overpowered by the grandeur of Upper Egypt's temples and other monuments, take time off to look at the life and landscape along the river. The Nile Valley often shrinks to the narrowest of green strips with the vast buff-coloured desert plateau looming beyond, and the colours of Nubia – pinks, ochres, ambers – are richer and deeper still. The horizontal line of the green fields of sugar cane or corn is interrupted by an occasional clump of palm trees and, back on a mound above the valley, the minaret of the village mosque or cross of a Coptic church. At sunrise, farmers in flowing white *gallabiya* emerge from their mudbrick houses to take their oxen to the field. One son rides the donkey to market. Another examines a malfunctioning ultra-modern electrical irrigation system and turns back to the old wood and tin lever-and-bucket hoist which had its prototype back in the days of the Pharaohs. The women wash their linen down by the river. Toddlers call out a word of greeting in English or German.

royal capital of Thebes. Over on the west bank, the rulers, nobles and a few privileged artisans had their tombs. This city of the dead, indeed a veritable kingdom of the dead, is known today as the Theban Necropolis, of which the Valley of the Kings is the most celebrated site.

Until the first tentative explorations of Napoleon Bonaparte's archaeologists, nothing but the towering Colossi of Memnon on the west bank were visible. The Luxor and Karnak temples remained concealed beneath the sands. In the first half of the 19th century, as we can still see from the famous coloured prints of British artist David Roberts, the temple pillars were still half or three-quarters buried in the sands. Lucky clients of Thomas Cook's first luxury package tours could wander around a hypostyle hall and practically touch the sculpted capitals at

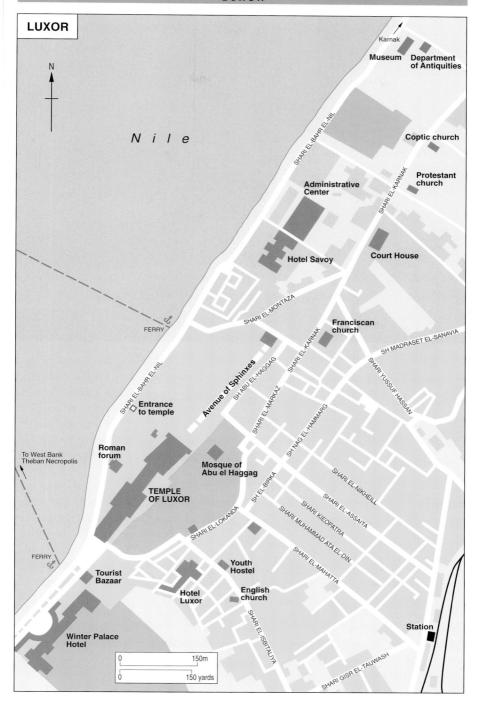

LUXOR

N

Nile

Karnak

Museum   Department
of Antiquities

Coptic church

SHARI EL-BAHR EL-NIL

Protestant
church

SHARI EL-KARNAK

Administrative
Center

Court House

Hotel Savoy

FERRY

SHARI EL-MONTAZA

Franciscan
church

SHARI EL-BAHR EL-NIL

SH MADRASET EL-SANAVIA

SHARI EL-KARNAK

Avenue of Sphinxes

SH ABU EL-HAGGAG

SHARI YUSSUF HASSAN

Entrance
to temple

SHARI EL-MARKAZ

Roman
forum

SH NAG EL-HAMMARG

To West Bank
Theban Necropolis

Mosque of
Abu el Haggag

SHARI EL-NIKHEILL

TEMPLE
OF LUXOR

SH EL-BIRKA

SHARI EL-ASSAITA

SHARI KIEOPATRA

SHARI EL-LOKANDA

SHARI MUHAMMAD ATA EL-DIN

FERRY

Youth
Hostel

SHARI EL-MAHATTA

Tourist
Bazaar

Hotel
Luxor

English
church

Station

SHARI EL-ISBITALIYA

Winter Palace
Hotel

0   150m

0   150 yards

SHARI GISR EL-TAUWASH

As you will see when cruising down the river, rural life in Upper Egypt is a balancing act, for man and beast alike.

the *top* of the giant columns. As compensation today, you get to see the whole thing.

The modern town is a thriving community, with an international airport, first-rate hotels and all imaginable facilities for tourists (except that there are few good restaurants outside the big hotels). The **Tourist Bazaar**, near the downtown hotels and Luxor Temple, is what you would expect it to be. The selection of statues and other craftwork is larger but perhaps not of such good quality as you may find in the artisans' workshops over on the west

bank. Less tidy but more colourful, the townspeople's own bazaar (*suq*) is in the backstreets north of the Luxor Temple. For nostalgics seeking something of the romantic atmosphere of tourism's early days, the garden terrace of the old **Winter Palace Hotel** offers a moment of calm at the end of the afternoon.

The footsore will find that there are plenty of taxis, but the most enjoyable forms of transport are the horse-drawn carriages popularly known by their French name, *calèches*, or the even more leisurely tall-sailed *felucca* boats. Fares may need to be negotiated, but they are in any case cheap enough to make tough haggling tasteless. Bicycles can be rented, and these are particularly useful for visiting monuments around the west bank – just put them on the ferry. For longer trips, a taxi-driver will happily tie your bike on the roof of his car.

Now in Luxor Museum, this is part of the reconstructed wall from a temple built by Akhenaten at Karnak before he moved to Tell El Amarna. It was destroyed by his successors.

Luxor Temple

Imposing but much simpler than the huge temple complex of Karnak to the north, for which it served as a kind of annex, the Luxor edifice is especially interesting as a clear exposition of the classic Egyptian temple. Built largely by Amenophis III around 1350 BC on the site of an earlier temple, it was the first step in the New Kingdom Pharaohs' deification that reached its climax with Ramses II. It was dedicated to the Theban triad of Amun, the Pharaohs' personal Creator-God, his wife Mut and son Khons. (Whenever the gods' names get too complicated, remember our READY REFERENCE on page 26.)

Raised on a platform above the usual level of the annual Nile flood, the temple is aligned parallel to the river, with its ceremonial entrance at the north end. To the left of the modern visitors' entrance, an **Avenue of Sphinxes** runs towards Karnak. The sandstone human-headed beasts date from the 30th Dynasty of Nectanebo (4th century BC). The excavation of the complete avenue linking the two temples has been interrupted by the presence of a mosque and Islamic cemetery.

The temple's ceremonial entrance is a massive twin-towered **Pylon** guarded by three **colossal statues** of Ramses II, two seated and one standing, over to the right (two others are in Paris's Louvre Museum

GIVING THEM THE NEEDLE

No, the French did not steal their obelisk. In fact, Mohammed Ali offered them *both* Luxor obelisks, in exchange for the ornate, rather tawdry clock in Cairo's Citadel, but the French gave up any rights to the second obelisk in 1980. Perhaps they recalled how, back in 1831, twelve years after the original offer, their ship had crossed the Mediterranean from Toulon to Alexandria and sailed up the Nile to reach Luxor five months later. The French crew had to fight off cholera as they – and a fair number of Egyptian labourers – lowered the great granite monolith on to the ship, another three months' work. After numerous delays, the ship, dubbed *Louxor* for the occasion and towed by the *Sphinx*, carried its obelisk through the Mediterranean, along the Atlantic coast and up the Seine River to Paris, two years after it left Luxor. Hoisting it on to the square at the bottom of the Champs-Elysées took three more years and 300 sweating, cursing French soldiers wondering how the hell those ancient Egyptians had managed it.

Offered at about the same time as the French obelisk, what the British nicknamed Cleopatra's Needle lay in Alexandria until 1875, when a British engineer worked out a way of getting it to London. He built a hollow metal cylinder for it, complete with cabin and sails, to be towed behind a tugboat. Taken from the sun-cult sanctuary of Heliopolis near Memphis, it was mounted on the Thames Embankment in 1878 and stands 21m (68ft) high, a bit shorter than Cleopatra's other Needle, also from Heliopolis, in New York's Central Park.

and a sixth has disappeared). Of two pink granite **obelisks** originally in front of the statues, one still stands on the left, 25m (82ft) high. Since 1836, the other has commanded traffic on Place de la Concorde in Paris.

On the pylon's towers are carved reliefs of Ramses II's historic battle of Qadesh (*see* page 67). Beyond the pylon, the square **peristyle court**'s arcade of papyrus-bud columns originally had a wooden roof. There are several **colossal statues of Ramses II** in red or black granite. Look to the left and you may get an idea of how the submerged temple must have appeared before the excavations. Some of the court's columns are still buried under the incongruous minaret and dome topped by the Islamic crescent and star of the **Mosque of Abu El Haggag**. Before the Moslems knew anything of the Luxor Temple, they built this mosque over the tomb of a revered 12th-century descendant of Mohammed's son-in-law Ali. The shrine is the object of an annual pilgrimage, with a ceremony that includes the parade of a sacred boat reminiscent of ancient Egyptian ritual. Even a new mosque built outside the temple precincts has not persuaded the devout to budge from the old one (a 19th-century reconstruction) and permit temple excavations to be completed.

A monumental **colonnade** leads through a rectangular court decorated with fascinating reliefs depicting the Nile procession of the gods' sacred barques between Karnak and Luxor. It leads to the great **Court of Amenophis III**, 45m (148ft) by 51m (167ft) with its majestic double rows of papyrus-bud columns beautifully preserved. Serving as a vestibule, the huge **hypostyle hall**, with its four rows of eight columns, has carved reliefs of Amenophis III making offerings to the gods, killing a sacrificial gazelle. One of the chapels off to the left is a **birth room** in which the reliefs of Amenophis III's divine birth stake the Pharaoh's claims as son of Amun. Two antechambers lead to the **Shrine of the Sacred Barque**, built or refurbished by Alexander the Great to honour his divine 'father' Amun as was revealed to him, too, at the oasis of Siwa (*see* page 239). Beyond a second 12-columned hypostyle hall with good but sadly scarred carvings, the inner **Sanctuary** is a small square room of just four columns.

Karnak

This vast temple complex was elevated by the Pharaohs to be Egypt's national shrine, comparable in prestige to the Acropolis of Athens or St Peter's in Rome. From the first buildings of the Middle Kingdom around 2000 BC to the last touches of the Ptolemies in 51 BC, countless rulers sought to enhance their glory by adding a personal monument at Karnak until it covered some 80 hectares (200 acres). Even if you limit your visit to the central **Great Temple of Amun**, we can sense the superhuman dimension of the whole gigantic enterprise.

Try to get your bearings with a first daylight visit before attending the sound-and-light show and, if the calendar allows it, add a romantic tour by moonlight.

Some 3km (nearly 2 miles) north of the Luxor Temple, an **avenue of ram-headed sphinxes** proceeds from what was the ancient riverside quay for the sacred barques of the Theban gods. It leads to the temple's western entrance, a **first pylon** left uncompleted by the first Ptolemies – parts of the mudbrick construction ramps are still visible behind the south (right-hand) tower. The **forecourt** was the work of a Libyan dynasty around 945 BC. Over to the right is the small **Temple of Ramses III**, fronted by two ponderous, ungainly colossi of the king.

In the context of Egypt's ancient religion, the temple at Karnak can be compared with the national cathedral of a Christian country in Europe.

Art and Architecture in Ancient Egypt

The miracle of art in the grandiose age of the Pharaohs is its ability to capture the essential warmth of real life. In their dialogue with the gods, the sculptors and painters treat the people and their kings with grace, dignity and even humour. Beyond the formidable size of the Giza pyramids or Ramses II's daunting colossi at Abu Simbel, the human dimension persists.

Religion and magic pervaded every aspect of life in ancient Egypt. It was the function of art to portray human beings, animals, birds and plants, so as to conciliate the supernatural forces in this world and above all in the world of the dead. Art was never, as we understand it today, the personal expression of a creative individual. What mattered was the skilful execution of a ritually established theme. This required proper mastery of materials, and in the ancient world Egyptians proved themselves supreme craftsmen in the fashioning of stone, metal and paint. It was nature's will that the aridity of the desert climate preserve their work, endowing it with the immortality which their rulers considered a birthright.

Architecture

The Pharaohs' edifices consciously reflect this quest to endure. Paradoxically, they also explain why we have no substantial remains of residential buildings. Expressing the eternal relationship with the gods and the afterlife, the pyramids and other tombs were built of lasting stone on escarpments away from the river. It was perfectly normal to ship the hardest, most durable granite all the way from Aswan up to Memphis and further north to the Delta. For the residences of the living world, on the other hand, whether workers' homes, noble villas or even royal palaces, the Egyptians used only mudbrick with reeds, wattles and, more rarely, wood. Built in the cultivated areas of the Nile Valley, the houses were carried away by the river's flood and the winds of time.

Next to King Djoser's Step Pyramid at Saqqara, we can get an impression of those structures of brick and wattles from the sanctuary's enclosure, modelled on the royal palace at Memphis (*see* page 149). The architects have imitated in stone the buildings' wooden beams, doors and walls. Subsequently, palm trunks, sheaves of papyrus plants and lotus flowers and stems continued to inspire the forms and motifs used for temple columns and their capitals.

Out in the country, houses today are probably taller than those of ancient Egypt, but still frequently built of sun-baked mudbrick.

Pyramids and Tombs

Egyptian tombs were furnished with the necessities of life after death, so that the deceased could act out their fates and acquit themselves appropriately towards the gods. Beside the burial chamber, chapels and storage rooms were added for food, clothes, jewels, weapons, tools and other commodities, in real or symbolic form. In time, the royal chapels became monumental mortuary temples built separately from the burial chamber.

The first royal and noble tombs were practically indistinguishable in size and materials, but with the unification of Lower and Upper Egypt, the power relationship changed. The Pharaoh asserted his supremacy by erecting a giant pyramid as a mausoleum. His family and closest courtiers had more modest tombs grouped at a respectful distance around the pyramid.

After Djoser's tentative, albeit revolutionary Step Pyramid, Kheops completed the first sheer-faced structure with his Great Pyramid at Giza. In fact, it seems his architects used the same basic technique as Djoser's man, Imhotep (*see* page 60), building up around a central core a series of stepped *mastaba*-like slabs of rough limestone, but then smoothed it all off with a finer limestone casing. While the 2,000,000 rough core and inner blocks (each weighing 2.5 tons) were quarried locally at Giza, the finer limestone casing was ferried across the river from Tura, facilitated by the Nile's annual inundation. Red granite and alabaster for the sculpture and other façade work were shipped from Aswan and Nubia. Hoisting by pulley had not yet been invented, and wheeled carts were not yet in use for transporting the blocks, which were most probably dragged on sledges up mudbrick ramps. Inside the pyramid, empty compartments were added as structural supports to relieve the huge pressure bearing down on the granite burial chambers of the king and queen. The dimensions and ritual orientation of the gigantic structures required a knowledge of highly sophisticated mathematics and astronomy (*see* Running a Tight Ship page 58).

The courtiers' tombs of the Old Kingdom may have been more modest than the pyramids, but they are nonetheless imposingly massive. Above ground, each has a long, flat-topped stone block, shaped like a gigantic gold ingot, with the burial chamber below at the bottom of a shaft. To the Egyptian workers helping French archaeologist Auguste Mariette excavate Saqqara in the 19th century, the superstructure looked liked a bench – *mastaba* in Arabic – and that has become the tombs' scholarly name. The *mastaba* housed chambers, a shrine with false door to the Afterworld, and other chapels decorated with friezes depicting worldly activities and offerings made to the deceased and his gods. The tombs grew with the power of the nobles, so that Mereruka's at Saqqara, for example, had an enclosure wall like the royal tombs, and as many as 21 rooms as votive chapels and burial chambers, including six for his wife and five for his son.

As ostentatious displays of wealth and power, the pyramids and *mastaba* had to be abandoned by the end of the Old Kingdom, not only because they cost too much, but also because they were attracting too many grave-robbers. Moving south to Thebes, the Pharaohs and nobles chose to be buried in the less accessible Valley of the Kings over on the west bank of the Nile. These tombs are less conspicuous, with no exterior edifice, just a doorway carved from the valley's limestone escarpment. Stairways and deep corridors lead past votive chapels down to the burial chamber. The splendour of the deceased's tribute to the gods lay, apart from treasure like that of Tutankhamun, in the wealth of sculpture and wall-decoration.

Other rock-cut tombs were created for provincial governors, at Aswan or in Middle Egypt at Beni Hasan. Aswan's tomb-chapels, notably those of Mehu and Sirenput, are elaborate labyrinths of corridors and chambers, while the Beni Hasan tombs are simpler in plan but splendidly fashioned chambers with carved columns, porticoes and barrel roofs, all finely decorated with mural paintings.

Temples of the Gods and Pharaohs

The Egyptians had two kinds of temple. Linked directly to the community, the cult temple provided for divine worship, with images of the gods, prayer halls and housing for the priests. The funerary or mortuary temple was a shrine for the cult of the dead Pharaoh, uniting his image with those of protective deities and located in the same area as his tomb.

Cult Temples

The first sanctuaries of the gods, dedicated to the sun deity Re at Heliopolis, were mere open courtyards with no main edifice. Worship focused on the *benben*, a large but stunted obelisk set to catch the sun on its passage across the heavens and anticipating in form the pyramid and later the full-fledged obelisk. At the Sun Temple of Niuserre (5th Dynasty, 2450 BC) at Abu Ghurab, isolated in the desert south of Giza, the massive base of the solar obelisk,

The Sacred Lake at Karnak, which was the scene of torchlight processions several thousand years ago, when sacred barques carried statues of the gods during the flooding of the Nile.

originally 70m (230ft) high, is still in position. A covered ramp (its friezes displayed in Cairo's Egyptian Museum) leads from a small chapel to an alabaster altar on which offerings were made to the sun-god.

The cult temple presents a journey through the Cosmos, with the temple floor as the earth, and star-studded ceilings as heaven. Progressively, the floor-level rises and the ceilings lower until they meet at the statue of the temple's chief deity in the innermost sanctuary, the Afterworld.

Imagine worshippers walking along an avenue of sphinxes (often from a landing-stage at the Nile, but at Luxor linking its temple with the one at Karnak) to the main entrance. They file through the twin towered pylon, between obelisks and colossal statues of the Pharaoh, across an open colonnaded court. On the far side, the procession continues through a hypostyle hall, a monumental columned basilica. Its sculpture and friezes glorify the names and exploits of the kings and honours their gods. Beyond the hypostyle hall is a smaller votive chapel immediately in front of the gods' innermost sanctuary, with a space for their sacred barque. Off to the sides are storage chambers for temple treasure and cult objects. Outside, a sacred lake or well provides water for the rituals. Other buildings in the temple precincts may include a *mammisi* birth-temple celebrating the Pharaoh's divine origin and the priests' hostels, kitchens and other offices.

The Karnak and Tell El Amarna sanctuaries of the monotheistic renegade Pharaoh, Akhenaten, were dismantled by his successors but were probably closer in spirit to the open worship-areas of early sun temples than the Luxor and Karnak shrine temples.

Seti I's temple at Abydos is remarkable for having two sets of pylons, two forecourts and two hypostyle halls and seven chapels dedicated both to Osiris and to Seti assimilated to Osiris. Ramses II's fantastic rock-cut sanctuary at Abu Simbel is in fact only the most gigantic example of the cult temple's same basic pattern: colossal statues guarding the façade with hypostyle halls and eight smaller chapels leading to an inner sanctuary of four divinities including Ramses II himself.

The Ptolemaic temples followed the Pharaonic conventions, but Kom Ombo is noteworthy for its twin sanctuaries serving the dual cult of Sobek the crocodile-god and Horus the falcon.

The temple at Kom Ombo was a popular pilgrimage sanctuary for the curative powers it offered the lame and the sick.

Funerary Temples

For the Giza pyramids, two temples were built for the funeral ceremony of the deceased Pharaoh. A valley temple was erected at the edge of the desert plateau to receive the king's body. From there, it was borne along a causeway to a mortuary temple adjacent to the pyramid, where it was prepared for the underground burial chamber.

At Thebes, the New Kingdom Pharaohs built most of their funerary temples on the edge of the Nile's west-bank escarpment. One exception is the spectacular temple of Queen Hatshepsut set inland, carved from the limestone rockface. Ramps link its three colonnaded terraces leading to the inner shrine set beyond a hypostyle hall in the cliff. Of Amenophis III's temple, only the Colossi of Memnon from the entrance and fragments of other royal sculpture remain to indicate how immense the original layout must have been. Ramses II apparently 'borrowed' the masonry and the groundplan for his Ramesseum. The entrance of two towering pylons leads to two vast open courts, a hypostyle hall and smaller sanctuary beyond. Ramses III's funerary temple at nearby Medinet Habu, smaller but better preserved, shows how it functioned. Conceived explicitly for homage and ritual devotion with offerings to the Pharaoh, it has no deambulatory or processional space around the halls for worship as in the cult temples.

The Houses of Nobles and Commoners

Apart from stone doorsteps, lintels, windows and column bases, perishable mudbrick and wood were used throughout houses and palaces alike. We get some idea of domestic architecture from the tomb-makers at Thebes who exploited the local materials to treat themselves to houses of stone. The homes of the artisans' village at Deir El Medinah have three or four rooms – bedroom, reception and storage cellar, an open-air kitchen, and a staircase leading to a rooftop sleeping area for the summertime. At Akhenaten's capital in Tell El Amarna, traces of the nobles' villas show some of up to 30 rooms, including bathrooms and toilets, some of them two-storey, supported by pillars. Tomb friezes at Thebes depict houses of several storeys, with windows placed high to limit the sunlight, and hooded roofvents to catch and circulate cooling breezes.

Sculpture

Each statue had a religious or magic function. Amenophis III's granite colossi of Memnon at Thebes or those of Ramses II at Abu Simbel were ritual expressions of the king's power. Tiny mummified *ushabti* figurines, often only 3cm (1 inch) long, were placed in the tomb to act as symbolic servants of the deceased.

The Old Kingdom established certain poses that became standard throughout Pharaonic history: standing with left foot forward; seated upright holding the symbols of office across the chest; the king protected by the wings of the falcon deity, Horus, at his rear; couples with the wife holding her right arm around the husband's back and left hand reaching across to touch his arm. If the poses were stereotyped, the sculptures did not lack the breath of life. In one of the earliest, a limestone statue of King Djoser, the prominent cheekbones and stern downturned mouth project a strikingly dignified authority.

These personal touches were added to sculpture's official canon of human qualities: youth, strength, beauty or

At the Luxor Museum, the limestone torso of Middle Kingdom Pharaoh Sesostris II (about 1890 BC) is portrayed after his death in the pose of Osiris, god of the netherworld.

venerable age. One classic pose was that of the scribe, seated cross-legged on the ground with a scroll of papyrus unrolled on his lap. If he was young, he was muscular; if older, he had folds of fat on his belly, a sign not of decrepitude but of mature wisdom. Within these conventions, the sculptor could inject an alertness in the scribe's posture, a watchful eye or head cocked to listen to his master's dictation.

No statue was portrayed with such individuality that it could be identified as a particular person unless specified by a hieroglyphic name. This is what enabled later Pharaohs, most notoriously Ramses II, to usurp the statues of predecessors by having their own hieroglyph engraved on them.

Accompanying the monumental sculpture of kings and nobles in their tombs were some splendid statuettes of their servants and labourers. Painted

limestone or wooden figures of butchers, brewers, cooks or farmers were as lively as the Dutch peasantry painted by Pieter Brueghel.

Khephren's Great Sphinx guarding the pyramids and temples of Giza (2560 BC) was the first colossus. The convention of a recumbent lion with a king's head to protect a royal sanctuary became common in the Middle Kingdom.

The disintegration of the Middle Kingdom was accompanied by a loss of psychological realism in the sculpture. Body lines were simplified by enveloping the figure in a voluminous cloak. This culminated in the bizarre convention of a cloaked figure seated on the ground with knees drawn up to the chin to form a block with only the head sticking out as if immersed in some kind of cubic hot-tub. These block-statues were mass-produced for pilgrims to the Osiris sanctuary at Abydos as votive offerings – with a space left to inscribe their own name.

More subtle carving skills were revived in the prosperity of the expansionist New Kingdom. Court sculptors produced vivid portrayals of Hatshepsut, more convincing as a queen than when masquerading as a false-bearded king. Luxor Museum's statues of Tuthmosis III are true masterpieces of regal art. Lesser mortals also had their share of impressive sculpture – Hatshepsut's steward, Senenmut, and Amenophis III's architect, Amenhotep, portrayed as a scribe, both young and old.

The prophetic powers of the Great Sphinx at Giza were commemorated by Tuthmosis IV who slept in its shadow and dreamed it told him he would become Pharaoh if he swept away the desert sand covering its paws. He cleaned up and got the job.

The sculptors' keen realism under Amenophis III heralded what became known as the 'Amarna' style of acute mannerism under Akhenaten. His break with traditional stereotypes was expressed with exaggerated depiction of bodily imperfections and idiosyncrasies – pot belly, fat hips and thighs, pendulous lips, elongated nose and cranium – a new stylization that achieved a mysterious grace rather than ugliness. Without resorting to distortions, the beauty of his beloved Nefertiti attained a sensuality unique in Egyptian sculpture. The new style was as much in choice of subject matter as in its treatment: scenes of touching intimacy such as Akhenaten kissing his daughter, or even charming banality, showing the king eating, then cleaning his teeth.

Just too big to attempt any psychological subtleties, the colossi of Ramses II at Abu Simbel and the Ramesseum at Thebes were at least an ultimate statement of Pharaonic might. Thereafter, just as the Egyptian empire declined, conventionalism set in. In the Late Period, the cult of animal deities did at least produce some startling statuary of crocodiles, hippopotami and baboons. The Ptolemies produced some interesting hybrids of ancient Egyptian and classical Greek sculpture.

Painting and Carved Reliefs

The Western eye has to make an important adjustment to the conventions of Egyptian two-dimensional art. Whether in painting or the relief carving adorning tombs and temples, the artist depicts not what he can *see* from one viewpoint but what he *knows* is there, what will present the subject to its best advantage. Thus, he paints the head in profile, but the eye is shown in full. Fine, broad shoulders are frontal while the torso shows off its muscles in

Carved reliefs on the façade of the Pylon gateway honoured the Pharaoh who built the temple and the deity to which it was dedicated. Note here the divine royal falcon spreading its wings to protect the Pharaoh.

three-quarter view. Legs stand in profile.

The many stereotyped scenes include the king smiting Egypt's enemies, usually seizing one of them by his hair; the deceased bearing offerings to the gods; a deity embracing the deceased with an often touchingly tender kiss; and the Pharaoh enthroned to receive offerings, with his family dutifully standing behind him.

Although the construction of funerary temples and tombs was begun long before their candidates' deaths, the deceased were very often buried before the decoration was completed. This has enabled us to see every stage in the process of preparing a sketch for the final painting and carving. Painting or carved relief was chosen as the medium, depending on the quality of the stone surface. The artist marked out the wall with a grid of horizontal and vertical red lines. Usually, 18 rows of squares served to frame a standing human figure. The preliminary sketch in red was corrected in black and then painted in tempera – powdered pigment mixed with a sticky base of egg or other glue.

Graphic skills were already highly developed in the earliest dynasties of the Old Kingdom, as can be seen in the Egyptian Museum's famous painted frieze of Maidum geese (2630 BC). Quite apart from the art historians, zoologists and botanists are astounded by the intricate detail in portraying animals, birds and plants. These are at their most striking in carved relief, as in the Saqqara tombs of Ptahotep and Ti.

Less refined but still very lively are the Middle Kingdom paintings in the rock-cut funerary chambers at Beni Hasan and the reliefs in the tomb of Menthuhotep II at Deir El Bahri.

In the New Kingdom, some of the finest relief carving can be seen at Seti

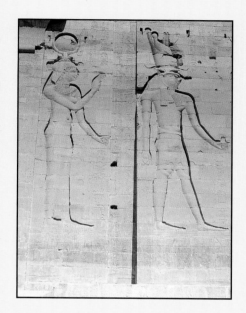

Blessings are bestowed by the sky goddess Hathor, known by her headdress of sun-disk and cow horns, and by the falcon-headed sun-god, Horus.

I's temples at Abydos and Karnak and his tomb in Thebes. For our knowledge of daily life at court and in the fields, hunting, playing games, music and cooking, we must thank the vivid paintings of 18th-Dynasty tombs in the Valley of the Kings. At Thebes and Abu Simbel, a characteristic bombastic but nonetheless splendid flourish is provided by Ramses II's battle-scene reliefs celebrating his 'victory' over the Hittites at Qadesh (*see* page 67). Equally lively and historically more justified are the Medinet Habu battle scenes of Ramses III over the Libyans and Sea Peoples.

One attractive oddity of painting is provided by the Greco-Roman mummies, decorated with brightly coloured facial portraits of the deceased in a style familiar to anyone who has seen the paintings of Pompeii.

Pass through the **second pylon** to the **Great Hypostyle Hall**, Karnak's monumental masterpiece. Covering 6,000m² (64,500ft²), the hall is a forest of 134 columns set in 16 rows. The taller columns flanking the centre processional aisle have capitals in the form of open papyrus blooms, while the others are more conventional closed papyrus buds. The effect is an apparently deliberate representation of the papyrus marshland that covered the primeval waters of the Delta. You have to imagine an original roof of sandstone slabs with light filtering through the upper walls' stone lattice windows, some of which are still in place. The columns of russet-brown stone, once brightly painted, are not monoliths but a series of cylindrical drums, the largest central columns measuring 10m (33ft) round and 21m (69ft) high.

Of the **coloured relief-carvings** on the walls, those of Seti I, in bas-relief, are the more refined (to the north or left-hand side as you enter). They show the king paying tribute to Amun, who wears a double-plumed headdress, the goddess Mut with a white crown or vulture headdress, and the moon-god Khons with a disk and crescent headdress. We also see him crowned by falcon-headed Horus and ibis-headed Thoth and presenting the temple's plans to Amun (a tradition continued in Christian iconography with kings presenting cathe-

These ram's-headed sphinxes provided an honour guard for deities brought by river in sacred barques from the temple of Luxor to the temple of Karnak.

dral plans to the Virgin Mary or patron saint). On the opposite wall, Ramses II is depicted in similar scenes, but more crudely carved in more deeply incised relief. While the inner walls are devoted to religious subjects, the reliefs on the outer walls celebrate the kings' military exploits: on the north wall Seti I's victories over Syrians, Palestinians and Libyans; on the south Ramses II's feats at the battle of Qadesh against the Hittites.

The reconstructed rear wall of the Hypostyle Hall is constituted by the **third pylon** of Amenophis III, leading to a court with fragments of three obelisks, and a fourth still upright, which stood at the entrance to an earlier stage of the temple. In the colonnade beyond the **fourth pylon**, much more impressively asserting her manhood, is the pink granite **obelisk of Queen Hatshepsut**. It measures 29.5m (97ft), the tallest in Egypt. This upset Akhenaten so much that he defaced inscriptions at upper levels. Tuthmosis III just preferred to cover it up, which obligingly preserved it for eternity. The second obelisk lies in fragments, its tip, once covered in gold, is out by the Sacred Lake (*see* below).

The **sanctuary** is almost completely buried in the rubble of the earliest Middle Kingdom temple. At the far end of this jumble of ruins is the fascinating **Festival Hall of Tuthmosis III**, unique among Egyptian temple buildings in its imitation of a king's field-tent for his battle campaigns. In the hall running transversally across the main temple, the two central rows of ten columns, taller than the rest, are tapered in inverted fashion like tent-poles. These are surrounded in a rectangle by 32 square pillars forming side aisles. Copts found this shape uncommonly suited to be a basilica and made a church

of it in the 6th century – traces of painting remain on the pillars.

South of this part of the temple is the great **Sacred Lake**, bordered by a stone terrace and the setting for the second half of the evening sound-and-light show. The lake – 130m (426ft) long, 80m (262ft) wide and 4m (13ft) deep – was the scene of quite another spectacle several thousand years ago. Torchlit and enveloped in clouds of incense, sacred barques carried statues of the gods, Amun, Mut and Khons, across the lake during the Nile inundation. At the north-west corner of the lake is a **giant granite scarab** dedicated to the sun-god Khepri by Amenophis III. The king had placed it originally near the Colossi of Memnon at his temple on the west bank.

Luxor Museum

On the waterfront north of the Luxor Temple, this modern, beautifully designed little museum makes a striking contrast to Cairo's vast but overwhelming and inevitably often chaotic Egyptian Museum. The collections culled from the Theban temples and tombs are modest in number but handsome in quality and subtly lit. When the museum opens at the end of the afternoon, it offers a moment's cool, quiet contemplation quite different from the sometimes strident experience of confronting the works of art in their open temple setting. To do justice to the huge reserves of antiquities, most of the works are exhibited on a rotating system. Of the few permanently in place, a prized exhibit is **Akhenaten's wall**, 18m (60ft) long, reconstructed here from a temple he built at Karnak when still bearing the name Amenophis IV. It has an early portrayal of the king with Queen Nefertiti paying tribute to Aten, deity of the sun's rays. Other works on display include the smaller but precious **treasures from Tutankhamun's tomb**, a great pink granite **bust of Amenophis III**, a green basalt **statue of Tuthmosis III** and a fine **statue of Isis**.

A separate wing, the **New Cachette Hall**, displays results of the 1989 excavations that revealed unsuspected treasures, in almost perfect condition, from Amenophis III's edifices at Karnak. Also exhibited on a rotating basis, they include an alabaster **sphinx of Tutankhamun**; a **statue of Horemheb** standing at the knees of his protector, Amun; an exquisite rich-burgundy-coloured statue of **Amun and Mut enthroned**; and **Amenophis III** himself, wearing the double crown of Upper and Lower Egypt.

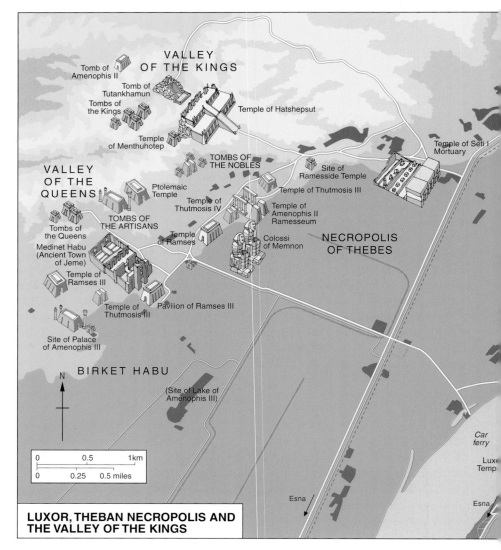

LUXOR, THEBAN NECROPOLIS AND THE VALLEY OF THE KINGS

Theban Necropolis

Even if the rocky escarpments across the river in the Western Desert did not provide the tombs of the Pharaohs and their entourage with the expected security from grave-robbers, the grandiose landscape should have consoled them with the notion that it was – and still is – the stuff that eternity is made of. Today, over and above the rewards of the tombs' magnificent friezes painted in colours that are still astonishingly bright, a walk among the formidable cliffs of the desert's endless craggy plateau imparts a sense of the ancient Egyptians' belief in an immortal destiny.

Habitués come here at different times of the day to see the changing colours – silver and pink at dawn, gold and dazzling white at noon, amber and russet at the end of the afternoon.

In any case, more than one visit would be necessary to appreciate the full scope of what is a veritable kingdom rather than mere city of the dead. The renowned **Valley of the Kings** is but one small part of the Theban Necropolis. With their equal share of artistic masterpieces, there are the **Tombs of the Nobles**, the **Valley of the Queens**, and by no means least, the fascinating **Tombs of the Artisans**. On a larger scale are the **mortuary Temple of Hatshepsut**, the **Ramesseum** of Ramses II and, as a grand final punctuation, the two **Colossi of Memnon**.

So start early. Ferries leave from the landing stages by the Luxor Temple. Taxis are available on the west bank if you do not have your own transport laid on. (Drivers may know the various sites by their Arabic names – *Deir El Bahri* for Hatshepsut's temple, *Deir El Medina* for the artisans' tombs – so we mention these in the text.) Take torches (flashlights) for some of the tombs that are not illuminated, your very best walking shoes, and a small wad of 50-piastre and one-pound notes to tip the tomb-guardians. As is so often the case, a tour-guide is invaluable for finding your way from one site to the other and negotiating entrance to the tombs when group-tours are present. Refreshments other than mineral water are in

meagre supply on the west bank, but it is not a bad idea to plan a full day with a picnic, if you take care to seek out some shade for a siesta.

WHAT'S IN A TOMB?

From the tomb's simple, deliberately unobtrusive entrance, a long corridor is cut down through the rockface to an antechamber which held real and symbolic offerings to the gods. Beyond that is the burial chamber with a sarcophagus originally and in some cases still containing the mummy. Off the main corridor are side chambers for the deceased's personal effects, treasure (all gone) and statues (some still there).

The walls are decorated (like those in the tombs of Saqqara and Beni Hasan) with brightly coloured paintings and carved reliefs of everyday life and ritual scenes. The décor almost invariably includes a ceiling of blue heaven studded with yellow stars, and a scene of the jackal-headed Anubis embalming the corpse. Other commonly depicted funereal themes are *Ka*, the deceased's spiritual power, symbolized by a pair of raised arms, often fashioned on a potter's wheel by the ram-headed creator-god, Khnum; and *Ba*, the soul of the deceased in the form of a human-headed bird released from the body. Hieroglyphic inscriptions are mostly texts from the Books of the Dead – religious prayers and hymns and magical incantations to prepare and protect the deceased for the afterworld.

Many of the tombs have a deep pit which guides like to say was a trap set for robbers, but archaeologists think it may just have been to catch rainwater. Of course, as their skeletons testified, some robbers did fall in. Many more, tipped off by the tomb-diggers or more often the tomb-diggers themselves, got away. Inscriptions show that some of the later ones were Christians who sought to save their souls by turning the burial chambers into churches.

Buy your tickets at the office on the west bank. You will need several depending on the number of tombs and other monuments you plan to visit.

Valley of the Kings

About 4km (2.5 miles) north of the ferry-landing, make a first stop for a look at the **Mortuary Temple of Seti I**. This porticoed shrine in white sandstone, completed by his son Ramses II, is typical of the conspicuous monuments that the Pharaohs allowed themselves here before being buried away more discreetly in the hills beyond. North of the temple are some of the valley's oldest tombs, dating back to 2050 BC, but with nothing left of great interest to the casual visitor.

A paved road running 5km (3 miles) south west from the Seti temple takes you to the Valley of the Kings at the foot of a pyramid-shaped hill.

There are some 70 tombs in this valley alone, not all of them worth visiting, not all of them open. They are numbered, roughly in chronological order of excavation. Since there is much to see and the best are not all grouped together, three or four seem to be the most that can reasonably be managed on one visit. We propose a half dozen in a certain order of accessibility from the rest-house.

First off (at the time of publication), the over-visited **Tomb of Tutankhamun** (62) has been closed indefinitely for renovation. Apart from the chance to say you were there, it must be admitted you are not missing much. In the historical scheme of things, he was an insignificant king who died so young that there was time for just a very small tomb and the décor is better in other tombs. Only the burial chamber is decorated – with scenes of Hathor giving him life, Isis and Anubis attending to his death and six baboon images of Thoth (the *Tut-* of his name). In the now glass-covered stone sarcophagus, his mummy lies in one of its mummiform coffins.

Behind the rest-house is situated the **Tomb of Ramses I** (16). It is small – like Tutankhamun, he reigned too short a time to get himself a bigger one – but its decoration is attractive. It has three chambers, of which the **burial chamber** has a brightly painted mural of brown and yellow figures against a turquoise background in procession with the sacred barque. The king makes an offering to the scarab-god Khephri. The lidded **sarcophagus** bears the protective image of Isis spreading her wings.

Next door to the left, the **Tomb of Seti I** (17), father of Ramses II, is one of the biggest of the royal tombs and boasts some of the finest decoration in vividly coloured bas-relief. Isis and her sister Nephthys protect the doorways as five connecting corridors lead over two pits and through four rooms to the splendid **burial chamber** with another long corridor beyond. As you follow the path taken by the king's coffin (the sarcophagus has found its way to London), notice Seti presenting his respects to the sun-gods symbolized by sun-disk, the ram-headed Re and the scarab Khephri. Vultures fly along the ceilings, past monsters, demons and ghosts. Interrupted work lets you follow the painting process of red and black guidelines preceding the final picture.

*I*t was among these rocks, overlooked by centuries of grave-robbers, that Howard Carter dug down to the fabulous treasures of Tutankhamun.

TUT'S LUCK

It was Tutankhamun's – and posterity's – good fortune that nobody cared much about his tomb. In 1140 BC, two centuries after his death, workers digging the tomb of Ramses VI tossed the debris out from their hole and covered up Tutankhamun's tomb lying neglected nearby.

Flash forward 3,000 years. British artist Howard Carter was hired by scholars in 1892 to sketch bas-reliefs at the temple of Menthuhotep east of the Valley of the Kings. He was convinced the valley still concealed unplundered tombs and persuaded an American investor to finance his excavations. He searched the tombs of Tuthmosis IV and Queen Hatshepsut, but found them empty. Back in Cairo, he found another backer in Lord George Carnarvon. The good lord, himself an ardent amateur Egyptologist, was immensely rich and more interested in fighting the boredom of a prolonged convalescence after a car accident than adding to his personal fortune. In any case, whatever treasure might be found would stay in Egypt. Carnarvon financed Carter for seven years, still without success, and returned to England with little hope that his man would find anything.

In November 1922, he received a telegram from Carter saying he had found a hitherto unknown tomb in the Valley of the Kings but would await Carnarvon's arrival before exploring it. Digging around the tomb of Ramses VI, Carter and his workers had uncovered a stairway of 16 steps leading down to a sealed door. Working by candlelight together with Carnarvon, he cleared rubble blocking the door and found at the bottom, unbroken, the seal of Tutankhamun. Beyond it was a corridor with more rubble to be shovelled away, some 9m (30ft), before reaching a second door. As Carter himself described it, 'with trembling hands', he made a small hole in the upper left-hand corner.

'Widening the hole a little, I inserted the candle and peered in. At first I could see nothing, the hot air escaping from the chamber causing the candle flame to flicker.' As Carter's eyes grew accustomed to the light, Carnarvon badgered him to say something. 'Can you see anything?' asked the lord.

'Yes,' replied Carter at last. 'Wonderful things!'

The first wonders he saw, in what was just an antechamber, included a jumble of two golden chariots, three gilded beds and two statues in black and gold. The rest, complete with massive shrines, mummiform coffins and fabulous death-mask, all of gold, is history – and displayed at the Egyptian Museum in Cairo.

Some four months later, Carnarvon died of a freak mosquito bite, five years before the excavations were completed, prompting the legend of Tutankhamun's curse. But Carter died in 1939 at the respectable age of 65. For him at least, Tut's luck had held good.

Double back for the **Tomb of Ramses III** (11), also known as the Tomb of the Harpists after one of its best-known pictures. From the Hathor-headed pilaster portal, descend some 10m (33ft) underground to a series of corridors continuing 125m (410ft) into the escarpment. The most interesting scenes are in the side chambers: butchers and bakers preparing meals; boats sailing on the Nile; a warrior's collection of spears, bows and arrows, helmets, armour and chariots; and the two harpists singing the praises of Ramses III before three deities. The eight-pillared burial chamber has lost its sarcophagus to the Louvre museum in Paris.

A short distance away to the north, the **Tomb of Horemheb** (57) rewards those who descend the long steep corridor to the

burial chamber with a splendid red granite **sarcophagus**. In the antechamber are fine reliefs of the soldier-Pharaoh Horemheb offering wine to Isis and ointments to Ptah.

Continue west to find the **Tomb of Amenophis II** (35), one of the deepest; to reach it, descend 90 steps into the bowels of the earth. Robbers plundered the tomb soon after the king's death in 1394 BC, but left the mummy. This prompted priests later to use it for 12 other royal mummies, a treasure-trove for modern scholars since they included Tuthmosis IV, Amenophis III and his queen Tiy, Seti II and Ramses IV. The plundered king's fine sandstone cartouche-shaped **sarcophagus** is still in the burial chamber. The walls have splendidly coloured scenes of offerings to Osiris, Hathor and Anubis. Notice, too, the yellow used to simulate papyrus for the inscriptions of the Books of the Dead – another prize for scholars as they represent practically a full text.

For the truly adventurous, the **Tomb of Tuthmosis III** (34) occupies an enthralling site in a narrow, sheer-faced gully at the far west end of the valley. Its approach was clearly intended to deter robbers and has a similar effect on faint-hearted tourists, but the trek is well worth the effort. There is a steep climb up a flight of wooden steps to the entrance and then a sloping corridor to another staircase and a corridor winding down to the core of the tomb. On the walls, scholars have counted the names of 740 different deities and evil spirits. Supported by two square pillars, the superb **burial chamber** has the rounded oblong shape of a royal cartouche. The beautifully carved red sandstone **sarcophagus** stands on an alabaster pedestal beneath a blue heaven studded with yellow stars. Scenes on the

*T*ucked away in the Valley of the Kings, the entrance to the tomb of Amenophis takes you down to burial chambers in which the priests stored 12 royal mummies.

pillars concentrate on the king's relationship with the women in his life, being suckled by Isis in the form of a sycamore tree, travelling with his mother in a boat, attended by three wives and a daughter, and the menacing alternative – a bunch of demons. The tomb's remoteness seems to have been at least partly successful in discouraging robbers as the king's mummy and much of the tomb furnishings of the side chambers survived for safe keeping in the Egyptian Museum in Cairo.

191

Temple of Hatshepsut

East of the Valley of the Kings, the queen's mortuary temple is in an area commonly known as **Deir El Bahri**, after the Northern Monastery that once stood here. Of all the monuments in the Theban Necropolis, the grandiose shrine dedicated to Hathor, goddess of the west, region of the dead, makes the most spectacular use of the desert landscape. For the design of the three terraces rising and receding to the sanctuary cut out of the escarpment, the queen's architect and lover, Senenmut, drew inspiration – and probably a lot of the building material – from Menthuhotep's mortuary temple, the first great monument to be built on Thebes' west bank, 600 years earlier in 2050 BC. You can see its remains immediately to the south. (For his efforts, Senenmut won the rare reward of a tomb at his queen's temple – situated to the right of the long avenue to the entrance, not easily accessible.)

Cross the **Lower Terrace**, originally, but alas no more, shaded by trees, to the **colonnade** divided by the ramp leading to the upper level. On the columns left of the ramp are some intriguing scenes of boat-building and how Hatshepsut's two great obelisks were transported from Aswan to Karnak. To the right of the ramp are

In keeping with her formidable character, Queen Hatshepsut chose for her mortuary temple the most spectacular setting in all the vast Theban Necropolis.

scenes of hunting and fishing and, with her image obliterated by subsequent enemies, making a calf-offering to the ithyphallic Amun.

At the rear of the **Middle Terrace**, another ramp divides a **second colonnade**. Left of the ramp are the important **Punt reliefs** of a trade mission south to buy incense and myrrh from the land now identified as Somalia. In the left-hand corner is the **Chapel of Hathor**, depicted variously as a queen with cow's ears on the columns or as a cow on the walls. Finely carved reliefs systematically obliterate the figure of Hatshepsut, replacing her with that of the Pharaohs who succeeded her, Tuthmosis II and III and Amenophis IV.

Right of the ramp are **scenes of Hatshepsut's birth**. In the one of her being blessed by Amun, whom she claimed as her divine father, the queen's figure is obliterated, but other finely carved scenes show her pregnant mother with Heket, the frog-headed goddess of midwives, and the ram-headed Khnum. In the far corner is the **Chapel of Anubis**, the jackal-headed god of embalming. A row of elegant fluted pillars leads from the chapel back along the right side of the terrace.

The **Upper Terrace** was defaced by Copts who installed their own monastery, Deir El Bahri, now completely removed. The terrace is undergoing prolonged restoration, notably for the ruined Hypostyle Hall, but may offer limited access to the rock-cut **chapels** and **sanctuary**, again with reliefs on which the queen's image is usurped by that of her successors. Of the sanctuary's three chambers, the third was added by the Ptolemies for Imhotep and Amenhotep, both architect-scribes deified as healers.

Tombs of the Nobles

Clustered around the hilltop village of **Sheikh Abd El Gurna**, of which you can see the mosque's minaret, the tombs are located south of Hatshepsut's temple, on the way to the Ramesseum. There are some 250 tombs here, each with a decorated chapel and a shaft descending to the burial chamber. The best of the decoration is of a quality equal to that of the kings' tombs and often more lively and varied in their treatment of everyday life. To fit them in with other sites, you may want to visit at least a couple. We propose a selection of four.

Appropriately for an agriculture minister for Tuthmosis IV, the **Tomb of Nakht** (52) has superbly detailed farm scenes of planting and harvest in its chapel. For the wine-making, the grapes are pressed in time-honoured fashion by dancing on them. At a banquet, we see Nakht and his loving wife (with a Rastafarian hairdo) entertained by a blind harpist, flute player and dancing girls.

The **Tomb of Menna** (69) shows the deceased, royal scribe to Tuthmosis IV, recording the crop yield. Clearly, he had his enemies, as a rival has sought to injure his afterlife by depriving him of offerings by 'blinding' his eyes and cutting the 'boomerang' he used in hunting, thus damaging the balance on which his behaviour was to be judged. Two vivid scenes show a couple of girls fighting while another removes a thorn from her friend's foot.

The **Tomb of Ramose** (55) is particularly valued for its celebrated funeral frieze of chairs, beds, musical instruments and board-games very similar to the treasure of Tutankhamun. Admire, too, the subtly carved reliefs fashioning the female figures' transparent robes and veils and

MAKING MUMMIES

You *really* want to know how they made mummies? Of course you do, but we should warn readers that parts of this tale are not for the squeamish.

In the earliest days of ancient Egypt, the dead were covered simply with an animal skin or matting, before being buried in a shallow desert grave where the air and sand were hot and dry enough to preserve the corpse with no bacteria to cause decay. But in the first Pharaohs' burial chambers, the rot quickly set in. The undertakers first tried wrapping the corpse tightly in linen, then reinforced that with plaster, but only the casing survived. By the 4th Dynasty, they learned to remove the quickly rotting internal organs. The process of mummification thereafter grew more and more sophisticated.

It took 70 days to prepare the body, including 40 days to dry it out. The brain and entrails were immediately removed. (The squeamish should stop reading here.) After breaking a bone at the top of the nose, the brain was drawn out through the nostrils. The viscera were extracted through an incision above the left hip. The heart, as the seat of understanding of what would happen to the deceased in the Afterworld, was left in place.

Dry natron crystals were used to dissolve body fats, dehydrate the body and keep the skin supple. Body cavities were packed with dried lichen, sawdust and linen. Lips of incisions were sewn back together and covered with patches of leather, metal or wax, known as an embalming plate, stamped with the eye of Horus for good luck.

A natural appearance was desirable, so eye-sockets were plugged with artificial eyes. Once the body was dehydrated, linen pads were inserted to fill out sunken cheeks, and mud or sawdust was packed into the limbs to make them pleasingly plump again. Such refinements occurred at the height of the embalmer's art in the 21st Dynasty (around 1070 BC).

In later, more decadent years, this beautification was neglected to concentrate just on a thorough bandaging. This, after rubbing the body with lotions, ointments and a thin coat of resin, took 15 days, keeping the bandages tight and following uniformly the contours of the body, keeping the shape and proper rigidity. Head, fingers, toes and limbs were each wrapped separately before being enveloped with the torso. The process took 325m² (3,500ft²) of linen.

A funerary mask was then fitted to the head and shoulders – linen or papyrus starched with plaster for ordinary mortals, gilded for aristocracy and the most precious metals for the likes of Tutankhamun.

The mummification of animals was more perfunctory. All that mattered for the sacred bulls, cows, cats, ibises and baboons was proper bandaging to preserve the silhouette.

beautifully detailed wigs. The tomb remained uncompleted when Ramose, governor of Thebes under Amenophis III, joined Akhenaten at Tell El Amarna, where he has a second tomb. Both Pharaohs are portrayed here, Akhenaten distinguishable by his familiar pot-belly. Notice in the funeral procession how the weeping women's mascara or *kohl* is running. Mourners slap clay on their heads, a custom that still continues.

The **Tomb of Rekhmiré** (100) shows that the chancellor of Tuthmosis III and Amenophis III also served as foreign minister, receiving gifts from envoys: Cretans bring their Minoan vases, Nubians, wearing dainty little leopard-skin loincloths, carry elephant tusks and gold, and Syrians chariots, horses, an elephant and bear. Another scene suggests he also manned the treasury, and was responsible for punishing tax-dodgers.

Ramesseum

South of the village of Sheikh Abd El Gurna, a splendid ruin is all that earthquakes have left of the mortuary temple and palace where Ramses II resided when attending west-bank festivities. (The name was coined by the hieroglyphics whizz-kid, Jean-François Champollion.) On the collapsed **first pylon** are scenes of the king's heroics at the battle of Qadesh. The hieroglyphic narration by his son, Banta-or, tells how enemy tricks led Ramses II into ambush. Near the pylon is the black granite base of the king's **seated colossus**, with the head and other fragments strewn around the second court. The statue is estimated to have been 17m (55ft) high and weighed 1,000 tons, which makes it about the same size as the standing (now recumbent) colossus in Memphis.

Town and Tombs of the Artisans

West of the Ramesseum at **Deir El Medina** (after the Town Monastery of which the ruins are still partially visible) is the home and last resting-place of the men who dug, built, carved and painted the tombs and monuments of the Theban Necropolis. Their honoured title was 'Servant in the Square of Truth', in other words holders of secrets with the privilege and unavoidable obligation to live, die and be buried here near their rulers.

They worked an eight-hour shift, nine days on, one day off, in compact teams of overseer, scribe, masons, artists and guards, in addition to serfs performing the menial tasks of cooking and cleaning up. Two teams usually worked inside each tomb, one on the left wall, the other on the right. Their **walled town**, dating back to the New Kingdom of Tuthmosis III and

Amenophis III (15th and 14th century), now comprises some 70 mudbrick and stone houses of one or two storeys, with a central court as reception area surrounded by bedrooms and kitchen.

Quite unlike those of royalty and the nobles, the **artisans' tombs** had a small pyramidal roof over their chapel, from which a deep shaft descended to the burial chamber. The artwork on these gives a much freer tone to the lively, down-to-earth pictures, less boastful than those of their masters, but with their own dignity and elegance.

The **Tomb of Sennedjem** (1) is that of an overseer. We see him in the sacred fields of Yalu. In this rather more workmanlike version of the Garden of Eden, there are wheatfields to be ploughed before the date-palms and other exotic fruit trees can be enjoyed. But he, too, has the right to an incarnation as Osiris, green-faced, protected by the eyes of the sun, and has the jackal-headed Anubis to embalm him.

The **Tomb of Innerkhau** (359) shows an overseer with his wife, both handsomely wigged, smiling with delight at the entertainment of an aged harpist. In another scene a sacred cat of Heliopolis kills the evil Apophis serpent.

Valley of the Queens

The tombs of the Pharaohs' wives and children have a valley to themselves tucked away in the south-west corner of the Theban Necropolis.

The most important, but not always accessible, is the **Tomb of Nefertari** (66), wife of Ramses II. Her name means 'beautiful companion' and she was the king's principal queen, honoured at Abu Simbel with her own temple and statues. The tomb's first chamber is a **banquet**

room, where food offerings were assembled for the deceased. In exquisite colour, we see Nefertari under a canopy playing the ancient board-game of *Senet* (of which a set can be seen among Tutankhamun's treasure in the Egyptian Museum). Other scenes show the queen's human-headed *Ka* spirit worshipping the sun-god, and her mummy attended by Isis and sister Nephthys in the guise of falcons. Her **sarcophagus** is found in the burial chamber.

In the **Tomb of Amun Hir Khopshef** (55), we see touching scenes of the prince, who died at the age of 9, being led through the Afterworld by his father, Ramses III. The king presents him to Isis, Thoth and Ptah. The little boy was honoured before his death with the title of Overseer of Horses. You can still see his **sarcophagus**.

SINGING FOR HADRIAN

Greek and Roman pilgrims came at dawn to hear one of the great statues sing. The colossi, they thought, represented Memnon, a warrior slain by Achilles in the Trojan war. More importantly, he was the divine son of Eos, goddess of the dawn, whom he greeted with a song at sunrise. She replied with tears of dew. On his tour of Egypt in AD 130, Emperor Hadrian camped overnight on Thebes' west bank in order to hear this wondrous song emitted by the northernmost of the two statues. Came dawn, nothing. The men who had brought him feared they would be punished for this embarrassment. Hadrian remained imperial and stayed another night. The next day, Memnon delivered. Not just once but three times, as a crack in the granite expanded in the morning sun, the wind moaned its mournful song. The court poetess Balbilla commemorated the divine honour in Greek verse now inscribed on the monolith's left leg.

Colossi of Memnon

These majestic statues are conveniently situated on the way back to the ferry from visits to any of the other major sites. Mistakenly named by the Greeks after a Trojan hero, they stand or rather sit alone at the edge of cultivated fields where once they guarded the entrance to the long destroyed mortuary temple of Amenophis III. The sandstone colossi of the 18th-Dynasty king are 21m (68ft) high, big enough to have been the only monuments in the Theban Necropolis visible through the ages until excavations began in earnest in the 19th century.

North of Luxor

Without abandoning your base at Luxor, there are a couple of day-trips to be made north before you start heading down to Aswan. The more important of the two is a combined visit to the west-bank temple towns of **Abydos** and **Denderah**, about 340km (212 miles) there and back – though they may be included as part of the package for a Nile cruise. Those interested in Coptic culture may want to visit two historic monasteries at **Sohag** further north on a separate trip.

In the great Temple of Seti I at Abydos, the Pharaoh's own effigy is constantly usurped by the images of his son Ramses II. The latter's megalomania, which included obliterating his father's name from reliefs, may well have stemmed from his lifelong need to outshine Seti I.

196

Abydos

On the west bank, about 150km (93 miles) north of Luxor, the temples of Abydos are surrounded by fields of sugar cane, barley and corn. An amphitheatre of Western Desert hills furnishes a dramatic backdrop. As the traditional burial place of earth-god Osiris, lord of Abydos, it was a funerary site for early dynasties and a popular place of pilgrimage under the Old Kingdom. Cemeteries and derelict *mastaba* tombs are in a scattered area south east of the main temples.

South of the modern village, the great limestone **Temple of Seti I** was the principal shrine of daily worship to Osiris and the memory of deceased Pharaohs. Its first two colonnaded courtyards, approached by ramps, were built by his son Ramses II, whom we see in carved relief welcomed by the gods. On the second colonnade, he worships Osiris and honours the god's sisters Isis and Horus. Battle scenes show him slaying Asian and Libyan foes in the presence of Amun.

The **first hypostyle hall**, with 24 papyrus-bud columns, is built of sandstone with finer limestone facing on the north wall. Though Ramses II has obliterated his name, Seti I can be seen, in carved reliefs to the right of the hall's entrance, planning the building of the temple and presenting the finished edifice to Horus. In the **second hypostyle hall** are paintings of Seti with the gods, but again usurped by his son. Notice the innovation of **seven chapels** leading in an L-shape off the rear of the hall. Between each of them is a niche for offerings. Their decoration shows the triad of Osiris, Isis and Horus and the daily ritual with sacred barques for the Theban triad of Amun, Mut and Khons and the creator-gods of Memphis, Re-Herakhty and Ptah, with Seti I deified.

In the temple's south wing off to the left is the **Corridor of Kings**, in which the names of 76 Pharaohs are listed, ending with Ramses II – and excluding Akhenaten, among other undesirables.

Beyond the temple is the **Osireion**, the sunken cenotaph of Osiris with whom Seti identified himself. The structure originally simulated the primeval mound set in the middle of a lake. Entrance was through a long passage at the far end. Preceding the main hall of square granite pillars is an arched-roofed transverse hall decorated with scenes of sky-goddess Nut. Closest to the Seti's temple is the god's symbolic burial chamber, which originally contained a sarcophagus.

A 15-minute walk across the sand north west of Seti's temple brings you to the **Temple of Ramses II**, distinguished on the north and west walls by some vigorous scenes of his battle against the Hittites at Qadesh.

Denderah

Some 60km (37 miles) from Luxor, on the west bank opposite Qena, Denderah's **Temple of Hathor** is one of the best preserved in Egypt, almost entirely built by the Greeks and Romans from 125 BC to about AD 60. A highlight is the climb to the roof, with particularly spectacular views at sunset, so it is best to make this the second of your visits if you are combining it with Abydos.

Hathor, the local sky-goddess – identified by the Greeks with Aphrodite – is portrayed throughout the temple with a headdress of cow's horns and sun-disk, or as a woman with dainty cow's ears. Entrance is through Corinthian columns on which the Roman emperors Domitian and Trajan appear as Pharaohs making offerings to the Egyptian gods.

Other emperors, Augustus, Nero, Tiberius, Claudius, have left their cartouches or effigies in the main **hypostyle hall**, which has 24 columns in four rows of six. Its most fascinating feature is the **ceiling** covered with its astronomical and astrological themes. We see the elongated sky-goddess Nut swallowing and giving birth to the sun. She arches her slim body over to form the vault of the heavens, with arms and legs outstretched to touch the four cardinal points. Other motifs show the course taken by the sun in 12 hours across the skies, the moon as a sacred eye, and the wind as a winged figure. Many of the zodiac signs are represented by now familiar Egyptian gods – Amun as Aries the ram, Apis as Taurus the bull, Osiris as Leo the lion, Isis as Virgo the virgin, and her sister Nephthys as Pisces the fish.

Beyond is a narrower small hall of six columns, leading to the antechamber of the gods' inner sanctuary. Surrounding this area are chapels and storage rooms for the temple's furniture, sacred perfumes and linen, much of it depicted or described on the walls if no longer present in the rooms. There are also 12 subterranean **crypts**, also used for storage, of which you can visit number 4.

Sohag

About 200km (125 miles) north of Luxor – more easily accessible for those driving south from Asyut – are the town's ancient Coptic monasteries founded in the 5th century. You may need a guide to help

B uilt out in the middle of nowhere, Coptic refuges such as the White Monastery at Sohag were built like fortresses, and made use of Greco-Roman pillars from the nearby temple of Athribis.

*I*cons of Jesus with Mary, at the Last Supper and as Christ Triumphant, decorate the sanctuary screen in the church of the White Monastery.

you locate the sites in the country on the outskirts of town, but local people are usually quite happy to oblige.

West of Sohag, the **White Monastery** (*Deir El Abyad*) takes its name from its fortress-like white limestone walls. Dedicated to its abbot, St Shenuda, it was founded around 440, but restored in the 13th and 19th centuries. The granite of the church's 19 columns and massive pulpit has been taken from the nearby Greco-Roman temple of Athribis and still bears its hieroglyphic inscriptions. The domes over the apses of the sanctuary have paintings of the Virgin Mary and two somewhat faded 12th-century Armenian works, notably of Jesus in majesty.

Further north, the **Red Monastery** (*Deir El Ahmar*), built largely of baked

*T*he Red Monastery, dedicated to St Bishai whose order once numbered 3,000 monks, is now deserted by all but its gate-keeper.

brick, is also a 5th-century foundation. The oldest part of the monastery is the chapel of the Virgin Mary in the southeast corner. In the opposite corner is the church of patron saint Bishai, of more recent construction. The iconostasis screen has portraits of St Shenuda, St Bishai and St Pjol.

Take advantage of your time in Sohag by crossing the river to the town of **Akhmim**, famous for its cotton manufacture, where printed cotton shawls and fine embroidery are on sale in its **bazaar**.

South of Luxor

The valley that runs south towards Aswan shrinks to a narrow strip as it approaches the ancient region of Nubia. Hemmed in by the Western Desert sands and the hills of the Eastern Desert, the villages have not changed in their simple appearance over the centuries, even though many of them have been relocated from lands submerged by the Aswan Dam. The temples here are interesting examples of the Greco-Roman assimilation of Egyptian architecture and of the animal cults inherited from the last period of Pharaonic civilization.

Esna

Just 54km (33 miles) south of Luxor, the town made its mark in history only for its worship of the local sacred fish, the *lates*, a kind of perch still found in the Nile and varying in size from a few centimetres to 1.5m (5ft). This won it the Greek name of Latopolis. (A half-hour visit will do it.)

In the middle of town, the **Temple of Khnum** makes a striking first impression from its situation in a depression 9m (30ft) below the surrounding houses. It is not the temple which has sunk, but the level of the town which has risen with each successive wave of superimposed construction over the centuries. The houses cover a large

Hamlets like this one have been reconstructed north of Aswan to replace homes submerged by the Aswan Dam.

unexcavated part of the temple – as well as two other temples which existed here in the time of Tuthmosis III.

Only the 24-column **hypostyle hall** begun under Emperor Tiberius is visible, but it is an impressive structure 33m (108ft) by 16m (52ft). Beneath zodiac signs on the ceiling, several Roman emperors are portrayed in carved relief as Pharaohs honouring the ram-headed Khnum, or have their names inscribed in cartouches. Titus and Trajan are seen smiting Egypt's foes. Hadrian and Marcus Aurelius are both represented by texts important to archaeologists studying the Greco-Roman assimilation of Egyptian religion. Less scholarly, Napoleon Bonaparte's soldiers left graffiti engraved on the temple terrace.

Edfu

Some 50km (30 miles) upriver, on the west side of the town of Edfu, is the best preserved and, after Karnak, biggest temple in Egypt. The grand **Temple of Horus** measures 137m (450ft) in length, its great pylon is 79m (260ft) wide and 36m (118ft) high. The Ptolemies took over a century, from 237 to 105 BC, to complete the sandstone reconstruction, including the reuse of ancient masonry from an earlier, perhaps Old Kingdom temple here. In its relatively impeccable condition, it serves as a model for imagining the progress of worshippers, priests and royalty (but not commoners) from the entrance to the inner sanctuary. It has the classical plan of a giant pylon at the entrance, a courtyard for offerings, two hypostyle halls, two vestibules and a sanctuary surrounded by

Ceremonial approach to the great pylon entrance of Edfu's Temple of Horus, rebuilt by the Ptolemies at the end of the 3rd century BC.

*T*he falcon guarding the temple entrance at Edfu wears the royal crown. Supreme among hunting birds, it was the symbol of divine kingship.

chapels and storage chambers. An enclosure wall leaves a narrow corridor around the main structure's periphery. The Greeks called the shrine Apollinopolis, identifying the sun-god Horus with Apollo. (A thorough visit takes two hours, but one hour may be enough.)

Hieroglyphic accounts of its rituals, found on scrolls in the temple library, have revealed in detail the colourful ceremonies dating back to the temple's earliest foundation, but portrayed for us less scholarly spectators in the carved reliefs.

The modern visitors' entrance is from the north, but make your way back to start out from the temple's main entrance, the gigantic **pylon** guarded by two black granite falcons, symbol of Horus. On the pylon's inside wall, to the left of the entrance, we see the all-important ceremony that took the sky-goddess Hathor from Denderah on her sacred barque upriver for her annual union with Horus at Edfu. This, the hieroglyphs tell us, was a festive journey lasting two weeks which people celebrated with great merriment all along the way as other gods sailed out in their boats to join the procession. To the right on this inner wall, we see Ptolemy, who renewed his coronation ceremony each year at Edfu, making offerings to Horus, guarantor of royal power, and Hathor. The hardy may want to climb the 145 steps to the top of the pylon for a truly magnificent view of the whole temple. As a bonus, see the French graffiti of Napoleon Bonaparte's troops who made the climb before you.

In the **forecourt**, surrounded by 32 columns, some of the reused blocks reveal on their undersides inscriptions and reliefs from earlier dynasties. Two more falcons, one of them wearing Upper and Lower Egypt's double crown, stand guard at the entrance to the **first hypostyle hall**. The 18 columns have lost most of their colour but the walls have some good reliefs of Ptolemy making offerings to the gods. Off to the right is the **library** which contained the scrolls of the daily ritual and annual festivals.

In the **second hypostyle hall** with its 12 more slender columns, 'dry offerings' – flowers, fruit and cuts of meat – were received from the west and 'wet offerings' – wine and milk – from the east. Surrounding it are chambers where sacred ointments and perfumes were prepared according to recipes inscribed on the walls. From a small **altar hall**, up a stairway to the right, the priests carried the sun-disk to the roof. They returned by the stairway to the left.

At the rear of the **inner sanctuary**, lit by a small opening in the roof, you can see the finely carved granite shrine, originally closed by bronze doors, which is attributed to Nectanebo II, one of the last Egyptian Pharaohs before the coming of the Ptolemies. In front of it is the granite pedestal on which was placed Horus's sacred barque.

In the **peripheral corridor** on the west (left) side of the temple are reliefs of the dramatic battles fought by Horus against his arch-enemy, Seth, lord of the underworld, in the form of a crocodile or hippopotamus. This ritual slaying was acted out on the temple's sacred lake.

Kom Ombo

About 60km (37 miles) south of Edfu or 43km (27 miles) north of Aswan, Kom Ombo's charming temple stands in a striking position on a small hill like a Greek acropolis, particularly picturesque when viewed from the river. (*Kom* means 'mound' in Arabic.) It is a not unique but rare example of a double temple, used for the dual worship of Sobek the crocodile-god and Horus the falcon-god. It is believed that, as the site of the primeval struggle between Horus and Seth – the latter is also symbolized by the crocodile – the temple was intended to propitiate these traditional forces of good and evil. Before their disappearance in the age of steamboats, hundreds of crocodiles gathered here, many of them basking on the sandbanks downriver beyond the bend. Some ancient specimens have been preserved as mummies at the temple.

The double entrance is on the riverside front of the temple, Sobek to the right, Horus to the left. In the courtyard, three vestibules and two hypostyle halls, the two cults are associated, rather than being divided into separate enclosures leading to the gods' two sanctuaries. You will notice in the carved reliefs that Horus and his family are hospitably honoured on Sobek's side of the temple just as Sobek and his triad have tribute paid to them in the Horus precinct.

Only the right side of the **pylon** still stands, with Roman emperor Domitian honouring Sobek. Off to the right side of the forecourt, a **Hathor Chapel** serves now as a storehouse for **mummified crocodiles** which were found in the temple. In the **first hypostyle hall**, the columns are well sculpted and some good wall painting shows the king's coronation in the presence of the falcon and crocodile deities.

In the **peripheral corridor** around the sanctuary, as we see from graffiti and drawings they have left on the paving stones, the temple was a favourite place of pilgrimage for invalids.

Aswan

The country's southernmost town has always had a vital role to play in Egyptian history. At the frontier with Nubia, Aswan was the gateway for trade with the rest of the continent. It was here that ancient Egypt exchanged its products for Africa's ivory, gold, spices, perfumes and other exotic goods. Indeed, the name *Aswan* in ancient Egyptian was the word for 'trade' or 'market' and even today, with the camel

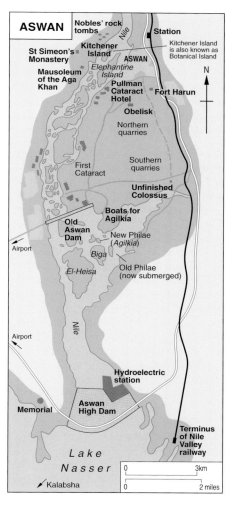

caravans long gone, Aswan's market thrives for the people of the region, not just for tourists. It was here, too, that the Pharaohs recruited their best policemen and mercenary soldiers while Aswan's granite and alabaster quarries were for Egypt's pyramids, temples and sculpture, what Carrara's marble quarries were for the Italian Renaissance.

In the religious sphere, Elephantine and other islands and rocks of the First Cataract at Aswan were regarded as the site where the Nile's inundation began, in the underwater home of creator-god Khnum and the Nile-god Hapy. The island of Philae was the home of Isis, Egypt's best-loved and most durable goddess. Like the colossi of Abu Simbel further upriver, her

beautiful temple was saved from submersion under the waters of Lake Nasser by the town's last great contribution to Egyptian history, the Aswan High Dam. That, too, is a monument to visit. (The Soviet-Egyptian enterprise of the 1960s supersedes the older Aswan Dam that bridges the Nile at the southern end of town, built by the British in 1912 and enlarged in 1934.)

Aswan's pleasant warm and dry climate, especially in winter, has long made it a favourite with European and American visitors. If you can spare the time, it is well worth a stay of three or even four days, to take in all there is to see, using it as a base for visiting Abu Simbel and perhaps sites to the north like Kom Ombo, but best of all, just to slow down the travel pace, relax, stroll around, take leisurely *felucca* cruises on the river and enjoy the charming Nubian townspeople.

The Town

Along the riverfront, the **Corniche** offers a delightful promenade, which is best of all – as always in Egypt – early in the morning and at sunset when the tall white sails of the *feluccas* gliding between the islands are a truly magical sight. More romantic still, even if you are not staying there, is afternoon tea or a cocktail on the terrace of the old **Pullman Cataract Hotel**, south of the Corniche looking across to Elephantine Island. This is a veritable monument in its own right, recalling the halcyon days of tourism in the more leisurely Edwardian age.

Just inland, running parallel to the Corniche south from the railway station, the **Bazaar** in and around Market Street (*Sharia El Suk*) is the place to buy spices, perfumes, and best quality henna hair-dye (jet-black, auburn or outright Titian red).

PUTTING IT ALL TOGETHER

Isis derived her immense popularity from an image of tender maternity, a merciful healing saviour and protective guardian at the all-important moment of death. After resurrecting her murdered brother and husband, Osiris, she gave birth to their son, the falcon-headed sun-god Horus.

But that task of resurrecting Osiris was complicated by the fact that he had been dismembered and the pieces tossed into the Nile. Why was it imagined that his envious murderer, the desert-god Seth, did this?

Scholars offer a somewhat cynical but not implausible explanation. To keep a hold on the lucrative pilgrimage market, like the relics trade in medieval Catholic churches, shrines throughout Egypt each claimed that they had a part of the revered lord of fertility and the nether world buried beneath their inner sanctuary. In the Delta, Busiris had the backbone and Mendes the phallus. In the Nile Valley, Abydos had the head. Aswan, at Philae, had a leg to promote the dual cults of Osiris and of his saviour, Isis.

*B*e careful when shopping in the market at Aswan – the spices and dyes are stacked side by side. You could end up making the world's first royal blue curry!

*A*t Aswan, forget the cruise ship or taxis and take to the feluccas, *easily the most graceful way to get around.*

207

For souvenir-hunters, the Tourist Bazaar is mainly at the north end of the street.

The Quarries

On the southern outskirts of town, in the **Northern Quarries**, can be seen the celebrated **unfinished obelisk**, which is still lying in its trench where the workers abandoned it after discovering a flaw in the red granite. Hewn from the rock probably in the 15th century BC, it would have been the biggest of Egypt's obelisks, 41.75m (137ft) high and 4.2m (14ft) thick at the base, but the flaw would have lopped 10m (32ft) off the top.

Its presence here has enabled us to learn how an obelisk was created. The block was separated from the rockface by drilling a series of preliminary slots, and then driving in wedge-pegs soaked in water to expand and form a precise split. Traces of burnt reeds and bricks when first discovered suggested that the surface was 'softened up' for smoothing with massive

hardstone pounders – also found here, weighing up to 7kg (over 15lb). Clamber up the quarry's rockface for a grand view across to St Simeon's Monastery over on the Nile's west bank.

Some 5km (3 miles) down the road to the Aswan High Dam, the **Southern Quarries** in a valley off to the west are also worth a visit for their unfinished works. Most notable are a formidable mummiform **colossus**, some 6m (19ft) long, lying in stately solitude on the side of the hill, another smaller **statue** and a couple of Ptolemaic **sarcophagi**.

After centuries of hit and miss with the Nile inundations, Egypt's farmers can at last count on the waters controlled by the Aswan High Dam arriving when they need them.

DAM FIT FOR A PHARAOH

As Pharaonic projects go, the Aswan High Dam has dimensions that would impress even a megalomaniac like Ramses II. It has a span of 3.6km (2.25 miles) at a point where the Nile is 550m (602yd) wide. The crest towers 111m (364ft) above the river-bed and the base is 980m (1,072yd) thick. The masonry would have built 17 Great Pyramids, with iron enough for 15 Eiffel Towers. The Lake Nasser reservoir created by the damming of the waters is the world's largest artificial lake, 500km (312 miles) long and an average of 10km (6 miles) wide. This doubles the combined water resources of the USA's Grand Coulee Dam and Russia's great Kuibishev Dam. The lake stretches into the Sudan, with whom Egypt shares water and power resources.

The six turbines of its hydroelectric plant have a total power capacity of 2.1 million kilowatts, well above Egypt's immediate needs. In addition to the obvious benefits of eliminating unpredictable drought and flood and creating more cultivated farmland, the lake has produced highly profitable new fisheries.

But the dam has negative aspects, too. The absence of the 'magic' silt that the Nile had always moved down to the sea has meant that farmers have to use costly artificial fertilizer that is often harmful to the environment. Fisheries in the Delta have declined for want of foodstuff that the Nile no longer brings them. The change has also led to a build-up of salt, which is visible around the edges of the lake and on many of the ancient monuments along the Nile. Underground chambers in Pharaonic monuments and crypts in Coptic churches have been flooded; even as far north as Alexandria, water in the catacombs has been attributed to changes brought about by the dam. There are plans afoot for new machinery to stir up the waters at the bottom of Lake Nasser to get that magic silt moving again. Even the weather has changed, with more rain in the south, but it is not yet clear whether this is a good or bad thing.

Aswan High Dam

Lacking the aesthetic beauty of the pyramids of Giza or the gigantic temples of Abu Simbel, the High Dam, built as a joint Soviet and Egyptian venture, is nonetheless a comparable feat of structural engineering. A dual-carriageway takes you clear across the dam, passing the hydroelectric plant at the east end to a palm-shaded **observation point** in the middle. From here, you get a great view south across Lake Nasser. Beyond the Sudanese frontier, the giant reservoir takes on the name of Lake Nuba. At the west end is a monstrously ugly **memorial** to Soviet-Egyptian friendship – proof that its Soviet sponsor, Nikita Khrushchev, may have done away with Stalin's policies, but not his artistic taste.

The Islands

Aswan owes a large part of its charm to the islands and the craggy outcrops of rock and shrubbery that form the river's **First Cataract** (there are a half-dozen others in Sudan). It is here that the Nile god Hapy, protector of the river's source, was believed to have his abode. Cruise out to the islands in a *felucca*, though a ferry serves Elephantine Island (from the Pullman Cataract Hotel) if you prefer.

On the way, you may be startled, at least at first, to see little boys paddling out furiously in tiny wooden boxes to sing you their amazing versions of *It's a Long Way to Tipperary*, the *Lorelei* or *Il était un petit navire*, depending on what they think is your nationality – they are definitely worth 50 piastres.

*F*resh from another Death on the Nile, *Agatha Christie's Hercule Poirot may appear any moment on the terrace of the grand old Cataract Hotel for a view of Aswan's islands.*

Elephantine Island

Directly opposite the modern town, the island, covered with lush groves of palm trees, was the site of Aswan's original settlement back in prehistoric times. At the south end is a sandstone **Nilometer**, originally built by the Romans and restored to use in 1870, when its marble slabs were installed. To the west are the ruins of the ancient town's **Temple of Khnum**. To honour the ram-headed god, the Ptolemies established a **Necropolis of Rams** nearby. Their stone sarcophagi are still in place, but the mummified rams, one of which is coated in gold leaf, have been moved, along with mummies of the temple's priests, to the island's **Museum**. This is housed in the villa of William Willcocks, the British engineer of Aswan's first dam. Other exhibits include prehistoric artefacts and jewellery, and small sculptures and pottery from the Middle and New Kingdoms. Some fascinating papyrus documents in Aramaic relate to the garrison of Jewish mercenaries brought here in the 6th century BC by the Persians then ruling Egypt. The Jews had a temple of Yahweh which caused conflict with the local worshippers of Khnum.

Kitchener Island

Also known as **Botanical Island**, it was a gift to the British soldier for his victorious campaign in Sudan. Its tropical flowers, shrubs and trees and the little tea-house make it a pleasant afternoon excursion.

*T*he botanical garden on *Kitchener Island – a peaceful memorial to the old imperial soldier's exploits in conquering Britain's enemies in the Sudan.*

Philae

The romantic island on which the **Temples of Philae** were built was known as the 'Pearl of Egypt'. When they were moved because of the threat of submersion by the building of the Aswan High Dam, the temples' particular magic turned the nearby island of Agilkia into another jewel. Landfill reshaped it to conform to the topography of the temples' original home and it has now deservedly taken over the name of Philae. *Feluccas* sail to the island from a landing stage 6km (nearly 4 miles) south of town. Ideally, try to visit it by day and return one evening for the superb **sound-and-light show**.

Philae was dedicated to the cult of Isis, the most beloved of Egyptian goddesses. It stood next to the burial place of her brother Osiris, on Biga Island, also an ancient cult centre but with few surviving traces (just south of the temples' new home). The island sanctuary of Isis was the last shrine to continue observance of the ancient religion. Hieroglyphic inscriptions here date to AD 394 and demotic texts as late as 452 are detectable among the graffiti and inscriptions attesting to the shrine's mass appeal to pilgrims. Other evidence shows that Nubians continued to worship Isis until the reign of Emperor Justinian (527-565).

The **Temple of Isis** is the largest of the island's monuments, built in its present form largely by the Ptolemies of the 2nd century BC with the last structures added

One of the Philae temples' less solemn deities is the dwarf-god Bes, who sticks his tongue out to ward off the evil eye.

by the Romans 500 years later. Pilgrims arrived at the south end of the island, and that is where our visit begins. The approach to the temple proper is through the **Hall of Nectanebo I** (30th Dynasty, 381-362 BC) to an agora-style courtyard bounded by two Roman colonnades with floral capitals. Adjoining the colonnade to the right are two small shrines to Nubian gods, Arensnuphis and Mandulis, and at the end a temple to Imhotep, the great architect subsequently deified as a healer.

At the north end of the courtyard, fronted by two lions, is the Ptolemies' **first pylon**, with deeply incised reliefs of the goddess wearing headdress of sun-disk and cow-horns on its twin towers. This monumental structure encloses the earlier Gateway of Nectanebo II (last of the 30th Dynasty, 360-343 BC). This is the main entrance to the temple of Isis. Beyond it

is the forecourt with a colonnade to the right, again with floral capitals, and over to the left, there is a Ptolemaic birth temple (*mammisi*) depicting on its north wall Isis cradling the newborn Horus in her arms.

On the **second pylon**, reliefs show Ptolemy XIII making offerings to Isis with the falcon-headed Horus to the right and with Osiris to the left. Like the first pylon, it is flanked by deep elongated niches originally holding giant flagstaffs. Its

*W*hen the Christians finally succeeded in ousting the worshippers of Isis from the island of Philae, they added Coptic crosses to the monuments to show that it was under new management.

MOVING PHILAE'S TEMPLES

The temples were already standing in water after the first Aswan Dam was built in 1902. The expansion carried out in 1934 raised the waters a third of the way up the pillars. For some, that made the temples look that much more romantic. But in the 1960s, without UNESCO's international rescue operation, they would have completely disappeared. A steel stockaded coffer dam was built around the old doomed island to pump out the water already there, before dismantling the temples, stone by stone, to be reconstructed on the new island in the same arrangement as before. The monuments were cut into 40,000 blocks, each cleaned, numbered and measured with millimetre accuracy to ensure their proper re-assembly, imperfections and all, no better, no worse than before. It was important not to 'improve' on the ancient construction. The transfer took 30 months.

doorway leads to the temple's main buildings: a columned court, **vestibule** (with Coptic crosses indicating its use as a Christian church) and antechambers culminating in the **sanctuary**. After seeing its reliefs of royal offerings to the gods and the stone pedestal for the statue of Isis, return to climb the stairs from one of the western antechambers for a **rooftop view** of the islands.

Take a look at two other shrines on the east side of the island over to the right of the main temple. The Ptolemies' **Chapel of Hathor** has charming scenes of musicians playing the harp and flute, an ape playing a lyre and the jolly god Bes practically a one-man band. And the elegant **Kiosk of Emperor Trajan**, with its 14 columns crowned by ornate floral capitals, has managed to usurp the Temple of Isis itself as the symbol of Philae.

The West Bank

A popular attraction over on the west bank is the handsome modern **Mausoleum of the Aga Khan**, which is situated at the top of a hill behind the white family palace facing the southern end of Elephantine Island. The Aga Khan (1877-1957) spent his winters here to help his rheumatism. Fabulously wealthy and not a slim man, he celebrated his diamond jubilee as the spiritual leader of the Ismaili sect of Shi'ite Moslems in Pakistan, India and East Africa by having himself weighed in diamonds. His last resting-place is a sober,

The mausoleum built for the Aga Khan's last resting place is located where he used to come in the winter to nurse his rheumatism.

simple structure in subtly ochre-tinted sandstone. Inside, the Aga's sarcophagus is of solid white marble, decorated every day with a single fresh red rose. The view from the hilltop terrace makes the climb worth the effort.

To the north, a 20-minute walk or mule-ride across the sand brings you to the **Monastery of St Simeon**, founded by the Copts in the 7th century. Its largely 10th-century buildings were in part destroyed by Saladin in 1173. The entrance on the east side of the fortress wall, 6m (nearly 20ft) high, takes you to the **church** in the lower precinct. Much of the roof of the aisled basilica has gone, but part of its decoration has survived, notably a **fresco of Christ enthroned** in a niche behind the main altar. In the upper precinct are the monks' residential quarters. The building comprises two storeys and includes a hall, cells and refectory.

Tombs of the Nobles

To visit the west bank's rock-cut tombs, take a *felucca* or ferry from the north end of the Corniche in front of the Tourist Information Office. Like those at Beni Hasan in Middle Egypt, the tombs were carved from the cliff face for provincial governors and military commanders.

Dating mostly from the Middle and New Kingdoms, their decoration is of uneven quality, but the most interesting are those of **Sirenput II** (31), a garrison commander whose mummiform statues

The camels that take you to and from the Monastery of St Simeon look as if they have been here as long as the fortified sanctuary itself.

are still in place, along with reliefs of the deceased with his son and with his mother; **Kakemet** (unnumbered), which has good ceiling paintings and reliefs of the deceased high priest with Osiris and Hathor; and **Sirenput I** (36), which has statues of the provincial governor at the doorway and reliefs in a six-pillared chapel of the deceased harpooning fish and receiving an offering of cattle.

Kalabsha

Less well known than Abu Simbel or Philae, the Nubian **Temple of Kalabsha** just south of the Aswan High Dam was the object of another important rescue-operation, carried out by the Germans in 1970. The original town of Kalabsha (ancient Talmis) lies submerged beneath the waters of Lake Nasser 50km (30 miles) south of Aswan. The temple dedicated to Mandulis, a Nubian god of healing linked to Osiris and Isis, has been resurrected high and dry in a fine state of preservation. (As a reward, the German archaeologists were able to take back to Berlin's Egyptian Museum a temple gateway which they ingeniously reconstructed from reused blocks found at the Kalabsha site.)

The approach to the sandstone temple is along a causeway that originally linked the temple directly to a quay at the river. Entrance through the sparsely decorated pylon leads up a stairway to the colonnaded forecourt and the handsome hypostyle hall.

Abu Simbel

The country's southernmost monuments, just 7km (4 miles) from the Sudan border, make a fitting climax to any visit to Upper Egypt. From all the photographs, you

may think you already *know* Ramses II's gigantic temples hewn from the cliffs and imagine you will be blasé when you see them. But, as with the pyramids at Giza, that sudden first view up close gives even the most seasoned traveller a jolt. For that marvellous experience of seeing the colossal statues greeting the rising sun, check in to an Abu Simbel hotel the night before. More exhilarating than flying, is the desert

At Abu Simbel, the colossal statues of Ramses II sit once more impassively facing the rising sun after being moved piece by piece from their original site, now under the waters of Lake Nasser.

those colossal statues of himself, and used them to store gold and other treasure massed from Nubia. (*Nub* in ancient Egyptian meant 'gold'.)

Almost completed buried in the sand, they disappeared from history until rediscovered by a Swiss traveller, Johann Burckhardt, in 1813.

drive from Aswan. It takes a good four hours or more and it is well worth starting out in the dead of night. The desert itself is a grand experience, offering good chances of seeing a Bedouin camel caravan on its way between Sudan and the Western Desert oases.

The temples of Ramses II and his queen Nefertari form the spiritual bulwark asserting the New Kingdom Pharaohs' control of the south. Tuthmosis I had extended and consolidated the Egyptian empire into Nubia – and the Sudanese Kush – south to the Fourth Cataract. Ramses II affirmed the imperial power with his great rock-cut temples, characterized by

Temple of Ramses II

This is the ultimate, almost sublime expression of royal megalomania. The Pharaoh raised himself to the status of sun-god by creating not one but **four colossi of Ramses II**, 20m (65ft) high, seated facing the rising sun. His face has a serene, not quite smug expression framed in the royal *nemes* headcloth, with the sacred uraeus cobra on the forehead, and the spade-like ritual beard and double crown of Upper and Lower Egypt. **Statues of the royal family**, appropriately minute, stand beside and between the king's feet. The torso and head of the second statue from the left have toppled, probably from an ancient earthquake; its fragments lie on the ground as they were when excavated. Graffiti of Greek and Phoenician mercenaries is inscribed on the legs of the two statues to the left.

On the sides of the thrones are images of the **Nile-gods** binding together in unity symbols of Upper and Lower Egypt. A **lower frieze** shows Egypt's captive enemies, with Syrians to the right and Africans to the left. Up in a niche between the two central colossi is a large but of course smaller statue of the falcon-headed god with a sun-disk headdress, **Re-Herakhty**, with whom Ramses II graciously condescends to share his temple. Across the top is a row of **baboons** praying to the rising sun. The whole trapezoid façade wall is the equivalent of a pylon in a free-standing temple.

Dispensing with the traditional forecourt, the doorway leads directly to a great three-aisled **hypostyle hall**. On eight square pillars along the centre aisle are formidable statues of the king assimilating the kilted mummiform figure of Osiris. Scenes on the pillars show Ramses II making offerings to the gods, together with his wife Nefertari and daughter. Flying vultures are portrayed on the ceiling over the centre aisle, with stars over the side aisles. On the walls are **painted murals and reliefs** of Ramses II as conqueror, killing his foes, attacking a Syrian fortress, valiantly charging in his chariot surrounded by enemy cavalry, and returning from the battle of Qadesh in triumph with Hittite prisoners.

In the **vestibule** for offerings of flowers, fruit and wine, Ramses II as a mere mortal is portrayed paying homage to Ramses II the god.

The rectangular **sanctuary**, to which only the king originally had access, is in every sense the culminating point of the temple. The whole edifice was oriented to let the first rays of the rising sun penetrate to this room at a specific time of year, probably key dates in the king's reign which scholars estimate to be 21 February and 21 October. There, beyond the pedestal for the sacred barque, the beams would illuminate four statues on the rear wall – creator-gods Ptah and Amun, the deified Ramses II, and Re-Herakhty. (Modern engineering has done its best for this still to work.)

Temple of Queen Nefertari

The smaller but still formidable temple a little to the north should not be neglected. Like her husband the queen has been deified and, as you will see from the façade's **six standing colossi**, has been granted the exceptional privilege of having statues equal in size to those of the Pharaoh. All the same, he chooses to flank each of hers with two of his. Each colossus, 11.5m (38ft) high, is accompanied by a couple of royal children.

The temple is dedicated to Hathor, whose cow-eared head decorates the pillars in the square **hypostyle hall**. Ramses II gallantly pays homage to Nefertari in inscriptions on the hall's ceiling, and among the **reliefs**, she is seen accompanying him into battle. In the **vestibule**, we see the gods receive wine from Ramses II and flowers from Nefertari. In the rear niche of the **sanctuary**, a statue of Hathor is protecting Ramses II. To the left, Nefertari offers incense to Hathor and Mut, wife of Amun. To the right, Ramses II offers incense and a libation to the queen and himself as deities.

Hieroglyphics

It may take a lifetime of scholarship to master the ancient hieroglyphic system of writing, but you can at least understand the principles of what remains one of the world's most fascinating and attractive puzzles, even after the scholars have solved most of it.

Egyptian hieroglyphs are a series of consonants, with a few vowels developing in the last period of the ancient civilization. The alphabet in fact combines sound-signs, *phonograms*, with sounds expressing meanings, *ideograms*, added to distinguish similar sets of consonants. Like Hebrew and Arabic, they read from right to left (with some older vertical texts reading from top to bottom). They first emerged around 3000 BC and found their classical form by about 2700 BC, in the Old Kingdom.

The sober, refined and separate sign-forms, important for their aesthetic value as much as for their clarity, were maintained for religious texts inscribed in stone for eternity. The word 'hieroglyph' comes from the Greek word for 'sacred, carved in stone', though some do appear on papyrus, if only as 'sketches' to be engraved in stone. For the most part, however, when the texts were transferred to papyrus or other more ephemeral surfaces, a more cursive form of linked signs developed, known as 'hieratic' (religious), while a highly simplified shorthand version evolved, known as 'demotic' (popular), for more mundane subjects such as administration and accounts. The writing of hieroglyphs was the activity of a tiny élite of priests and eminent scholars. Most scribes of demotic writing were humble clerks, pen-pushers who never learned to read the exalted and arcane script of the sacred tablets.

The hieroglyphs inscribed in the oval cartouche frames spell out the names of the Pharaohs and the deities participating in the act of homage.

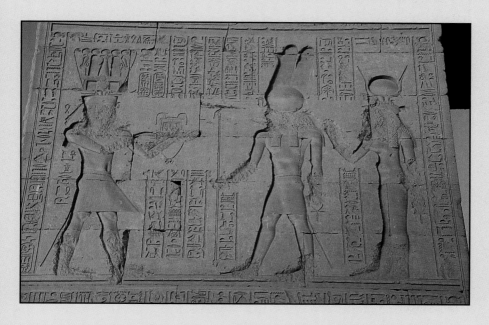

Notice the Ankh amulet held by the falcon-headed god Horus in his left hand reappears in the cartouches bearing his name as the hieroglyph for life: 'nkh'.

The Equipment

As you will see in their statues, scribes used a palette, sometimes slung over one shoulder, as a portable writing-case. It contained what we would call a couple of inkwells for the pigment (black carbon and red ochre, to which water was added for writing) and a 'pencil-box' of reed writing instruments, though the scribe, like any good modern draughtsman, usually tucked spare reeds behind his ear. Standing or sitting cross-legged on the ground, he mashed one end of the reed to absorb the pigment for writing.

Besides papyrus, the scribes wrote on leather, large flakes of white limestone, white-plastered wooden boards and fragments of pottery (*ostraca*). Papyrus, believed to come from the ancient Egyptian word *pa-per-aa*, 'material for the Pharaoh' and the origin of our own word, paper, was made from the stem of the flowering marsh-plant of the Delta which had largely died out by the end of the Roman period. The stem's hard outer fibres were peeled away (for use as rope, sandals, mats and baskets) and

The hieroglyphs accompanying this Pharoah's portrait describe his qualities: 'Rich in years, mighty in conquests', 'Beloved of the sun-god, great in justice and virtue .'

the pithy inner fibres were cut in strips of up to 50cm (20in), for some reason never longer. The strips were placed side by side in one layer, and then a second layer was placed crosswise on top and beaten so that the natural juices glued the two layers together in one smooth, light buff-coloured sheet. The sheets could be joined together to form a scroll. Indeed, the image of a scroll tied with string was the ideogram hieroglyph for writing.

Deciphering the Ancient Script

The last known example of hieroglyphic writing was found at Aswan on the island of Philae's Temple of Isis, dated AD 394. For the next 15 centuries, nobody knew what the hieroglyphs meant. Early Egyptian Christians abandoned the ancient script, not because it was inefficient, but because of its 'pagan'

Once Champollion cracked the hieroglyphics code, it was possible to decipher whole chapters of the Pharaohs' Book of the Dead *as inscribed here over the entrance to a sanctuary.*

idolatrous origins. In fact, the Copts' transcription of their ancient Egyptian language into the Greek alphabet with six additional letters proved more confusing because it no longer had the additional ideogram signs to clarify meaning. In any case, conversion to Islam ended all links with this Coptic language outside the church liturgy.

Attention to hieroglyphs themselves was only resumed with the expedition to Egypt of Napoleon Bonaparte's soldiers and scholars in 1798. The next year, in the process of restoring a fortress for the purpose of defending the Delta against imminent Anglo-Turkish attack, Lieutenant Pierre Bouchard found at Rashid (Rosetta to Europeans) an ancient slab of black granite recycled as part of the Arab fortifications. Its inscriptions made it worth passing on to the new French Institute of Egyptology in Cairo. The scholars made several copies from rubbings and sent them to fraternal scholarly institutions back in Europe before the victorious British seized what became known as the Rosetta Stone and presented it to the British Museum. The growing international community of Egyptologists pored over the stone's three pieces of writing – in hieroglyphs, demotic and Greek. For the decipherers, the most important part of the Greek text was the last sentence stating that all three inscriptions repeated the same text. (It was a proclamation of 196 BC, after Ptolemy V's coronation at Memphis, listing his achievements in the face of domestic unrest and decreeing him a god to be worshipped throughout Egypt.)

In 1819, the British scholar Thomas Young made the vital discovery that the demotic script was a cursive form of hieroglyphics, but believed the latter's signs were purely symbolic, without any phonetic elements. It was left to the young French linguist Jean-François Champollion (1790-1832) to crack the code. Obsessed by ancient Egyptian texts since childhood, he had studied the Coptic language as a link with the Pharaonic past. In 1822, he presented a letter to the Académie Française expounding his theories. He recognized the dual function of hieroglyphs as sound and meaning. He worked out sounds for signs by comparing the Rosetta texts, well-known royal cartouches bearing the names of Tuthmosis III and Ramses II, and elements of the Coptic language.

In Coptic, *ra* means 'sun'. The sungod had as its hieroglyph the sun-disk and might be pronounced *Ra*. The 's' sound could be gleaned from the Rosetta text by tracking down the hieroglyphic equivalent of the last letter of the Greek for Ptolemy, *Ptolemaios*. All this provided the name *Ra-?-s-s*. How to nail down the missing letter? The first hieroglyphic sign for Tuthmosis was an ibis bird, sign of the ibis-god Thoth. This left *-mosis* with a similar hieroglyphic configuration to the last part of *Ra-mses*. Bingo! With *Tuth-mosis*: 'son of Thoth' and *Ra-mses*: 'son of Ra', Champollion got the missing letter 'm'. Applying roughly the same principles, he built up a dictionary and even grammar of ancient Egyptian.

Thus Kheops is the Greek for *Khufu*. You can read the hieroglyphs on the Pharaoh's cartouche at his Great Pyramid in Giza as follows: a barred circle for *Kh-*, a bird for *-u-*, a viper for *-f-*, and another bird for *-u*. Now learn the signs that make up your own name. Goldsmiths in Cairo and Luxor will be happy to engrave them on your own cartouche emblem as a pendant for a necklace, bracelet or key-chain. For Ruby, take a mouth-sign for *R-*, a bird for *-u-*, a foot for *-b-* and a reed for the *-y*.

Apricots, Bubbling Brooks and Alexander's Oracle

To complete your sense of Egypt, you may like to consider spending some time in what does after all make up more than 95 percent of its surface: the desert. Or at least experience it from the more comfortable vantage point of the green and pleasant oases in the Western Desert. After a surfeit of traffic and crowds, and monuments and museums, enjoy a prolonged moment of contemplation in the wilderness, the fabulous constellations of the skies at night, and the bubbling springs and lush orchards of the oases themselves.

Many foreign conquerors have tried to penetrate the desert's mysteries, some, like the Persian Cambyses in 525 BC, losing whole armies in the process. These days, four-wheel-drive will get you out safely. The whole vast but sparsely populated region – 130,000 inhabitants for an area of 360,000km² (145,000 square miles) – is now known as New Valley. You can fly out from Luxor to its capital, **Kharga**, as a gateway for exploring other oases further west at **Dakhla** and **Farafra**. With-

*N*o, this is not some kind of mirage, there really are enchanted oases like this one out in the Western Desert.

out rushing, you would need at least a week. For a briefer excursion, the northern oasis of **Bahariya** can be reached by road from Cairo. The **Siwa** oasis, close to the Libyan border, is accessible with special permit from the Mediterranean coastal resort of Mersa Matruh. The accommodation offered is simple but acceptable.

The people are largely Berbers of North African origin or Bedouins from Arabia, but the nomadic life with herds of goats and camels is dwindling. With the advent of motorized transport and national borders, most have given up wandering the desert with tents, blankets and carpets and only those utensils, tools and weapons that can easily be transported. Instead, they have chosen to settle down in the oases and rear poultry or tend their orchards of

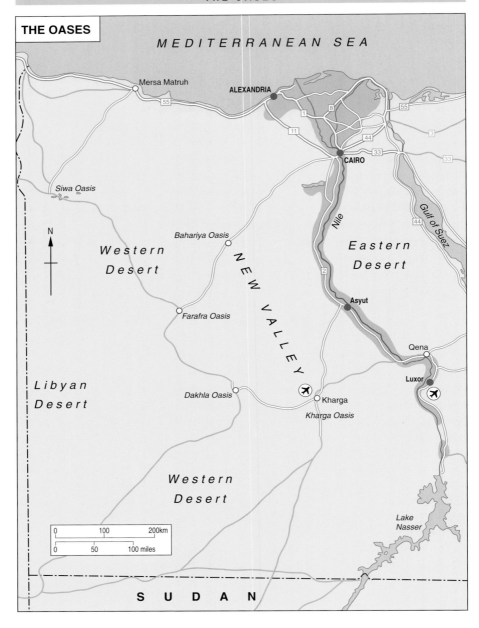

THE OASES

MEDITERRANEAN SEA

apricots, mangoes, and mandarines and groves of date-palms and olives. The abundant water of the oases comes through hundreds of springs fed by the rains seeping through the sandstone from the African tropics. Cultivated land in Kharga alone can count on 50 million litres (11 million gallons) a day.

In the shade of their orchard at the Farafra oasis, a family of Berber origin invites you to share a cool refreshment.

229

Kharga

This fully fledged administrative capital of some 50,000 inhabitants is at first sight disappointingly modern, but seek out the fascinating ancient neighbourhood of **Darb El Sindaliya**, situated on the east side of town, around the bazaar at the junction of Port Said Street and El Nada Street. This was Kharga's original settlement, dating back to the 10th century. Its narrow alleys zigzag to foil enemy incursions – riders on horses and camels could not duck through the low covered streets. Houses of mudbrick and palm-tree beams may be of several storeys but all windows face on to the shady inner courtyard, making it impossible to scale the sheer exterior walls.

North of town and west of the road to Asyut is the **Temple of Hibis** – *Hibis* means 'town of the plough' in ancient Egyptian. The shrine dedicated to Amun was built by late-dynasty Pharaohs, with additions by the Ptolemies, and completed by Persia's Darius I around 500 BC. The structures left in place and their carved reliefs have been well preserved by the desert climate, but over the centuries some of the inscribed slabs have been carted off by villagers to form the walls of their houses. Worshippers entered the gateway of Darius to a portico and a succession of three hypostyle halls leading to the sanctuary at the far end. Christians occupied the temple in the 4th and 5th centuries,

W*orkers in the bazaar at Kharga prepare spices not only for consumption within the oasis region, now known as New Valley, but also for the rest of Egypt.*

leaving traces of a church on the north side of the portico and defacing statues and carvings, notably the ithyphallic fertility god, Min.

Out in the desert north of Hibis, the **Bagawat Cemetery**, also dating back to the 4th and 5th centuries, is one of the world's oldest surviving Christian burial sites. It comprises over 260 tomb-chapels of baked brick, many of them with a shaft descending to a burial chamber. Some are designed with domes and finely detailed arcaded façades, with well preserved wall paintings inside. One of the best known is the **Chapel of Peace** with dome paintings of Adam and Eve, Abraham, Sarah and Isaac, and Noah's Ark shaped like a Pharaonic sacred barque. The **Exodus Chapel** is among the oldest here, its paintings in the dome showing the Pharaoh and his army pursuing Moses, Joshua and the Israelites. Down in a hollow north of the cemetery are the remains of the fortified **Monastery of Mustapha Kashif**, named after the 11th-century Moslem governor who appropriated it as an office for collecting taxes.

Dakhla

With a population of some 70,000, the Dakhla oasis is the largest in the New Valley. The road west from Kharga takes you past fascinating rock formations. Many in the shape of sphinxes or camels have prehistoric inscriptions and it is not clear whether the 'sculptures' themselves were fashioned by the hand of man or by desert sandstorms. At the eastern edge of the Dakhla oasis, off to the right as you approach from Kharga, is the attractive **Islamic cemetery of Tineida**, which has gravestones in the form of small baked-

brick houses topped by tiny crenellated battlements.

The village of **Bashindi** has hidden among its houses Pharaonic-style **Roman**

tombs. Further along the Kharga-Dakhla road is the charming little village of **Balat**, whose narrow covered streets are like those of Kharga's old town, where you

Many of the tombs at Bagawat are over 1,600 years old, making it one of the most ancient Christian cemeteries in the world.

The narrow covered alleys of Balat, with its tunnels forcing all comers to stoop as they pass through, are a customary feature of old oasis villages to hamper invaders.

must duck through tunnels to get from house to house. Hospitable elders may invite you to share the shade of their courtyard figtree and drink mint-tea as they study the Koran.

In Dakhla's main town, **Mut**, is a small **Ethnographic Museum** displaying the artefacts of life at the oasis – clothes, tools and utensils, many of which have not

234

*T*he oasis of Dakhla has grown into a major agricultural enterprise as well as an attractive gateway for camel safaris into the Western Desert.

235

There is a risk of eating up the profits when a man grows thirsty smoking a narguileh *water-pipe while selling oranges and tangerines from the oasis orchards.*

changed since the days of the Pharaohs. In the midst of the burning desert, the great joy of Dakhla is its cool green **gardens**, shady olive groves and orchards of man-goes, apricots, apples and mandarines, irrigated by swiftly flowing streams from the gushing springs.

The ultimate luxury in the desert wilderness is a barbecued kid-goat – for which the magic word is meshwi.

*C*raftsmen who have settled in the New Valley have maintained the ancient arts of pottery and/or basketware with shapes identical to those scenes on frescoes of Pharaonic monuments.

*A*fter his visit to the
oracle at Siwa oasis, Alexander
the Great was never the same.
Before the visit, he only thought he
might be divine, afterwards he was
totally convinced.

Farafra

Further north, this small village of wide
open streets with mudbrick walls is also
surrounded by its share of delightful shady
gardens and orchards where guava, oranges and apricots abound. The grand at-

traction here is a camel or jeep safari out into the magical wilderness of the **White Desert** north east of the village. Amid endless stretches of powdered white chalk 'sand' are monoliths of the most fantastical shapes – giant humans, monstrous animals. Take warm clothes and plenty of blankets to spend a night out there and experience the sunset, the starry night and the dawn.

Bahariya

The Northern Oasis, as its Arab name implies, is 334km (208 miles) from Cairo. Its population of 6,000 grows citrus fruits, dates and olives, runs poultry farms, and brews a heady date-palm toddy – not a drink for drivers. The oasis town **Bawiti** has attractive whitewashed houses decorated with red and blue motifs and a **bazaar** of locally made basketware and pottery. Out in the desert, half buried in the sands, are a couple of late-dynasty temples.

Siwa

Access by special permit, issued by government offices at the Mediterranean town of Mersa Matruh, depends on the current state of relations with nearby Libya. It is also necessary to have a convoy of at least two vehicles for the 4- or 5-hour expedition. Desert-lovers find the trip worthwhile for the unspoilt nature of the oasis community, which is ethnically more Libyan than Egyptian. The long journey is rewarded by a cool dip in one of the dozens of Siwa's celebrated **bubbling springs**. Best known are **Cleopatra's Bath**, where the famous lady is said

to have refreshed herself on her visit to the local shrine, and **Aïn Tamousi**, a spring favoured by brides – both situated on the loop road departing from either end of the town bazaar.

Just 1km (over ½ mile) east of town amidst the abandoned village of **Aghurmi** on a solitary spur of rock is the **Temple of Amun**, dating back to the 26th Dynasty (600 BC). Famous throughout the classical Greek world, it is also known as the Temple of the Oracle, which Alexander the Great visited before setting out on the journey of conquest that took him to India. It lies in ruins now, but two courtyards can be traced to the **sanctuary** where the fateful interview took place.

GETTING THE GOOD WORD

Alexander's pilgrimage to the Temple of Amun at Siwa is shrouded in mystery and legend. After turning inland from the Mediterranean coast and getting lost in a sandstorm, he and his friends were apparently saved by a miraculous rain-shower which replenished their four-day supply of water. But they were still lost, until two crows appeared among the dunes to guide them through the wilderness to the Siwa oasis. There, amid lush palms, pomegranates and other fruit trees, grassy meadows and ponds where quail and falcon nested, the priests of Amun received Alexander at the temple. The oracle, Amun's spokesman, was one of only four in the ancient world reputed to tell the 'real truth' (untainted by bribes and political expediency). Alexander emerged from the shrine without saying what he had heard, but later allusions suggest he had been told he was the true son of the god Amun, whom the Greeks equated with Zeus. Not a bad job reference for someone setting out to conquer the world.

Memories of a Golden Past, a Battlefield and Beach Resorts

The city's ancient grandeur has gone, but not its proud spirit. Facing as it does the European world across the Mediterranean, something of Alexandria's cosmopolitan atmosphere remains. That and its milder summer climate attract many Cairenes to spend their holidays at the beach and other resorts along the coast. At El Alamein, veterans of World War II and their families visit the famous battlefield.

There are flights to Alexandria from Cairo, or it is a morning's drive along the well-paved desert highway. Besides touring the old and new city of Alexandria and the resorts along the coast, you may like to see some of the interesting Coptic monasteries just off the Cairo-Alexandria road in the region of Wadi Natrun. They can be visited on a day-trip from Alexandria or on the road journey to or from Cairo.

*T*his monument at the El Alamein Museum pays tribute to the fallen of both sides in the momentous desert battle of World War II.

Alexandria

The once great capital of Alexander the Great lies some 220km (137 miles) north west of Cairo. If the town, founded in 332 BC, has lost its monumental and cultural grandeur to war and careless modern construction, there is real pleasure in getting to know its spirited people, independent-minded in a town that sets itself defiantly apart from the Cairo authorities. Nasser, for instance, was never so popular here as in the rest of Egypt.

Alexandria remains Egypt's chief seaport, with two deepwater harbours. With a population of over 3,000,000, the city is the main focus of the national cotton industry and fisheries.

The city's sights take just one full day, but it's worth staying overnight to

241

ALEXANDRIA

Ras El Tin Palace
Fort of Qaitbay
Naval Museum
Mosque of Abu El Abbas
Eastern Harbour
Pullman Cecil Hotel
Mosque of Ibrahim
Museum
Roman Baths
Kom El Dik
Roman Amphitheatre
Pompey's Pillar
Catacombs of Kom El Shuqafa
SH AL MITWALLI
SH EL-GUEISH
SH SIDI GABER
GAMAL ABDEL NASSER (EL HOREYA)
SH MOSTAFA KAMEL
SH EL-GUEISH
SH MAHMUD ESAWI
GAMAL ABDEL NASSER (EL HOEYA)
Montazah Palace
MAAMOURA MONTAZAH
ABOUKIR BEACH
EL-MANDARA
SH MAHATTET
N
MEDITERRANEAN SEA
0 1km
0 1 mile

F or all its modernization, Alexandria still offers the old-fashioned pleasures of a shoeshine with your haircut – and a shave with cut-throat razor, if you like.

enjoy a leisurely dinner at one of the many good fish restaurants on the seafront, or longer if you want to enjoy its beaches and hang out in the cafés.

In the centre of town, **Saad Zaghloul Square** offers interesting sport for people-watchers from the café terraces around the bustling bus-terminus. The colourful members of the Levantine port's cosmopolitan community celebrated in Lawrence Durrell's *Alexandria Quartet* are only a distant memory since the 1952 revolution and subsequent conflicts drove the last of them away, but nostalgics can track down their old haunts. The ghosts of Justine, Balthazar, Nessim and Cleo have all been spotted by the gin-and-tonic crowd at the bar of the **Pullman Cecil Hotel** or a couple of blocks away at the terrace of the **Pastroudis Café**. They may also like to rummage among the expatriates' old books, photo-albums, chinaware and other paraphernalia in the **flea market** of antique shops south of Sidi El Mitwalli Avenue between Mahatter and Masgid El Attarin streets.

I n those, for him, blessed years of the monarchy, Egypt's playboy-king Farouk tried to walk off some of his puppy fat in these gardens of his Montazah palace.

The Corniche

Start at the western end of the Corniche, officially known as 26 July Street, where it hugs the curve of the eastern harbour. If the sweep of the bay when lit up at night might recall a seafront on the French Riv-

iera, its **promenade** is more reminiscent of an English seaside town, the clear product of British town planning at the turn of the century.

On the peninsula at the Corniche's western end is the ornate Turco-Baroque

*O*n the horizon,
a fisherman's view of
Alexandria's Corniche
reveals all the trappings of
a modern city with its
ancient monuments a long-gone
memory.

royal palace of **Ras El Tin** where King
Farouk signed his abdication in 1952 before taking his yacht, moored nearby, to
exile in Italy.

Most of Alexandria's mosques are
modern structures. One of the most attractive, a couple of blocks back from the
Corniche, is the **Mosque of Abu El Abbas**. Rebuilt in 1943, it has elegant
minarets and ornate domes over the tombs
of the 18th-century Andalusian sheikh and
other holy men.

*T*he Mosque of Abu El
Abbas is a graceful 20th-century
edifice that captures the best
elements of traditional Islamic
architecture.

Sultan Qaitbay, who built this fort, gave rebellious generals two choices: either be flogged to death or go and meditate on the wisdoms of Islam in a retreat.

Fort of Qaitbay

Out on a narrow promontory in the old harbour, Sultan Qaitbay's 15th-century fortress stands on the site of Alexandria's ancient Pharos lighthouse, once one of the wonders of the ancient world. Ptolemy II's beacon, built in 279 BC, stood 120m (nearly 400ft) high, topped by a huge statue of Poseidon (Neptune to the Romans). Earthquakes progressively toppled it into the sea, finishing it off in 1307. The fort now houses a **Naval Museum**, displaying, among other memorabilia, weapons, ammunition and coins from the French frigate *L'Orient*, which was sunk by Anglo-Turkish forces at the battle of Aboukir. Take a stroll along the fort's **ramparts**.

In the eastern neighbourhood of Zizinia is the popular **Jewellery Museum**, housed in a royal palace of the Farouk family. Besides its extravagant collection of jewels, the grandiose bathrooms are a major attraction.

Greco-Roman Monuments

Despite its name, the **Greco-Roman Museum** (off El Hurriya Street) is also rich in Pharaonic relics from the Delta and Middle Egypt. Among the exhibits are **mummies** from both the Pharaonic and Roman periods, the latter with painted wooden face masks, and the toes peeping out; a white marble **statue of Isis** stands with her left foot on a crocodile; a red granite **statue of Ramses II**; posthumously sculpted **busts of Alexander;** and fine sculptures of **Julius Caesar** and the **Emperor Hadrian**.

Roman baths and an **amphitheatre** (3rd century AD) have been excavated and nicely restored in a strange setting of tenement housing south west of the museum at Kom El Dik. Further south west are the **Catacombs** of Kom El Shuqafa. The burial site dates from the 2nd century AD, and the paintings in its tomb-chambers offer a bizarre mixture of Pharaonic and Greco-Roman styles. The **hall of Caracalla** still contains skeletons of men and their horses. The nearby **Pompey's Pillar**, which stands 30m (95ft) high with its fine Corinthian capital, was erected on the site of the Ptolemaic Temple of Serapis. The column of pink Aswan granite was raised not in honour of the Roman general, Pompey, as you might think, but to Emperor Diocletian in AD 300, for saving the city from famine – before driving out the Christians.

Montazah

The coast road continues from the centre of town all the way to the resort area around **Montazah Palace** 8km (5 miles) to the east. This strange mixture of Ottoman Turkish and Italian medieval styles was originally the summer palace of the 19th-century monarchy, and is now part hotel, part casino. The **gardens** have beautiful shady umbrella pines and other Mediterranean trees.

The few relics of Alexandria's ancient glory are to be found in its Greco-Roman Museum (following page).

ALEXANDRIA AND THE MEDITERRANEAN

*M*ore relics from when Alexandria reigned supreme in the Mediterranean, in the Greco-Roman Museum.

The Beaches

Alexandria's beaches start in the centre of town, but many of the best are to the east beyond Montazah at **Maamoura** and **Aboukir**. This last, at the site of Nelson's victory over Napoleon's fleet in 1798, is now more famous for its seafood.

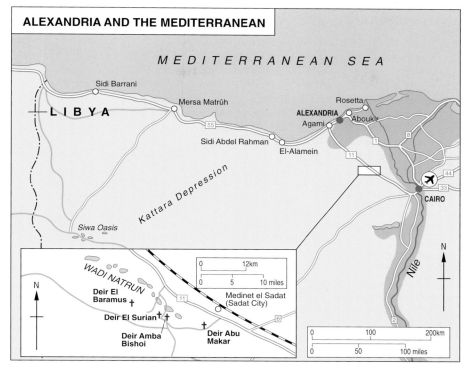

ALEXANDRIA AND THE MEDITERRANEAN

The Mediterranean

West of Alexandria, the Mediterranean coast stretches some 500km (over 300 miles) to the Libyan frontier. There are several resorts along the way, all accessible by public transport. A particularly popular Egyptian resort, now practically an extension of Alexandria, is **Agami**.

El Alamein

A 90-minute drive from Alexandria, what is now an attractive beach resort earned its place in the history books as the theatre of the savage desert battles of 1942. Commemorating the decisive victory of Montgomery's British, Commonwealth and Allied forces over Rommel's German and Italian armies are a **museum**, with tanks and other armoured vehicles in its

The fallen heroes of the British Commonwealth battle against Rommel's Afrika Corps have their last resting place in the cemetery at El Alamein.

WORDS OF WAR

The Eighth Army of British and Allied forces at El Alamein numbered 230,000 men against the German-Italian force of 80,000 men. The Allies outnumbered enemy tanks 3 to 1 and enjoyed vastly superior air-power. But it was will-power as much as armour that won the day. The observations of the chief actors in the battle express the inexorable advance to its momentous outcome. At the beginning of July 1942, with his supply-lines over-extended back to Libya and under constant air attack, Rommel's advance towards Alexandria had stuck in the sands just west of El Alamein. 'Things are unfortunately not going as we would like,' he wrote in a letter back to Germany. 'The resistance is too great and our strength is exhausted.' As if he had read that letter, British commander, General Auchinleck wrote in his orders the same night: 'The enemy should be given no rest ... Eighth Army will attack.'

A first assault failed on the German panzers, but British tanks and infantry had more success against the Italians. 'The enemy is using his superiority,' wrote Rommel, 'especially in infantry, to destroy the Italian formations one by one and the German formations are too weak to stand alone. It is enough to make one weep.' By September, as Field Marshal Montgomery patiently built up striking power for what Rommel himself called a 'battle without hope', the German commander had to return to Germany for hospital treatment for severe stomach ailments.

As the fateful day approached for the battle code-named 'Lightfoot', British commander-in-chief General Alexander confidently cabled Prime Minister Winston Churchill: 'Since there is no open flank, the battle must be stage-managed so that a hole is blown in the enemy front.' The Allied attack was set for 23 October, the night of the full moon, to be signalled to Churchill by the simplest of code-words: 'Zip!'

Rommel's temporary replacement, General Stumme, died of a heart attack in the opening hours of combat. The Desert Fox was back on the front on 25 October. A couple of days later he wrote to his wife that he was unable to sleep: 'I haven't much hope left. What will happen if things go wrong here? I can see no way out if that happens.' It did happen.

On 4 November, Alexander informed Churchill of the 'severe defeat' inflicted on the enemy and two days later, he cabled: 'Ring out the bells! Prisoners estimated now 20,000.' Churchill had the last word: 'It may almost be said: before Alamein, we never had a victory. After Alamein, we never had a defeat.'

gardens, and impressive **cemeteries** of the war-dead from both sides (*see* page 86). If you venture off the highway into the desert where the battles took place, be aware that there are still hundreds of unexploded mines buried beneath the sands. Local guides who claim they can take you over a 'safe' route are indulging in perilous wishful thinking.

Sidi Abdel Rahman, 20km (12 miles) beyond the town, has a fine beach and hotel as a relaxing base from which to visit the battlefield.

Mersa Matruh

Two hours' drive further west, not far from the Libyan frontier, is the region's administrative capital and main fishing port. Mersa Matruh also has its share of resort hotels and some of the coast's best beaches for swimming and other water sports. It is also the starting point for visits to the Siwa oasis (*see* page 239).

Wadi Natrun

The region, which takes its name from the natron mineral found here (and used in mummification and glass manufacture), provided a convenient refuge for Copts to found their monasteries well away from the major cities. Some 120km (75 miles) from Alexandria, turn south at the Rest House near Sadat City. A paved road passes through **Bir Hooker** to a signpost to the monasteries about 6km (3.5 miles) from the main road. Their accessibility to the public may vary from time to time, so be prepared to visit more than one.

Another 6km (3.5 miles) further south, **Deir El Baramus** (Monastery of the Romans) is named after two Roman soldier-saints Maximus and Domidius. It is the oldest of the Wadi's four monasteries, founded in 340 by the hermit St Makarios. The walled fortress you see today was erected by Patriarch Shenuda in the 9th century. Of its five churches, the oldest is the **Church of the Virgin**, at the centre of the monastic buildings, with recently discovered **frescoes** of Biblical scenes and relics of an ancient criminal-turned-saint named Moses the Black. The monks' **refectory** is at the rear of the church, its benches and tables all of stone. The monks farm the land irrigated by its artesian wells and raise sheep and poultry.

Many Berber and Bedouin women like these have settled with their families in the Wadi Natrun region after years of a more nomadic existence in the desert.

Standing aloof in the desert like some Crusader fortress, Deir El Baramus monastery was built in its present form during the 9th century.

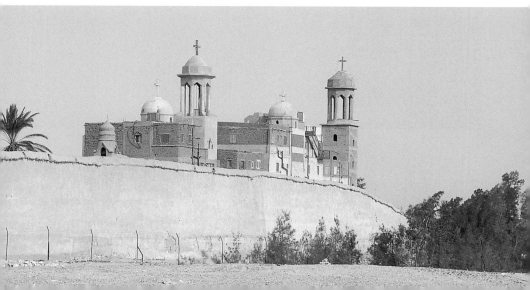

*D*eir El Surian, the Syrians' Coptic monastery in Wadi Natrun, is said to have been originally built to the specifications in the Bible for Noah's Ark.

The telltale white mark on the threshold suggests that the monks of the Deir El Surian monastery still use this millstone to grind their flour, as they have probably done since the monastery was first occupied.

In the middle of the Wadi are two monasteries facing each other, **Deir Amba Bishoi**, where the relics of St Bishoi are an important object of pilgrimage, and **Deir El Surian**, named after the Syrian monks who occupied it in the 9th century. Its **Church of the Virgin Mary** has an interesting marble foot-bath in the nave.

Deir Abu Makar, which is dedicated to St Makarios, is the most southerly of the region's four monasteries and was actually the most important of the ancient foundations. Through repeated destruction by hostile Berbers originating from Libya – its present shape, partly modernized, dates right back to the 9th century – it provided the Coptic church with most of its early leaders. Recent excavations have led to the discovery of a headless skeleton which some like to believe is St John the Baptist (his head can be found in the Omayyad Mosque in Damascus). After all those raids, it is now a red fortress approached by a **drawbridge** up to the first storey above the well, flour-mill and store-rooms.

On the upper floor you will find three churches, the most important of which is the **Church of Archangel Michael** with its nine Corinthian and Doric columns and fine iconostasis screen in front of the haikal sanctuary.

A Time for the Bible and Time Out for the Beach

The ancient region in which the people of Israel parted company with the Pharaohs of Egypt is today both a place of memory and a playground for the holidaymaker. Deep-sea diving and lazing on the beach at a comfortable modern resort on the Red Sea or the South Sinai's Gulf of Aqaba can be coupled with tracing the steps taken by Moses up Mount Sinai, and a tour of the Monastery of St Catherine. Throughout the region, the seafood is excellent.

Domestic flights inside Egypt serve both the Red Sea resorts through Hurghada and the Sinai resorts through Sharm El Sheikh. If you are combining a tour of the region with your visit to Cairo, you may prefer to take the land route, crossing the Suez Canal and down the Sinai peninsula's west coast. Because of the Sinai's military importance, the Egyptians (and the Israelis) have built excellent roads, so that driving is easy, though the distances can be long. If you take off from the main

St Catherine's Monastery stands at the foot of what is believed to be Mount Sinai, from which Moses brought the Ten Commandments.

highways into the desert – often discouraged for reasons of military security – four-wheel-drive is usually essential.

Sinai West Coast

Road access to the west coast of the Sinai peninsula is through the **Ahmed Hamdi Tunnel**, which is 12km (7 miles) north of Suez City (*see* page 276) and named after an Egyptian hero of the 1973 war against Israel. The debris of tanks and aircraft from that and earlier Sinai campaigns can still be seen from the coast road as you drive south.

This is the route that Moses is said to have taken when leading his people on the Exodus from Egypt. Tradition has it that **Uyun Musa** (Springs of Moses), 45km

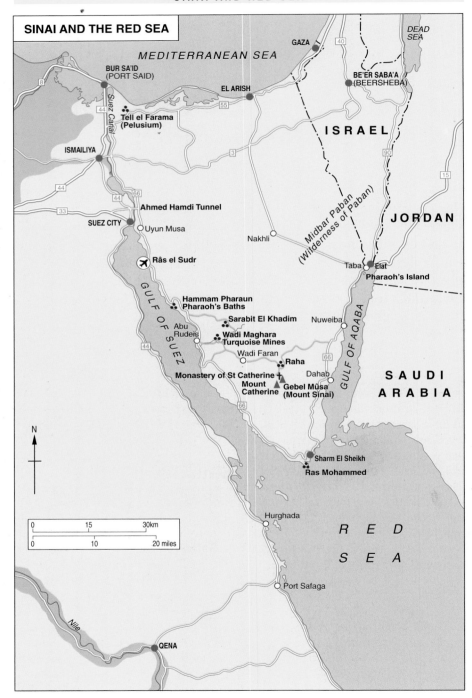

SINAI AND THE RED SEA

MEDITERRANEAN SEA

GAZA

DEAD SEA

BUR SA'ID
(PORT SAID)

BE'ER SABA'A
(BEERSHEBA)

EL ARISH

Tell el Farama
(Pelusium)

ISRAEL

ISMAILIYA

Suez Canal

JORDAN

Ahmed Hamdi Tunnel

Midbar Paban
(Wilderness of Paban)

SUEZ CITY   Uyun Musa

Nakhli

Râs el Sudr

Taba   Elat
Pharaoh's Island

GULF OF SUEZ

Hammam Pharaun
Pharaoh's Baths

Sarabit El Khadim

Nuweiba

Abu
Rudeis

Wadi Maghara
Turquoise Mines

GULF OF AQABA

Wadi Faran

Raha

Monastery of St Catherine   Dahab

Mount
Catherine   Gebel Musa
(Mount Sinai)

SAUDI
ARABIA

N

Sharm El Sheikh

Ras Mohammed

0   15   30km
0   10   20 miles

Hurghada

RED

SEA

Port Safaga

Nile

QENA

(28 miles) south of the tunnel, is the spot where the prophet found drinking water for the parched Israelites. It is now a rather sorry-looking well surrounded by a few palm trees and Bedouins selling trinkets. Another 80km (50 miles) further south, **Hammam Pharaun** (Pharaoh's Baths) is a hot spring coming from deep inside a hillside cave to spill out on to the sandy beach, at 72°C (161°F) – plenty hot enough to cook an egg.

Wadi Maghara and Serabit El Khadim

This fascinating all-day excursion to the **ancient turquoise mines** and the Sinai's most important Pharaonic temple runs inland from the coastal highway and requires a four-wheel-drive vehicle. The best route, signposted to Serabit El Khadim, turns east from the highway just south of the important oilfields of **Abu Rudeis**. It winds 25km (15 miles) inland to the ancient mines, many of whose workings are still visible. As inscriptions on the rocks at Wadi Maghara have testified, the turquoise mines were exploited in Old Kingdom times all the way back to Djoser, builder of the first pyramid, and continued to be worked under Queen Hatshepsut and Tuthmosis III.

The track winds north to Serabit El Khadim, site of the **Temple of Hathor** which dates from the Middle Kingdom (2000 BC). A series of courts and porticoes lead to the rock-cut **sanctuary**, the oldest

A deserted beach on the coast of the Sinai peninsula is the perfect place to ponder on the wonders of Egypt or on nothing at all.

part of the shrine. Along with Hathor are dedications to Thoth and Snopdu, god of the Eastern Desert. Inscribed stelae attest to the interest of Hatshepsut and Tuthmosis II in the region. Evidence of other ancient mining activity can be seen in adjoining valleys.

Mount Sinai and the Monastery of St Catherine

About 20km (12.5 miles) south of the Abu Rudeis oilfields, a good paved road turns inland from the coastal highway to the **Wadi Faran oasis.** It winds through spectacular landscapes of purple, golden and vermilion-coloured mountains closing in on the oasis of green acacias and cascades of date palms. From here, Biblical tradition takes over. Some 55km (34 miles) beyond Wadi Faran, the mountain road curves south into the **Plain of Raha** where the Israelites are said to have camped on their journey from the Red Sea. A mound on the left-hand (east) side of the road has been dubbed the **Shrine of Aaron**, where, it is believed, Moses' brother made the golden calf from the Israelites' jewellery.

At the southern end of the road is the complex of hotels, hostels, camping and parking areas serving Mount Sinai and St Catherine's Monastery.

Monastery of St Catherine
At an altitude of 1,570m (5,149ft), the monastery stands at the head of a narrow valley in the shadow of the mountain where Moses is believed to have received the Ten Commandments. The Greek Orthodox monastery was founded by

Emperor Justinian in AD 527, and part of the masonry from that era can still be seen in the massive walls of what was truly a fortress, complete with battlements.

The **Church of St Catherine** was built in 552 by Emperor Justinian, though it was dedicated to the Alexandrian saint only after her relics were discovered (on Mount Catherine, next to Mount Sinai) 300 years later. It was built near the spot where Moses is believed to have confronted the Burning Bush, which event is commemorated by a chapel which was subsequently incorporated into the church. The rich decoration of the interior – the nave's marble floor, the **wooden pulpit** to the left, the wooden ceiling, the **bishop's throne** to the right and the monumental **candlesticks** in front of the iconostasis screen – is nearly all 18th-century. The richly gilded and carved **iconostasis** itself, with paintings of Jesus, Mary, St Catherine and John the Baptist, was the work of Jeremias of Crete in 1612. Beyond the screen, flanking the door of the **sanctuary**, are two sumptuous **silver chests** with gold figures of St Catherine. The marble-canopied **tomb of St Catherine** (18th-century), containing her skull, stands in the sanctuary to the right.

In the dome and arch of the **apse** is the church's great art-treasure, **6th-century mosaics** created for the foundation of the church. With exquisite artistry, the **dome mosaic** portrays Christ Transfigured, with Moses and St James to the right and Elias and St John to the left, and St Peter kneeling before them. In the **arch mosaic**, Moses is seen in the left-hand corner before the Burning Bush, taking off his sandals, and in the right, receiving the Ten Commandments.

The simple **Chapel of the Burning Bush** is in the north-east corner of the church, to the left of the sanctuary. A silver plate below the altar marks the spot of the Burning Bush.

West of the front entrance of the monastery church is an old pilgrims' hostelry, converted into a **mosque** in the 11th century at the pressing request of Islamic authorities, for equality of worship. The three-tiered **bell-tower** was donated by the Russian orthodox church in 1871.

With barely a dozen monks left to run the establishment, it is difficult (but not impossible if you write ahead of your visit) to get the special authorization for access to the precious **library** and monastic treasure in the **museum**.

Be sure to visit the **garden** with its cypresses and grove of olive, cherry, apricot and plum trees. People also like the somewhat ghoulish **ossuary** of monks' skulls and bones – only archbishops have their skeletons kept intact, one of them the 6th-century St Stephen, still wearing his monk's habit.

Mount Sinai

Controversy still rages as to whether the real Mount Sinai is the nearby **Gebel Musa** (Mount Moses) 2,285m (7,494ft), its taller sister **Gebel Katherina** (Mount Catherine) 2,642m (8,665ft) or some other Sinai mountain altogether. At any rate, the pre-dawn climb is still a wonderful, truly spiritual experience – or can be if you get up before the crowds begin to gather on the slopes. Dress very warmly for the bitter desert cold – a flask of hot tea or coffee is a good idea – and you may want to pay a little extra to a Bedouin to lead you up the first part of the slope on camelback. You will not easily forget your first view of a sunrise in the Sinai.

In the Ossuary, for the past 14 centuries, Archbishop Stephen has been sitting quietly among the skulls of lesser monks of St Catherine's Monastery.

Sharm El Sheikh

Biblical scholars feel this may have been the site of Ophira from where King Solomon transported the gold for his throne. More mundanely, but no less important for them, scuba buffs insist that this southern end of the Sinai peninsula is

THE JEWS IN EGYPT

It comes as a blow to Jewish pride to learn that all those thousands of hieroglyphic inscriptions on stone and papyrus make absolutely no mention of the Old Testament giants, Abraham, Jacob, Joseph and Moses. Abraham went to Egypt, he even had his first son by an Egyptian girl, Hagar – it's in the Bible. And what about Joseph? For a while, he ran the whole country. His father Jacob brought the family to live in the Delta, the Biblical land of Goshen, for over 200 years. And Moses? Those hardships, the plagues, the parting of the Red Sea, and no mention in the hieroglyphics? Come on!

The fact is that in Biblical times Egypt was much more important to the Jews than the Jews were to Egypt. Momentous as the Exodus was for the Jews, for Egypt it was just another walkout by unpaid labour.

So what *were* the facts or at least well-informed conjecture? Outside the Bible, there is no written record of Abraham, but it was perfectly normal in time of drought – 'famine was grievous in the land' – for Semitic cattle-herders like him to cross into the Delta in order to use its rich pastures. There was just no reason for the Egyptians to notice. Scholars hazard a date of around 1800 BC.

Similarly, it was quite feasible and not uncommon in the 17th century BC for a Hyksos Pharaoh to have chosen as chief counsellor someone such as Joseph, an Egyptianized Semite like himself. The economic measures he recommended for the distribution of land, harvest and cattle in time of famine corresponded exactly to the chronicled practice of the times.

The Jews identify with the Hebrews of Jacob's clan, the descendants of Joseph and his brothers who stayed in the Delta. For the Egyptians, 'Hebrew' appears to have covered a much broader range of marginal nomads in their territories. During the reigns of Tuthmosis III and Amenophis III, people described by the hieroglyph *apiru* as 'dusty' or 'covered in sand' stirred up trouble in the Palestinian colonies. Occasionally they were pressed into service in Egypt as soldiers or construction workers, and it was from the latter, reduced to slave-labour, that Moses chose the people he led across the Sinai to found the land of Israel.

Again, there is no written record of Moses, but much of the Biblical account of his time in Egypt can find a historical basis. The key phrase in *Exodus* 'And they built for Pharaoh treasure cities, Pithom and Raamses' indicates the dates. Most Egyptologists agree that this refers to Pi-Ramses, the new capital built in the Delta by Ramses II (1279-1212). Moses' name is derived from *mes* or *mesu*, a root meaning simply 'child', with a prefix subsequently dropped, perhaps because it was the name of an Egyptian god, as in *Ra-mses* itself – 'child of the sun-god'.

The Ten Plagues with which Moses persuaded Pharaoh to let the Hebrews go all have a factual explanation. Blood is the blood-red waters spilled by the Nile in flood, coloured by silt brought down from Ethiopia and long regarded as a curse. Others are vagaries of the Egyptian climate: frogs, mosquitoes, flies, murrain cattle-disease, boils, hail (rare, but not unknown), locusts and darkness (caused by blinding sandstorms blown in from the Western Desert). Even the slaying of the first-born, including the Pharaoh's, has a plausible historical background. It seems to refer to the personal catastrophe of Ramses II who buried many a crown prince before finding in his 13th son, Merneptah, an heir to survive him.

Californian archaeologists have convincingly demonstrated that the parting of the Red Sea waters for the Hebrews' escape may in fact have occurred at the sea's northern tip in the marshy Bitter Lakes area of the Suez Canal. To avoid the Philistines and Egyptian fortresses on the northern route along the Mediterranean – and to undergo the spiritual purge of 40 years in the wilderness – the Hebrews probably travelled south along the Gulf of Suez, then cut inland at

THE JEWS IN EGYPT (continued)

modern Abu Rudeis via the turquoise mines near Serabit El Khadem and turned south to Mount Sinai, most commonly identified today as Gebel Musa (Mount Moses). The Ten Commandments brought down from the summit may have developed from ideas which Moses debated with disciples of the monotheistic Pharaoh, Akhenaten. From the sacred mountain, the Hebrews turned north to cross the Midbar Aran (Paran in the Bible) and enter Israel through the Negev.

The only known mention of Israel in ancient Egyptian – an inscription found in the mortuary temple of Merneptah — jumps to a hasty conclusion. The heir to Ramses II boasts in 1207 of victories over the Libyans and various Palestinian peoples and adds: 'Israel is annihilated, its seed exists no more.'

one of the best places in the world for deep-sea diving. So that they may appreciate the wonders of the Red Sea's coral and exotic fish, even inexperienced swimmers can get on-the-spot training at resort hotels equipped for every kind of water sport. Non-swimmers can get a glimpse of the marvellous marine life in a glass-bottomed boat. In addition to its superb sandy beaches, the resort enjoys a magnificent backdrop of the Sinai mountains, perfect at sunset.

Long before they carved steps in the rock for the pilgrims, the prophet had a tough climb to the top of Mount Sinai, and with no Bedouin's camel to help him.

Ras Mohammed National Park

Among the exotic creatures you could spot if you left the aquarium and took a dive would be this prickly puffa fish.

For a perfect day-trip from Sharm El Sheikh, drive 25km (15 miles) south to this wonderful marine nature reserve at the very tip of the peninsula where the sea is magically translucent. From the park's quiet, carefully protected and unspoiled beaches in the coves and creeks, you can explore underwater wonders that include over 1,000 species of fish, **coral** in some 150 different varieties, and fossilized marine life that may be anything from 75,000 to 20 million years old. Friendly rangers are on hand to direct you to the park's coves and other vantage-points, where you will find telescopes for the often spectacular panoramas.

Among the different species of **fish** you may see around the coral reef are damsel-, parrot- and butterfly-fish, hump-head wrasse, orange grouper and plain old snapper. Even for waders unable or unwilling to snorkel or scuba-dive, many of the fish are visible in the shallow waters just offshore. Three types of **turtle** come to breed at the park – hawksbill, green and leatherback.

Ras Mohammed owes its marine riches in part to the exceptional confluence of the relatively shallow waters of the Gulf of Suez – 75m (246ft) deep – to the west, and the abyss that plunges 1,800m (5,900ft) in the Gulf of Aqaba to the east.

*If you cannot get the waters of the Red Sea to part at the wave
of a rod, Hurghada will let you windsurf across.*

This is part of the great rift that stretches from the Dead Sea to the African Rift Valley. One of the park's more remarkable phenomena is the small **tropical mangrove forest** growing in the shallows and hosting fish-breeding grounds and a habitat for **birds**. You can spot black and white storks, ospreys, falcons, buzzards and kites.

Remember the park's two golden rules: 'Look, but don't touch' and 'Take nothing with you, leave nothing behind.'

East Coast Resorts

Further north on the Gulf of Aqaba, other resorts are springing up fast, notably **Dahab**, **Nuweiba** and **Taba**. The latter, on the Israeli border, has the best-equipped hotels. Out in the bay just south of Taba is the picturesque **Pharaoh's Island** – an apparent misnomer as it was used by Romans and Byzantines for a lighthouse, *pharos* in Greek. Today, you can visit the nicely reconstructed 12th-century fortress of the great sultan, Saladin. In Biblical times, the Old Harbour was probably used by King Solomon as a shipyard for his spice and gold trade with Ofira (modern Sharm El Sheikh). The island was also on the route for Moslem pilgrims from Cairo on their way to Mecca. The view gives food for thought. Four countries are visible from here: besides the Egyptian mainland, Israel lies to the north, Jordan and Saudi Arabia to the east, so close and so far apart.

The boatyards at Port Safaga build and repair fishing boats and other launches for seafarers along the whole Red Sea coast (previous page).

The North Coast

The Sinai has been a battlefield throughout Egypt's history, ancient and modern, and the Mediterranean coast road was the

route habitually taken by the Pharaohs on their expeditions into Palestine and Syria – and by Egypt's invaders, from the cavalry of the Hyksos, Persians and Crusaders to the tank corps of the Israelis.

On the coast of the Sinai peninsula, the mountains seem to be tumbling their crags into the Gulf of Aqaba.

Solitary fishing in the Red Sea can be a soothing experience, and they will barbecue your catch when you get back to the hotel.

You will see that the desert has preserved their traces, whether it be the stones and bricks of fortifications or the twisted metal of 20th-century military hardware.

El Arish

The Sinai's main Mediterranean port is a popular resort with Cairene and Ismailiya holidaymakers in the summer. The lively **sheep and camel market** is held every Thursday, near the old fort, but the **fishing harbour** is picturesque every day. The beautifully arranged **Sinai Heritage Museum** is well worth a visit for its fine collection of Bedouin jewellery, cos-

tumes and handicrafts. Beside the usual pottery and cooking utensils, there are some magnificent coloured woollen camel saddle-bags and a splendid **goat's wool tent**, warm and rain-proof and divided by a curtain wall into two compartments – men on the right, women and children on the left.

Pelusium

At the west end of the coast road, the maps indicate **Tell El Farama**, but the Egyptians call their nearby village **Balousa**, an Arabic version of Pelusium, classical antiquity's name for the ancient **fortress** guarding the approaches to the Delta. Remains of the rectangular fortress with lookout towers at each corner can still be seen poking out of the sands between the highway and the sea – uniting the Pharaohs' red and grey Aswan granite pillars, the Romans' redbrick ramparts, and the arches of the Arab invaders' mosque. In an eery telescoping of the

region's troubled military past, you may also come across the half-tracks and chassis of an armoured personnel carrier from the Arab-Israeli War of 1967 or 1973.

*E*ven if you cannot bear the idea of taking the hook out of the fish's throat, you may like to go along for the trip.

Red Sea

Many people threatened by an excess of pyramids and temples in the Nile Valley like to relax body and soul with a little mindless beach-bumming on the Red Sea. No brutal sightseeing schedules, at most a **camel safari** into the desert (organized from your hotel) to have a barbecued supper prepared by the local Bedouin, with a little folk music and dancing thrown in.

Hurghada
This coastal resort is developing rapidly, with direct flights from Cairo or Luxor or a not too tiring coach-ride across the Eastern Desert via Qena. It offers first-rate hotel facilities and holiday-villages with endless stretches of fine white sand and cool snorkelling or deep-sea fishing. In town, the **bazaar** has a good array of Bedouin and other traditional folk art. You can also visit the **Aquarium** to get an idea of the exotic tropical fish that you see swimming free among the coral. Remember when scuba-diving or snorkelling among these natural wonders: look, but don't touch.

Safaga
What began as a commercial and fishing port is being opened up as a resort with new holiday-villages. Both the water-sport facilities and the seafood are good.

271

Industrious Northern Gateway to Commerce – and Invasion

If Upper Egypt is the nation's heartland, the northern land of Lower Egypt formed by the fertile triangle of the Nile river delta confronts the outside world. It attracted the Hyksos ancestors of Ramses II, the Biblical nomads of Israel, and the empire-builders of Persia. At its eastern edge, the Suez Canal linked the western world of the Mediterranean to the trade routes of Africa and India.

Those wishing to tour the area of the Suez Canal will find good hotels at Ismailiya or Port Said. (For those coming to Egypt by sea, Port Said may be the port of entry.) Most of the main points of interest in the eastern Delta – the ancient sites of Tanis, Bubastis and what may be Avaris – can all be visited on day-trips from Cairo. Over to the west, Rosetta is most easily accessible from Alexandria.

With churches like this, Ismailiya evokes for many Europeans a nostalgic air of the old colonial days when the French were building the Suez Canal.

Suez

The canal, cutting for most of its length straight as an arrow through the isthmus between the Delta and the Sinai peninsula, is the symbol of Egypt's commerce with the modern world. It was natural that after Rommel's German army failed to get there in 1942, its strategic importance continued to make it a natural target of three more wars, in 1956, 1967 and 1973. Since the peace treaty with Israel, its recovery from the repeated bombardments has been quite spectacular and its cities are flourishing, both as commercial centres and as burgeoning resorts. They are worth a look.

Port Said

Founded in the 19th century at the time of the construction of the Suez Canal, the

273

town is the key strategic link between the Mediterranean and the Red Sea. The ravages of war have for the most part disappeared and it thrives now as a lively duty-free zone with some of the cheeky port-city atmosphere of a miniature Hamburg or Naples. Bargain-hunters will find Egyptians exercising their ancient trading talents from the *suk* on the latter-day electronic exotica of modern audio and video technology from Japan, Korea and Singapore.

The town's landmarks are the famous green-domed **Suez Canal Building** on Filastin Street and, as a link to the ancient past, an **obelisk** on Shuhada Square.

You can take a **harbour cruise** to see the ocean-going vessels being piloted into the canal. The **Port Said National Museum** has assembled an important collection of some 10,000 pieces of art from pre-Dynastic and Pharaonic times to Greco-Roman, Coptic and Islamic. Egypt's accomplishments in war are celebrated in the **Military Museum**. The town has a quite prosperous suburb across the canal at **Port Fuad**.

T his Ismailiya tea room is a left-over from the era when Britain's civil servants and officer corps were welcome stars among Suez society.

Ismailiya

Midway down the Suez Canal, some 120km (75 miles) on a direct highway north east of Cairo, the town has preserved a certain faded colonial charm amid green parks on the western shore of **Lake Timsah**. The lake offers good opportunities for windsurfing and sailing along its handsome beaches.

Take a late afternoon promenade along the **Mohammed Ali Quay**. The local **museum** houses the private collection of Ferdinand de Lesseps, builder of the Suez Canal, and gives pride of place to the granite stela (column) erected by Darius, de Lessep's ancient Persian predecessor, to mark an earlier canal linking the Red Sea to the Nile.

I n the more sedate neighbourhoods of Ismailiya, the gardens spill over with bougainvillaea, oleander and rhododendron.

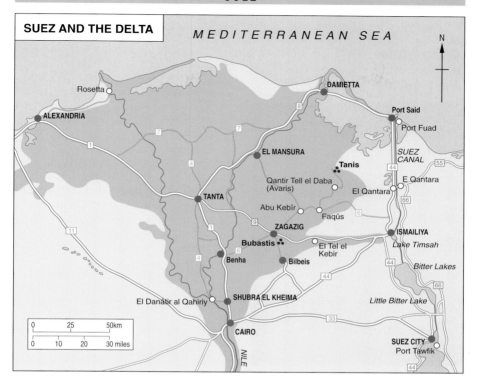

SUEZ AND THE DELTA

MEDITERRANEAN SEA

N

Rosetta

ALEXANDRIA

DAMIETTA

Port Said
Port Fuad

8

7

7

SUEZ
CANAL

1

EL MANSURA

Tanis

44

55

4

Qantir Tell el Daba
(Avaris)

E Qantara

El Qantara

TANTA

Abu Kebir

Faqûs

66

6

1

9

ZAGAZIG

ISMAILIYA

11

Bubastis

El Tel el
Kebir

Lake Timsah

4

Benha

Bilbeis

Bitter Lakes

44

44

66

El Danatir al Qahiriy

SHUBRA EL KHEIMA

Little Bitter Lake

33

0   25   50km
0   10   20   30 miles

CAIRO

SUEZ CITY
Port Tawfik

NILE

44

Since the peace treaty with Israel, Suez City has recovered enough to turn its coastline into resort beaches.

Suez City

Badly damaged in successive Arab-Israeli wars, the town has been attractively reconstructed with plenty of greenery and a couple of pleasant **beaches** around **Suez Bay**. In the summer months, the city is host to a colourful parade of pilgrims passing through on their way to Mecca.

Port Tawfik is the place to watch great freighters coming in and out of the canal. On a promontory overlooking the mouth of the canal is an eloquently empty pedestal for the statue of Ferdinand de Lesseps which was removed after his fellow Frenchmen had staged their abortive invasion of Suez in 1956. Graffiti, always eloquent on Egypt's monuments, include here a 1960 inscription in Russian Cyrillic letters, the name of a Soviet engineer on his way to build the Aswan High Dam.

SUEZ CANAL

Ever since the Pharaohs, men have been planning a canal linking the Mediterranean and the Red Sea, either via the Nile or directly through the isthmus east of the Delta. Around 600 BC, Necho II abandoned work on a canal from the Nile to the Red Sea after oracles warned him the work would only serve the trade interests of foreign invaders. A century later, the Persian ruler Darius dug a canal roughly along the bed of the present one from Ismailiya to Cairo. It silted up and was restored by Roman Emperor Trajan around AD 100 but had disintegrated again by the time of the 8th-century caliphs.

Napoleon Bonaparte's engineers were the first to conceive a channel along the present bed of the Suez Canal, but abandoned it after mistakenly calculating that the Red Sea was 10m (32ft) higher than the Mediterranean, necessitating a costly system of locks. Ferdinand de Lesseps, French consul in Cairo, persuaded a reluctant Mohammed Ali and his successors to revive the project. In 1869, ten years after work began from Port Said, the Suez Canal, a supremely imperialist effort, was inaugurated in the presence of royalty from France, Austria and Prussia, with Britain getting into the act six years later. Nasser got them all out of the act in 1956.

The Delta

The seven branches of the Nile which formed the Delta in ancient times have been reduced to two – the Damietta to the east and the Rosetta to the west – supported in the land's irrigation by an elaborate network of canals. The curved northern band of its fan-like shape, assimilated in Pharaonic art to the Delta swamps' papyrus flower, has grown with the land-reclamation created by the mud brought down by the Nile. The drive out

from Cairo or Alexandria will give you an instructive view of an industrious Egypt, both on the Delta's rich farmland and in the associated industries of foodstuffs, cotton and other textiles.

At the end of a long day's work, the Delta's fishing boats lie at rest on a branch of the Nile River.

Many of its ancient sites are still undergoing extensive excavation as archaeologists feel that this region still conceals important treasures. It was the ancestral land of Ramses II, who built with the help of the Hebrews his capital of Pi-Ramses, a second Karnak long-lost and identified variously as Tanis or Avaris.

Eastern Delta

Cairo's northbound highway passes through the industrial city of Shubra El Kheima to **Benha**, a vital junction for traffic between the Nile Valley and the Delta, and famous in ancient times for its sacred sycamore fig trees. Turn east to **Zagazig** where the local **museum** displays some

If Otis Redding had come to the Delta, he would know San Francisco Bay is not the only place where young men enjoy sitting on the edge of the dock.

After too many years sending its raw materials overseas for manufacture, the Delta's textiles are once more a home-grown industry.

interesting archaeological finds from the area. The ancient site of **Bubastis**, which was an important Lower Egypt capital for the Libyan dynasty in 945 BC, is located at **Tell Basta**, 3km (2 miles) south east of Zagazig. The ruined granite **temple** there was dedicated to Bastet, the cat-goddess of love and joy. An ancient **cat cemetery** was found nearby. Some of the site's major findings are on show at the Zagazig museum.

From Zagazig, the road runs 25km (15 miles) north east via Abu Kebir to Faqus. The road turning north from here passes through **Tell El Daba** which archaeologists identify as the site of the ancient Hyksos capital of **Avaris**; neighbouring **Qantir** is thought to be the area where Ramses II built his Delta residence of Pi-Ramses.

The most important of the region's ancient sites in terms of what there is actually to see is further north at **San El Hagar**. French archaeologists still digging there have identified it as **Tanis** – and the Egyptians share the belief, their village name meaning Stones of Tanis. Its origins date back to the Old Kingdom, but

its heyday was under the Hyksos. In a romantic setting at the edge of the desert, a great gateway leads through a forecourt to the **Temple of Amun** built under the 19th Dynasty of Ramses II. Two **cemeteries** have been uncovered, one royal and one for commoners. Finds, including sculptures, amulets, jewellery and pottery, are exhibited in the site's **museum**; the more precious gold and jewellery found by the site's great excavator, Pierre Montet, in 1939, is displayed back at the Egyptian Museum in Cairo. The scholars have many years of work ahead of them and, if you are not in too big a group, they will gladly let you watch them and discuss their progress.

Rosetta

A short excursion of 56km (35 miles) from Alexandria takes you to the town on the western branch of the Nile, named **Rashid** in Arabic. Best known now for its inscribed stone that permitted the mystery of hieroglyphics to be solved (*see* HIERO-GLYPHICS page 221), it was historically important under the Ottoman Empire when for 300 years it eclipsed Alexandria as Egypt's main Mediterranean port until the 19th century.

The principal charm of the town today is in the Ottoman merchants' tall four- or five-storey **mansions** built in handsomely ornate brick still lining the streets near the port, most notably the **Arab Keli house**, converted to a museum. Notice particularly the finely carved *mashrabiya* grills on the windows and the mosaics of terracotta and brick around the doorways. Of the town's many imposing mosques, the most elegant is the **Zaghlul Mosque**, at the end of the main street running south from the railway station.

In **Fort Rosetta**, which is a largely 16th-century edifice 3km (2 miles) north of town, is the bath house in which the famous Rosetta Stone was found.

In the labyrinth of canals that link up the towns and farms of the Delta, the boats operate an informal taxi system, not as fast as a Venetian vaporetto but with their own Egyptian charm.

After a Long Day's Sightseeing Something Entirely Different

There comes a time when even the most receptive sightseer faces a serious case of overdose. The eyes blur, the mind swims. You just cannot *see* another sight. It is time to *do* something, a little sport, a little shopping, a little entertainment, join in with the Nubian dancers, anything. Here are a few ideas.

As when you are visiting Egypt's monuments, try to avoid the heat of the day for your more energetic activities. Most entertainment is laid on in the evening anyway, but the cool of early morning and late afternoon are best for sport and shopping alike. In any case, at any unreasonably hot hour, you will find few Egyptians to assist you – they take a siesta and so too should you.

This may be a vacation, but deciding what equipment to use for deep-sea diving in the Red Sea is a serious business. If you're not up to scuba-diving, try snorkelling over the coral reefs.

Sports

All over the country, practically all the first-class hotels have excellent facilities for relaxation. Many have a health club, in addition to a swimming pool, tennis and sometimes squash courts. Cairo and Alexandria have many sporting clubs once patronized only by wealthy foreigners and Egyptian nobility. Today they are much more democratic, and tourists are invited to use the facilities as short-term members – your hotel will give you details. In the heart of Cairo on the island of Gezira are dozens of tennis courts, a racetrack, golf course, squash and handball courts, several swimming pools and every other imaginable sports facility. Besides the island's more exclusive Gezira Club, it is possible to gain temporary access to the

Cairo Yacht Club, Heliopolis Sporting Club, Maadi Sporting Club, Maadi Yacht Club, Mena Golf Club and the Shooting Club.

Watersports: When on the Nile, the only **swimming** you should risk is in the little swimming pool you may find on your cruise-boat. Otherwise stick to the hotel pool, or the many beaches on the Mediterranean, Red Sea and Sinai coasts.

At the Red Sea resorts of Hurghada and Port Safaga, you will find superb conditions for **scuba-diving** and **snorkelling**. In

The capital's sporting clubs have a genteel bourgeois atmosphere that is more European than Egyptian.

the Sinai, the best watersports facilities are available at Sharm El Sheikh, especially the **deep-sea diving** down at nearby Ras Mohammed. Fierce competition is offered by the resorts of Dahab, Nuweiba and Taba up the coast of the Gulf of Aqaba.

284

Fishing: All the Red Sea and Sinai coastal resorts offer boats for hire for deep-sea fishing. Many of the hotels provide a beach-barbecue to cook your catch.

Riding: Horses can be rented by the hour or for a day, or, most romantically, at night when you can ride by moonlight. Rates are reasonable and may include the company of a guide. One of the most exciting trails in the country takes you from the stables at the pyramids of Giza along the edge of the desert to the pyramids at Abusir and Saqqara. Across from Luxor in the Valley of the Kings, you can combine sport and sightseeing by touring the tombs and temples by **camel**. The Sinai resorts and Dakhla, Farafra and Bahariya oases offer **camel safaris** to explore the desert.

If you get seasick easily, your hotel should be able to help you rent equipment for fishing from the jetty.

Shopping

Yes, it is an Egyptian custom to bargain when making your purchase. Indeed, some merchants display almost hurt surprise if you accept the first suggested price. But be careful not to overdo it. It is one thing to bargain for a carpet or piece of jewellery or even a souvenir costing 40 or 50 Egyptian pounds or more, but quite another to haggle over something that is only 10 or 15 pounds. Despite the inflation brought about by years of tourism, prices in Egypt are still relatively low, and the people have to make a living. So join in the traditional sport of the bazaar, accept the mint tea without any sense of obligation to buy – the price *will* go down – but try not to feel you have to triumph over the merchants, who are by and large an honest bunch in this country.

Cairo's world-famous bazaar at **Khan El Khalili** is of course a convenient place to group your purchases, but spare some time – and money – for the markets at **Alexandria**, down in **Aswan** and **Luxor** (and across the river at the artisans' village on the west bank), and at **Hurghada** on the Red Sea. If you take a guide or interpreter when you go shopping, remember it is standard practice for them to get a percentage on every purchase. Sometimes, a detour to the workshop in a back street or roof-top room will give you the chance to buy at a reduced price.

Here are some of Egypt's best buys:

Alabaster: Egypt has always been a major centre of this fine-grained translucent gypsum, which is quarried around Aswan and carved up at Luxor. (The word itself is said to derive from the name of a long-forgotten Egyptian town.) Ranging in colour from buttermilk yellow to coffee

He will sell you anything from henna hair-dye to a colourful narguileh *water-pipe. Your price is his price is your price.*

brown, it is used for fine statuary (good copies of Pharaonic antiquities), pyramids, eggs, bowls and vases. Beware that some shoddy goods may be an amalgam of alabaster dust and wax. If you doubt that your purchase is solid alabaster, hold it up to the light to see that its grain is visible through the stone and not just 'painted' on.

Whatever you decide to buy, make sure you have room to pack it. The big brass is attractive, but who is going to carry it?

Amber: This is available in delicate polished lemon-yellow or rich orange brown for necklaces, bracelets, worry-beads, cigarette-holders and key chains. If you are in the market for a serious piece, note the prices back home for comparison, as the better designed objects are not always cheaper here.

Not all Egyptian carving comes up to the refined standards required by the Pharaohs, but these rustic pieces can be a lot of fun.

Antiquities: Quite simply, it is illegal to take genuine Egyptian antiquities out of the country without a government permit (which is almost impossible to obtain). The best way to check the authenticity of a proferred antiquity is to discuss its export problems. If the merchant says there is no problem, there is a problem. That said, there are good-quality copies at the major museums and in the artisans' workshops on Luxor's west bank. Plaster casts of Pharaonic reliefs acquire their

G allabiyas *are designed
for Egyptians happy to envelop a
generous paunch. They make good
beachwear or even nightshirts
back home.*

ancient patina by being dipped in tea. One place to find genuine, exportable 'antiquities' is in Alexandria's flea market (*see* page 242) of bric à brac, largely Victoriana, left by the town's cosmopolitan community forced to leave in a hurry after the 1952 revolution.

Baskets: You will find these everywhere, but the best are made in Faiyum and at the Western Desert oases.

Bedouin Costume and Jewellery: Originals or copies of dresses, hats, bracelets, anklets, necklaces and rings are sold at Sinai and Red Sea resorts and the village of Kerdasa near the Giza pyramids.

Clothes: Egyptian cotton's long fibres and smooth finish make it among the best in the world – great for T-shirts. Mohammed Ali built the wealth of his dynasty on cotton. *Gallabiyas*, the long, loose collarless Egyptian caftans, are comfortable and attractive both for men and women. Since 1952, the tasselled burgundy-coloured **tarbush** or fez has been considered counter-revolutionary, symbolic of the monarchy and the colonial era, but is still sold at Khan El Khalili to people who are unbothered by such considerations. **Belly-dancing outfits**, yes, those great transparent veils, scarves and sequinned bras, complete with the little **finger-cymbals** to complete the effect, are also available there.

Coins: Collectors will find coins of all Arab countries and occasionally Greco-Roman medallions.

Copper and Brass: The tinkling of coppersmiths' hammers is a familiar sound in Khan El Khalili. It takes about a day and

*Y*ou can watch the proud, centuries-old craft of fashioning
brassware in the workshops of Khan El Khalili bazaar.

a half to chisel the arabesques into a small copper serving tray. The best trays, Turkish coffee sets, samovars and other items are of course the older ones, but new copper and brass trays make good buys, especially those with portable wooden folding trestles to turn them into tables.

Games: For backgammon, chess and dominoes, pieces and boards are available in alabaster, ebony, inlaid mother-of-pearl and Egyptian ivory. Do not feel ecologically bad about buying Egyptian ivory, just make sure the price is right – it is nearly always camel- or donkey-bone, and very good quality, too.

Jewellery: Gold and silver jewellery is often sold by weight, with only a small mark-up for the detailed workmanship. Take your pick from Pharaonic styles inspired by King Tutankhamun's treasure, arabesques, or modern pieces. Popular as gold and silver pendants or earrings are the **hieroglyphic cartouches** prepared on the spot with the wearer's name. Precious and semi-precious stones – notably brandy-coloured topaz, blue lapis lazuli, purple amethyst and greenish-blue aquamarine – are also sold by weight and can be set as rings or pendants in the shop.

Leather Goods: Handbags, satchels and shoulder bags can be of very uneven quality, generally of sturdy leather, but the sewing is not always good. The camel saddles are first-rate, but these are more ornamental than useful, unless you are also in the market for a camel.

Music Cassettes: For those who have developed a taste for Arab music, especially the golden oldies of the divine Oum Khalsoum, numerous cassettes are on sale.

Papyrus: The plant died out after the Roman occupation and did not come back into Egypt until the 1970s, at first imported from Sudan but now locally grown again. Dr Hassan Ragab has resumed the ancient art of paper-making (*see* HIEROGLYPHICS page 221) at his Papyrus Institute on a houseboat near the Cairo Sheraton, and the process has spread, with shops throughout the tourist areas. They sell hieroglyphic scripts, calendars, bookmarks and Pharaonic pictures, which are more expensive hand-painted than printed.

Perfumes and Cosmetics: Scent and the art of make-up are among the most ancient of Egyptian traditions. Types on sale include very good copies of the most celebrated French and Italian brands. The top 'nose' in Paris, say the merchants, is an Egyptian. Look out for incense, too, kohl eyeliner and, especially down in Aswan, henna hair-dye, both for jet-black and subtle auburn tints.

Rugs and Tapestries: The best bets are the flatweave kilim rugs with geometric patterns, or the rough but handsome goat's wool rugs of the Western Desert in red, black and green – check that the colour will not run by wetting it with your finger. Harraniya tapestries (made in factories in the village between Giza and Saqqara) have attractive patterns for wall-hangings or table-covers. The genuine article can be quite expensive.

Water-pipes: Also known as *narguileh*, *shisha* or *hookah*, these elegant, fierce-looking instruments may be coveted by that (perhaps literally) dying breed of tobacco smokers. Lit by coals and drawn through water, the tobacco mixture comes straight (*tombaq*), honey-flavoured

(*ma'asil*) or apple (*tuffa*). An essential accessory is a set of dominoes or backgammon (*see* GAMES page 290).

Woodwork: The Egyptian speciality is making the *mashrabiya*, the intricate screens of lathe-turned wooden lattice which traditionally covered Egyptian windows, shielding women from the curious stares of strange men. Screens, room-dividers and tray-stands are all very reasonably priced, considering the workmanship. More easy to transport back home is a small box of cedar or sandalwood inlaid with mother-of-pearl and ebony.

Festivals and Entertainment

Festival time in Egypt finds everyone outdoors, following processions in the

When footsore from sightseeing in Cairo, take a sunset cruise on the Nile for cocktails, or dinner in a floating restaurant.

streets, strolling along the Nile, or filling the parks and gardens. Vendors sell snacks and refreshing drinks, and the crowds eagerly pay court to itinerant performers. Wrestlers, dancers and singers all put on open-air shows, with a hat passed round for coins at the end of the performance.

A favourite diversion is the mock battle called **El Tahtib**: two men, armed with stout reed staffs, size each other up as they prowl around in a circle, swinging the staffs above their heads. It looks like a courtly dance, but each combatant is just waiting for the opportunity to take a swing

Nubians are among the country's finest musicians and dancers, continuing a tradition that dates back to an age when their kingdom was independent of Egyptian rule.

at his opponent. When the players are equally matched, El Tahtib becomes a graceful ceremony of smooth movements and mutual respect.

In Upper Egypt, **Nubian folklore and music** is very different from the Arabic folklore of Cairo and the Delta. The music

sounds surprisingly Far Eastern in its tonalities and rhythms. In floorshows in hotels and cruise-boats, guests are invited to join in the dances.

All Egyptians are united in the celebration of major Islamic and traditional festivals. The National Spring Festival, **Sham En Nessim**, comes on the Monday following Coptic Easter. It's an excuse for everyone to get outdoors or into boats on the Nile, because an old legend has it that, 'He who sniffs the first spring zephyr will have good health all year'.

Another major holiday is **Mulid En Nabi**, the Prophet's Birthday, when a mammoth procession winds through Cairo's streets, while smaller ones take place in other cities.

Ramadan is a period of 30 days in the early spring, the ninth month of the Moslem lunar calendar. During this time, all good Moslems observe strict fasting between the hours of sunrise and sunset. The rules are strict: beginning at first light there must be no food or drink, no smoking or even licking a stamp. Working hours are also reduced. The fast is broken at sunset, and special dishes fill the feast tables for the early evening breakfast meal of *iftar*. Children, pregnant women, travellers and the infirm are exempted from the fast, and everyone else takes advantage of shorter working hours. Tourist hotels and restaurants keep normal, year-round hours for the convenience of non-Moslem visitors, though many stop serving alcoholic drinks. At the end of the holy month comes **Ramadan Bairam** *(Eid El Fitr)*, a three-day celebration marked by gifts of greeting-cards, and visits among friends.

Perhaps the most sacred of Moslem festivals, the summer **Qurban Bairam** *(Eid El Adha)* comes in the middle of the month of Zu'l-Hegga, when many Moslems make the *hajj*, or pilgrimage, to Mecca. The four-day feast commemorates the biblical sacrifice by Abraham, when a ram was at the last minute substituted for his son – Moslem families relive the moment by sacrificing a ram. After the ritual slaughter according to Koranic law, the meat is cooked and a feast is prepared for family and friends, with a generous portion going to the poor.

August used to be a time of elaborate festivals in Cairo. As the waters of the Nile rose in the annual flood, Nilometres all along the river would be checked and rechecked, and the readings sent off to Cairo by messenger. When the water level reached a certain point, all the canals would be unblocked and the precious water would surge deep into the fields carrying valuable silt to replenish the soil. Now that the Aswan High Dam controls the Nile's flow at an even level all year round, the August festivities have only the faintest echo of their former gaiety and importance.

The **Cairo Film Festival** was first organized in 1977 and has proved a great success, a major event in the Middle East. The festival is generally held in November, when award-winning films from all over the world are shown at some of the major hotels.

Sound-and-Light Shows

The grandeur of the Giza pyramids is enhanced at night by powerful floodlights bathing the ancient stones in rich colour. A stirring commentary – at alternating times in English, French or German – is accompanied by orchestral music from hidden loudspeakers.

At Luxor, the show is held at Karnak's Great Temple of Amun. After following the light-effects and commentary through the temple, spectators sit in banks of seats behind the Sacred Lake. At Aswan, an enthralling spectacle dramatizes the Temples of Philae.

Remember to bring a sweater to counter the evening chill.

Cinemas

Check local English-language newspapers for current film showings. You can usually find something in English or at least with English subtitles. In Egypt's cinemas everyone has a reserved seat. Purchase your tickets an hour or more in advance (especially on Thursday, Friday or Saturday nights).

Clubs

Clubs in the large hotels and along Cairo's Pyramids Road offer nightly variety shows, with both Western song-and-dance reviews and fiery Egyptian music and belly-dancing. Music for less acrobatic dancing follows. Though exciting and entertaining, hotel shows are good clean family fare.

Opera

Cairo's Opera House was an official gift from the Japanese government in 1988. The complex, which also houses several art galleries, is well worth a visit. Operas, with foreign and Egyptian performances, are staged from October to May. Semiformal or formal dress may be required.

Casinos

Officially, foreigners are the only ones allowed into Egypt's gambling houses – gambling being an Islamic taboo. You should bring along your passport. Only foreign currency may be used at the tables. Most luxury hotels have casinos, offering

Dining in Egypt is a colourful, savoury affair and you can see from Egyptian diners that it is as much for gourmands as for gourmets.

roulette, blackjack, baccarat and, increasingly, one-armed bandits.

If you see 'Casino' on a sign by a Nileside restaurant, that does not mean it has gambling. In the Middle East, a casino is a waterside establishment, which can be anything from a snack bar to a restaurant with a floor show, but no gambling.

National Circus

Egypt's National Circus was started with the help of Soviet circus masters some

WHAT TO DO

time ago and has been, along with the Aswan Dam, one of the more welcome legacies. The clowns, acrobats and animals perform in Cairo's Agouza quarter during most of the year, before moving on to Alexandria for the hot months of July and August.

Eating Out

Modern-day Egyptian restaurants bring to the same basic ingredients that tickled the palates of the Pharaohs a cuisine inspired by the diversity of their subsequent conquerors: Persian, Greek, Arab and Turkish. You eat the same Mediterranean and Red Sea fish. The Nile Valley and the Delta yield the same sheep, beef, rabbit, quail, pigeons and ducks, grain and vegetables that appear in the old wall paintings. Italian, French and British influences are also to be found in Egyptian cookery, and international dishes range from chow mein to Wiener Schnitzel, fast-food hamburgers, fried chicken and pizza, to Indian chicken tikka.

In your hotel, the normal continental **breakfast** of coffee or tea, toast and rolls, butter and jam may be supplemented with salty white or pale yellow cheese, and fresh fruit juice. Larger hotels lay on copious buffets of cooked American or Egyptian dishes.

Lunch is the main meal of the day, though many hotels cater to foreign habits and serve a big dinner in the evening. One o'clock until three or four in the afternoon is the usual lunchbreak, though you may prefer to emulate the Egyptians in their habit of eating much later – before the siesta.

Dinner in Egyptian homes is also traditionally served quite late, perhaps not until 10pm. During Ramadan all these hours, and many of the foods served, change completely.

Egyptian Cuisine

Your hotel is likely to serve more European dishes than Egyptian ones, but you should not miss any chance to savour the local fare. In the hotels with more adventurous buffets, you may like to experiment with combinations of Egyptian, European and even Chinese dishes.

Starters

For an interesting sampling, many restaurants offer *mezzeh* – a selection of local salads, cheese, stuffed vine leaves and, sometimes, meat. An enjoyable first course for a group of friends, *mezzeh* can be a light meal in itself.

The best Egyptian meal begins with a good plate of mezzeh, *an infinite variety of hors d'oeuvres that can end up being a whole meal.*

ONE MAN'S CAMEL MEAT

Cuisine set the tone for Egypt's subtle relations with the rest of the Arab world from the very earliest days of the Islamic conquest in 641. It took some time for the rough, desert-dwelling Arabs to adjust to the more sophisticated ways of their new colony. Governor Amr chose to honour the refinement of the Egyptians with a three-day banquet. On the first day, he had a meal served Bedouin style: camel meat boiled in salt water. His Egyptian guests could barely touch it. On the second day, the guests were invited to respond with a feast of Egyptian culinary delicacies which the Arab officers had an equally difficult time handling. On the third day, Amr ibn al'Asi let the Egyptians know how much real importance he attached to this business of gourmet cuisine by staging a formidable military parade in full battle array.

Or begin with *molokhia*, a savoury soup of the green leafy vegetable cooked in broth with garlic, pepper and coriander, usually eaten with rice and chicken. No Egyptian would do without *ful*, thick and tangy bean-stew, flavoured with tomatoes and spices. It is commonly served with oil and the juice of a lime or with deep-fried *taamia*, a paste made of the same beans plus other vegetables, mixed with parsley and spices.

Makhallal (turshi), spicy pickled vegetables, are an important accessory on Egyptian tables, and a taste you may acquire to resist dehydration in the dry desert climate. If it is too salty for your palate, cool off with *taboulah*, a refreshing combination of *bulgar* (crushed wheat), parsley, mint and chopped tomatoes and onions.

Bread of the flat Middle Eastern *pitah* type is especially well-suited for scooping up mouthfuls of *leben zabadi* (yoghurt),

297

Nine times out of ten, the fruit served as dessert is freshly picked from the tree, like these bananas from the Delta.

tahina (sesame seed purée) or its variation, *baba ganoug* (*tahina* with a purée of baked aubergine, lemon and garlic), and *megdra* (puréed black lentils and rice).

Meat
Some restaurants specialize in *kebab*, succulent chunks of lamb or mutton marinated in spices and grilled over charcoal on a spit. A variation is *kofta*, which is minced or ground lamb spiced and wrapped around a flat skewer to be grilled in the same way, over charcoal, then served on a bed of fresh parsley or coriander leaves. *Shwarma* is lamb roasted on a vertical spit, sliced thinly and served with bread or rice.

Egyptians love to dine on pigeon (*hamam*) or quail (*somon*) from the Delta, the birds being split and grilled or stuffed (*meshi*), and served on rice.

Fish
From the Mediterranean and Red Sea come sea bass, sea bream, red or grey mullet, and freshwater tilapia from Lake Nasser. It is pan-fried, sometimes spiced with a pinch of cumin added during cooking. Large Alexandrian shrimps or giant prawns are a speciality, grilled on a skewer over a fragrant charcoal brazier. A monkfish *kebab* is first marinaded in olive oil, lemon juice and cumin before being grilled over the coals. In some seafood restaurants, you may find the dried, salted roe of the grey mullet (*betarek*), but deep brown in colour. This is a delicacy appreciated since Pharaonic times, apparently for its aphrodisiac powers. Have it on bread dipped in olive oil. The Red Sea or Sinai resorts serve spiny lobster (*langouste*). Squid or cuttlefish (*subeit*) are also popular, deep-fried or in cold salads.

Salads are served before and during the main course. Boiled cold beetroot is popular when it is in season, as are the excellent ripe sliced tomatoes and cucumbers with a dash of lemon juice or vinegar. Green salads may contain a tart, almost peppery green leaf called gargir mixed with the lettuce.

Egyptian **cheese** is generally quite salty. This, like those pickled vegetables, may be good for water retention in a desert climate, but is no treat for an unaccustomed palate. More boring processed cheese wrapped in foil is widely available.

For **dessert**, try the Delta's fine fresh bananas, oranges, figs or guavas. You will find many varieties of date, most quite different from the sweet dates you may know back home. The great local delicacy is *om-ali*, a baked dessert of rice, milk, raisins and pistachios or other nuts. Its fans insist it is delicious even when made badly, it is unquestionably heavenly when made well.

Look for the many delicious Egyptian pastry-desserts, mostly of Turkish origin – impossibly sweet, but let yourself go. Try *baklava*, a many layered flaky pastry stuffed with nuts and honey; an alternative is *atayeef*, a deep-fried pastry with either sweet or cheese filling, served principally during Ramadan. If you want something less sweet, *mahallabiyah* is a smooth pudding of rice and milk garnished with nuts.

European Cuisine
In Egyptian tourist hotels, local cuisine is too often banished from the menu almost entirely and its place taken by 'international' cuisine, with only the best hotels employing foreign-born chefs. Depending on a number of factors, therefore, this cuisine can be bland or merely undis-

In this Moslem land, local wine growing was once the preserve of Greeks and Italians living in Alexandria. Today it is still carried on by several Coptic families.

tinguished, only occasionally sublime. Things are improving. Both inside and outside the hotels, you will find a wide variety of cosmopolitan cuisine – Chinese, Indian, Japanese and Italian, though it is generally best to avoid the French (outside the French-run hotels it is too often just pretentious and expensive, too rarely French). For a full list, *see* page 307.

Beverages

Moslems are forbidden to drink alcohol. Though many Egyptians enjoy a glass of beer, the religious prohibition of alcohol means that soft drinks are very popular, and found everywhere.

The good news is that you do not have to worry about the water. Perfectly good, safe water is bottled under licence from local wells by French mineral water companies. Fruit juices are almost always available – the cautious just have to remember to say 'no ice'. Be sure to try the Egyptian speciality called *karkadeh*, a deep-red infusion of hibiscus petals with an agreeable flavour, served slightly sweetened. It is delicious cold at breakfast-time, but can be a bracing pick-me-up served hot as well.

EATING OUT

Egyptian vineyards in the Delta have been cultivated for centuries. Of the reds, Omar Khayyam and Chateau (or Kasr) Gianaclis are soft, fairly dry, and have a good deal of tannin. Pharaons is less tasty and slightly more dry. White wines – Nefertiti, Cleopatra, and Gianaclis Villages – are often better than the red, but have them chilled. If you prefer rosé, ask for Rubis d'Egypte.

Several imported brands of beer are relatively expensive. Local beer, a light lager called Stella, comes in large bottles which easily serve two people. Some prefer the upmarket Stella Export, in smaller bottles at a higher price.

Zibib, the Egyptian version of aniseed-flavoured *arak* (like ouzo or pastis), may be made from either grape brandy or date brandy.

Tea and Turkish Coffee

Coffee can be a problem. French- or American-style here is not that great, espresso may be available, otherwise many prefer instant. The best solution is Turkish coffee. It is served on the slightest pretext. In his shop, office or home, an Egyptian host will nearly always offer coffee to visitors – even on a five-minute visit. Most foreigners come to prefer Turkish coffee when it is brewed *mazbut* (with a medium amount of sugar). If it tastes too bitter, order it *ziyada* (with lots of sugar). *Saadeh* is with no sugar at all. *Arrihah* means your tiny cup will come flavoured with just the slightest pinch of sugar. In practice, you can never quite be sure exactly how the coffee will come, as one coffee-maker's *arrihah* is another's *mazbut*.

Tea (*shay*) is popular with Egyptians and tourists alike. As a refresher served in the best local coffee houses, it will come with sprigs of mint.

TO HELP YOU ORDER

In an Egyptian restaurant, it is always useful to have a few words at your disposal to be able to communicate your order. For more comprehensive help with reading a menu or for making yourself understood in restaurants where they speak little English, we recommend BERLITZ ARABIC FOR TRAVELLERS, but here are a few words to start with:

beer	bira
boiled	maslook
bread	esh
butter	zibda
cheese	gibna
chicken	firakh
chickpeas	hommos
coffee	ahwa
dates	balah
eggs	baed
figs	teen
fish	samek
fried	makli
fruit	fakha
fruit-juice	aseer-fakha
garlic	toam
grilled	mashwi
lamb chops	riyash dani
lemon	laymon
meat	lahm
milk	laban haleab
mineral water	mayya madaniyya
mustard	mostarda
olives	zayton
onions	basal
pepper	filfil
pigeon	hamam
potatoes	batatis
rice	roz
salad	salata
salt	malh
soup	shorba
sugar	sokkar
tea	shay
vegetable	khodar
watermelon	battikh
wine	nibit

The Right Place at the Right Price

Hotels

Our selection of hotels in three price categories covers all major Egyptian destinations: Cairo; Upper Egypt (Luxor, Aswan, Abu Simbel); Middle Egypt (Faiyum, Minya); the Oases (Kharga, Dakhla, Siwa); the Red Sea (Hurghada, Safaga); Alexandria and the Mediterranean (El Alamein, Mersa Matruh); the Suez Canal (Port Said, Ismailiya, Suez City) and Sinai (St Catherine, Sharm El Sheikh, Dahab, Nuweiba, Taba, El Arish). Prices will vary according to season, travel agent's package and unpredictable inflation. For booking directly with the hotels, we include phone and, wherever possible, fax numbers.

At last inspection, these hotels met reasonable standards of cleanliness and comfort, with air-conditioning usually available in all but the very cheapest rooms. Following local practice, current prices are quoted in US dollars. For our three price-range categories, we have used the following symbols (double occupancy with bath, meals extra):

▌	below $40
▌▌	$40-$80
▌▌▌	above $80

Cairo
(international tel/fax code 20.2)

Al Manyal Youth Hostel ▌
135 Abdel Aziz Al Saud Street
Manyal
Tel. 840 729

Atlas Zamalek ▌▌
20 Gamaet El Dowal El Arabia St
Mohandessin
Tel. 346 4175, fax 347 6938
Good small hotel located in chic neighbourhood of Cairo; 74 rooms, popular with Middle Eastern bourgeoisie, good local cuisine, renowned Tamango nightclub.

Baron ▌▌▌
Horriya
Heliopolis
Tel. 291 5757; fax 290 7077
Convenient for airport, well-run business hotel, also popular for its disco and banquet facilities; 126 rooms, health club and shopping centre.

Cairo Marriott ▌▌▌
Saraya El Gezira Street
Zamalek
Cairo
Tel. 340 8888; fax 340 6667
Originally Khedive Ismail's palace built in 1869 on Gezira Island, the hotel has been renovated and expanded, retaining grand artwork, marble statues, and Oriental carpets; 1,147 rooms and bungalows, swimming pool amid landscaped gardens, shops, terrace restaurant, casino, nightclub, good business-centre.

Cairo Mövenpick Jolie Ville ▌▌▌
Cairo-Alexandria Desert Road
Tel. 385 2555; fax 383 5006
Giant 412-room hotel away from city bustle. Swimming pool, good European and Egyptian restaurants.

Cairo Sheraton ▌▌▌
Galaa Square
Giza
Tel. 348 8600; fax 348 9051
Twin towers on Nile west bank; 660 rooms, friendly and helpful service, swimming pool, casino, Oriental nightclub and efficient business-centre.

Carlton ▌
21 July 26th Street
Ezbekiya
Tel. 755 181
Modest, old-fashioned charm is offered in this bustling city-centre hotel; 60 rooms.

Forte Grand Pyramids
Alexandria Desert Road
Giza
Tel. 383 0383; fax 383 1730
Spectacular luxury hotel just a walk from the Pyramids; 523 rooms, swimming pool, tennis, health club and business centre.

Gezirah Sheraton ▌▌▌
Gezirah Island
Tel. 341 1333; fax 341 3640
Round tower dominating south end of Gezirah Island, superb river and city views; 520 rooms, open-air riverside restaurants, swimming pool, casino, first-class business-centre.

Grand Hotel   I
17 July 26th Street
Ezbekiya
Tel. 757 700; fax 757 593
*Situated in the heart of the busy
shopping district, amiable hotel; 97
rooms, most of them big with balcony, antique or at least old-fashioned furnishings.*

Heliopolis Mövenpick   III
Airport Road
Heliopolis
Tel. 291 9400; fax 667 374
*Situated close to the airport, but the
412 rooms are well soundproofed;
the impressive business-centre is
conducted with Swiss efficiency. A
selection of European and Egyptian
cuisine is offered, swimming pool,
shops and disco.*

Heliopolis Sheraton   III
Oruba Street
Heliopolis
Tel. 290 2027; fax 290 4061
*Handy for the airport, completely
renovated after fire; 90 rooms,
much appreciated restaurants, and
a good business-centre to serve all
the needs of the business traveller.*

Helwan Shepheard's   III
Corniche El Nil Street
Garden City
Tel. 355 3900; fax 355 7284
*Modern riverside construction
bearing only the name of an old
Cairo landmark originally near
pyramids (burned down in anti-
British riots); 281 rooms, good
views of Nile and Gezirah Island;
European and Middle Eastern
cuisine, swimming pool, business-
centre.*

Le Méridien   III
Corniche El Nil Street
Garden City
Tel. 362 1717; fax 362 1927
*Offering a superb Nile view from
north end of Roda Island; 275
rooms, swimming pool, great health
club with all the facilities needed to
keep you trim, appropriately good
French restaurant, fine business-
centre.*

Les Trois Pyramides   II
229 Pyramids Road
Giza
Tel. 582 2233; fax 582 3700
*Convenient access to pyramids;
230 rooms in modern 12-storey
building, swimming pool, health
club.*

Manial Palace Hotel   II
Kasr Mohammed Ali
El Manial
Tel. 844 524; fax 363 1737
*On Roda Island in the palace
grounds once owned by a cousin of
King Farouk, Club Méditerranée offers 190 rooms and bungalows
(available for local booking); garden of shady banyan and palm trees,
giant swimming pool, legendary
mammoth buffet.*

Mena House Oberoi   III
Pyramids Road
Giza
Tel. 383 3222; fax 383 7777
*Set in 40 acres of gardens right be-
side the Great Pyramid, originally
built in 1869, it has been renovated
and expanded but the older part is
more charming than the new; 20
minutes from downtown Cairo; 520
rooms, casino, Indian restaurant,
giant swimming pool, tennis, gold,
horseback riding, good business-
centre.*

Méridien Heliopolis   III
51 Oruba Street
Heliopolis
Tel. 290 5055; fax 291 8591
*Conveniently close to the airport
with added asset of the hotel chain's
traditional first-class cuisine; 302
rooms and well-organized facilities
for business conferences.*

Nile Hilton   III
Tahrir Square
Cairo
Tel. 765 666; fax 760 874
*A Cairo institution, handiest for the
Egyptian Museum; riverside loca-
tion, 434 rooms, swimming pool,
casino, fine business-centre;
renowned people-watching café
terrace.*

Oasis   II
Cairo-Alexandria Desert Road
Pyramids
Tel. 383 1777; fax 383 0916
*Pretty garden of palm and orange
trees 5km (3 miles) from pyramids;
260 rooms, swimming pool.*

Pullman Maadi Towers   III
29 Corniche El Nil
Maadi
Tel. 350 6092; fax 350 6209
*Riverfront location with panoramic
view of Giza Pyramids; 176 rooms,
swimming pool, health club, good
restaurants and efficient business-
centre.*

Ramses Hilton   III
1115 Corniche El Nil Street
Maspero
Tel. 777 444; fax 757 152
*Soaring 36-storey tower with grand
riverside views, centrally located
but separated by major highway
from downtown area; 849 rooms,
rooftop piano bar, swimming pool,
first-class business-centre.*

Semiramis Intercontinental   III
Corniche El Nil Street
Garden City
Tel. 355 7171; fax 356 3020
*Great riverside views from tower
centrally located south of Tahrir
Square; giant complex of 840
rooms, but efficiently run; French
cuisine, disco, good business-centre
and shops.*

Siag Pyramids   III
Saqqara Road
Ahram
Tel. 385 6022; fax 384 0874
*On edge of the desert within view of
Giza pyramids; 352 rooms, swim-
ming pool, tennis, fine Middle East-
ern dining room.*

Upper Egypt

Luxor
(international tel/fax code 20.95)

Akhetaton Village   II
Khaled Ibn El Walid Street
Tel. 580 850; fax 580 879
*Club Méditerranée's 144-room re-
sort hotel, superb swimming pool,
disco and good shopping facilities.*

Etap Luxor Hotel   II
Corniche El Nil Street
Tel. 374 944; fax 374 912
*Centrally located riverside hotel
with easy access to Luxor temple,
museum and market; 306 rooms,
swimming pool, disco.*

Horus   I
Karnak Temple Street
Tel. 372 165
*North side of town, handy for Kar-
nak Temple; small, clean hotel, 25
rooms.*

Isis Hotel   III
Khaled Ibn El Walid Street
Tel. 373 3366; fax 372 923
*Giant riverfront luxury hotel at south
end of town; 500 rooms, swimming
pool, efficient business-centre.*

Luxor Hilton IIII
New Karnak
Tel. 374 933; fax 386 571
*Near Karnak Temple, prettily
situated amid gardens leading
down to river promenade; 261
rooms, swimming pool, casino and
disco.*

Luxor Sheraton IIII
El Awameya Road
Tel. 374 544; fax 374 941
*Set back from nicely landscaped
riverfront gardens at south end of
town; 298 rooms and bungalows,
open-air poolside grill restaurant,
good business-centre and shopping
mall.*

Luxor Youth Hotel I
Corniche Street

Mövenpick Jolie Ville IIII
Crocodile Island
Luxor
Tel. 374 855; fax 374 933
*Quiet location 7km (4 miles) from
town centre in beautiful gardens;
320 rooms, swimming pool, tennis,
sailing, reputedly best hotel food in
town.*

Savoy I
El Nil Street
Tel. 580 522; fax 581 727
*Modest but clean riverfront hotel;
108 rooms and airconditioned
bungalows.*

Winter Palace II
Corniche El Nil Street
Tel. 580 422; fax 374 087
*Grand old-fashioned hotel situated
right next to Luxor Temple. Agatha
Christie atmosphere remains in the
bar and delightful terrace for tea
overlooking exotic gardens and
swimming pool; offering 370 rooms
in Old and considerably less
charming New Winter Palace next
door.*

Aswan
(international tel/fax code 20.97)

Amoun II
Amoun Island
Aswan
Tel. 322 816; fax 322 555
*Club Méditerranée's hotel situated
on a private island in pleasant
gardens facing Cataract, with
transport by felucca to town and
local sights; offering 56 rooms,
swimming pool.*

Aswan Oberoi IIII
Elephantine Island
Aswan
Tel. 323 455; fax 323 485
*Giant tower at the north end of
Elephantine Island with fine view
of other islands and Cataract.
The hotel has its own boats for
excursions; it offers 244 rooms
and a swimming pool in which to
relax.*

Aswan Youth Hostel
Abtal El Tahrir
Tel. 2313

Happi Hotel I
Abtal El Tahrir Street
Tel. 322 028
*Happi-go-lucky establishment
set back from river, popular
with backpackers; 60 rooms,
some with river view.*

Isis Aswan Hotel II
Corniche El Nil Street
Tel. 315 200; fax 315 500
*Facing Elephantine Island;
100 rooms, swimming pool,
good open-air terrace
restaurant.*

Isis Island Hotel IIII
Isis Island
Aswan
Tel. 317 400; fax 317 405
*The hotel consists of luxury
bungalows on an island in the
middle of the Nile; it offers 406
rooms, swimming pool, health club,
tennis, squash court and disco.*

Kalabsha Hotel II
Abtal El Tahrir Street
Tel. 322 999; fax 325 974
*Modern building at south end
of town with fine view of
Cataract; 120 rooms.*

Pullman Cataract Hotel IIII
Abtal El Tahrir Street
Tel. 316 002; fax 316 011
*This is a splendid British
monument of Moorish pastiche
architecture, renovated but
retaining old colonial charm; it
has 136 rooms, a grand
riverfront terrace facing
Elephantine Island and the Aga
Khan's mausoleum. The
neighbouring giant hotel called
New Cataract, (Tel. 323 434; fax
323 510) has 144 rooms, and is
comfortable but characterless;
nevertheless it has a good
business-centre.*

Abu Simbel
(international tel/fax code 20.97)

Nefertari II
Abu Simbel
Tel. 324 836; fax 282 5919
*Well located, easy 400m (440yds)
walk to temples; offering
comfortable air-conditioned rooms,
swimming pool.*

Nobaleh Ramses I
Abu Simbel Tourist City
Tel. 311 661
*Modest but comfortable govern-
ment-run hotel 1.5km (1 mile) from
temples.*

Middle Egypt
Faiyum
(international tel/fax code 20.84)

Auberge du Lac II
Faiyum
Tel. 700 002; fax 700 730
*Handsome resort location amid spa-
cious lakeside gardens; 77 rooms,
swimming pool, tennis, squash,
health club, disco.*

Panorama Shakshouk I
Shakshouk
Faiyum
Tel. 701 314; fax 701 757
*Small resort hotel, gardens leading
to lakeside jetty; 30 rooms, swim-
ming pool.*

Minya
(international tel/fax code 20.86)

PLM Azur Nefertiti/Aton IIII
Corniche El Nil Street
Tel. 331 515; fax 326 467
*Set back from Nile with attractive
riverfront garden bungalows; offering 96 rooms, swimming pool, riverside cocktail-terrace.*

Western Oases
(international tel/fax code 20.88)

Kharga
El Kharga Oasis I
El Kharga
El Wadi El Guedid
Tel. 93766
*Simple modern establishment; offer-
ing 30 rooms with shower, pleasant
garden.*

Dakhla

Mebarez Tourist Hotel |
2 El Tharwa El Khadraa Street
Dakhla Oasis
Tel. 9414524
Modern, in centre of town, convenient for bus to Farafra; 27 rooms, restaurant.

Siwa

(international tel/fax code Mersa Matruh 20.3)

Arousa El Waha |
Siwa
Tel. Mersa Matruh Tourist Office
394 3192
Modest, with baths but no air-conditioning, restaurant.

Red Sea

(international tel/fax code 20.65)

Hurghada

Coral Beach Village |||
Hurghada-Safaga Road
Tel. 442 160; fax 443 577
Vast resort complex over 140 acres of grounds; 174 rooms and bungalows, swimming pool and water sports facilities.

Magawish Tourist Village ||
Magawish
Hurghada
Tel. 442 620; fax 442 759
Formerly Club Med, now government-run in similar club style; 314 bungalow-rooms, swimming pool, elaborate diving, fishing and other water sports facilities, seafood restaurant, disco.

Mashrabia Village ||
Hurghada
Tel. 443 330; fax 443 344
152-room resort, private beach, 3 swimming pools, water sports.

Sheraton Hurghada |||
Hurghada
Tel. 442 000; fax 442 033
Luxury resort complex, 125 rooms, disco, good restaurants, swimming pool, plus every imaginable water sports facility.

Sonesta Beach Resort |||
Hurghada
Tel. 764 633; fax 443 661
Cheerful resort complex built village-style; 132 rooms, first-class diving and fishing facilities.

Safaga

Menaville ||
Safaga
Tel. 451 761; fax 451 765
Sprawling resort complex; 152 rooms, shopping centre, European and Middle Eastern cuisine, swimming pool, tennis, water sports.

Alexandria and the Mediterranean

(international tel/fax code 20.3)

Alexandria

Agami Palace |
Al Bittash Beach
Agami
Tel. 433 0230; fax 430 9364
Beachfront resort hotel but not too far from downtown; 56 rooms.

El Shatbi New Youth Hostel |
23 Port Said Street
Shatbi
Tel. 75459

Montazah Sheraton |||
Corniche Road
Montazah
Alexandria
Tel. 548 0550; fax 540 1331
Giant luxury hotel opposite Farouk's old palace; 305 rooms, good seafood restaurant, swimming pool, efficient business-centre.

Palestine Hotel |||
Montazah
Alexandria
Tel. 547 4033; fax 547 3378
Amid beautiful royal gardens leading down to Mediterranean harbour, promenade and long jetty; 208 rooms, swimming pools, business-centre.

Pullman Cecil ||
16 Saad Zaghloul Square
El Ramleh
Tel. 807 055; fax 483 6401
Friendly old-fashioned institution in city centre, host to Churchill and Lawrence Durrell; 86 rooms, casino, nightclub, health club, seafood restaurant, café terrace, good business-centre.

Ramada Renaissance Hotel |||
544 El Gueish Street
Sidi Bishr
Tel. 866 111; fax 431 1690
Convenient downtown location, efficient modern hotel for businessmen; 171 rooms.

San Giovanni Hotel |
205 El Gueish Street
Stanley
Tel. 546 7774; fax 546 4408
Cosy seafront hotel, offering 30 rooms and a good seafood restaurant.

Windsor ||
17 El Shohada Street
El Ramleh
Tel. 808 700; fax 809 090
Stylish old-fashioned seafront hotel in city centre; 56 big rooms, many with balcony.

El Alamein

Hotel El Alamein ||
Sidi Abdel Rahman
El Dabaa Centre
El Alamein
Tel. 492 1228; fax 807 250
Handsome beach resort hotel conveniently located for visiting battlefield and museum; offering 209 rooms and chalets, swimming pool, beachfront gardens, tennis, and water sports.

Mersa Matruh

Beau Site ||
El Shatee Street
Tel. 934 012; fax 933 319
A family resort hotel located on the seafront; offering 103 rooms, good restaurant.

Suez Canal

Port Said

(international tel/fax code 20.66)

Helnan Port Said ||
El Corniche Street
Tel. 320 890; fax 323 762
A giant modern waterfront hotel; offering 203 rooms, good business facilities.

Ismailiya

(international tel/fax code 20.64)

ETAP Forsan Island ||
Ismailiya
Tel. 222 292; fax 222 220
Occupying a beautiful island location on Lake Timsah linked to mainland by causeway; 152 rooms, pool, terrace restaurant, swimming pool, tennis, windsurfing and sailing, business-centre.

Suez

(international tel/fax code 20.62)

Red Sea Hotel
13 Riad Street
Port Tawfik
Tel. 223 334; fax 227 761
On quiet side street with nice views across port to Red Sea; 81 rooms, seafood restaurant, business-centre.

Sinai

(international tel/fax code 20.62)

St Catherine

Daniela Village
St Catherine
Tel. 749 7732; fax (Cairo 20.2) 360 7750
Modest, clean accommodation handy for visiting monastery and mountain; 42 rooms, restaurant.

St Catherine's Village
Wadi El Raha
St Catherine
Tel. 770 456; fax 770 221
Superbly designed in local granite with spectacular views of Mount Sinai, a few minutes from monastery; 100 chalets, gardens with desert flora, tennis, panoramic restaurant.

Sharm El Sheikh

Hilton Fairouz Village
Na'ama Bay
Tel. 770 501; fax 770 726
Fine resort complex; 150 rooms, first-class deep-sea diving and fishing, tennis, squash, horseback riding, good seafood restaurant, safaris.

Mövenpick Sharm El Sheikh
Na'ama Bay
Tel. 600 100; fax 600 111
Easy-going resort atmosphere; 210 rooms, very good restaurants, pool and all water sports facilities.

PLM Azur Aquamarine
Sharm El Sheikh
Tel. 770 474; fax 770 556
Family resort complex; 152 rooms, shopping, tennis, swimming pool, good diving and other water sports facilities, decent seafood restaurant.

Sanafer Village
Na'ama Bay
Tel./Fax 770 868
Lively offbeat atmosphere in Moorish-style architecture; 47 rooms, very good beach.

Dahab

PLM Azur Holiday Village
Dahab
Sinai
Tel. 776 736; fax 770 788
Dazzling white against dramatic mountain backdrop, sprawling resort complex; 141 rooms, swimming pool, tennis, horseback riding, water sports; disco and shopping mall.

Nuweiba

Nuweiba Holiday Village
Nuweiba
Sinai
Tel. 770 393; fax (Cairo 20.2) 392 2228
Simple rooms, friendly service, beachfront bar and restaurant.

Taba

Salah El Deen Hotel
Taba
Sinai
Tel. 771 345; fax (Cairo 20.2) 356 4005
Dramatically situated in bay of Pharaoh's Island (direct boat access to ruined fortress); 50 rooms, handsome chalets of Sinai granite, first-rate seafood restaurant.

Taba Hilton
Taba Beach
Sinai
Tel. 763 544; fax 747 044
Mammoth resort hotel on Israeli border; 326 rooms, private beach, swimming pool, tennis, desert safaris, good variety of restaurants, seafood, Middle Eastern and European, good business-centre.

El Arish

(international tel/fax code 20.62)

Egoth Oberoi El Arish
El Farik Abu Zekri Street
El Arish
North Sinai
Tel. 351 321; fax 352 352
Pleasant gardens leading down to Mediterranean; 221 rooms, swimming pool, water sports, health club, tennis and squash.

Nile Cruises

The current official guide of the Egyptian Hotel Association lists over 160 vessels cruising the river between Cairo and Aswan, some on Lake Nasser. Classification runs from modest 2-star riverboats up to luxury 5-star cruise-ships. Prices vary enormously according to the nature of the package (tie-ins with flights, land-excursions for sightseeing, number of days on the river, individual or group booking, etc.). Our selection includes most of the leading cruise organizers, many of whom have a fleet of several vessels in different price categories. For those not booking through their local travel agent, we provide Cairo addresses, telephone and fax numbers (international code 20.2).

Abercrombie & Kent
5A Bustan Street
Tel. 761 324; fax 757 486

Alexander the Great
23 Kasr El Nil Street
Tel. 393 9390; fax 391 1808

Belle Epoque
17 Tunis Street
New Maadi
Tel. 352 4775; fax 353 6114

Cataract Nile Cruises
26 Adan Street
Mohandessin
Tel. 361 6231; fax 360 0864

Club Méditerranée
48 Mossadak Street
Dokki
Tel. 361 4441; fax 360 1912

Florence
15 Hassan Sabry Street
Zamalek
Tel. 340 6820; fax 341 0432

Hilton Cruises
Nile Hilton Hotel
Tahrir Square
Tel. 754 999; fax 574 0880

Memnon Cruises
18 Hoda Shaarawi Street
Tel. 393 0195; fax 391 7140

Nile Crocodile
41 Abdel Khalek Sarwad Street
Tel. 391 4554; fax 392 8153

Nile Pullman
9 Menes Street
El Korba
Heliopolis
Tel. 290 8804; fax 290 8803

Oberoi Cruises
Mena House Hotel
Giza
Tel. 383 1225; fax 383 1227

Presidential Nile Cruises
13 Maraashli Street
Zamalek
Tel. 340 0517; fax 340 5272

Pyramids
56 Gamaet El Dowal El Arabia Street
Mohandessin
Tel. 360 0146; fax 360 4399

Ra
13 Kasr El Nil Street
Tel. 753 305; fax 743 482

Sheraton Nile Cruises
4 Ahmed Naguib Street
Garden City
Tel. 355 6664; fax 355 8100

Sonesta Cruises
4 El Tayaran Street
Nasr City
Tel. 262 8111; fax 619 980

Restaurants

We appreciated the food and service in the restaurants listed below; if you find other places worth recommending, we would be pleased to hear from you.

We have given a special emphasis to restaurants serving Egyptian or Middle Eastern cuisine, but also include, for the sake of variety, a few Italian, French, Indian or other oriental establishments.

Apart from a few addresses in main cities like Cairo, Alexandria or Ismailiya, you will find most restaurants attached to the major hotels. They welcome outside visitors as well as their own guests.

We note as 'formal' a few more elegant places where men are expected to wear jackets, and some which do not serve alcohol. With usual warnings about changes due to fluctations in exchange rates and inflation, our symbols cover the following price-range:

I	below $10
II	$10-15
III	above $15

Cairo

Abou Shakra II
69 Kasr El Aini Street
Tel. 848 811
Simple traditional Egyptian fare, good kebabs and kofta, popular with Cairo residents. Friendly service, no alcohol.

Abu Aly's I
Nile Hilton
Tahrir Square
Tel. 767 444
Great people-watching café terrace serving good spicy Egyptian snacks and om ali dessert.

Aladin III
Cairo Sheraton
Galaa Square, Giza
Tel. 348 8700
Good Lebanese and Middle Eastern dishes with evening floor show.

Al Fanous III
5 Wissa Wassef
Riyadh Tower, Giza
Tel. 737 592
Refined Moroccan cuisine in Oman restaurant-complex. No alcohol.

Alfredo III
Heliopolis Sheraton
Oruba Street
Heliopolis
Tel. 290 2027
Comfortable setting for standard Italian dishes – veal, pasta and pizza.

Al Sarraya III
Heliopolis Mövenpick
Airport Road
Tel. 291 9400
French cuisine with good seafood, dinner only.

Al Shabaka
Forte Grand Pyramids
Alexandria Desert Road, Giza
Tel. 383 0383
Refined seafood restaurant right near the Pyramids.

Al Walima
Forte Grand Pyramids
Alexandria Desert Road, Giza
Tel. 383 0383
Traditional Egyptian cuisine with a spectacular view of the Pyramids.

Andrea I
59 El Maryoutia Canal Road
Pyramids
Tel. 387 1133
People travel out to this Cairo institution to try its renowned barbecued chicken or grilled pigeon.

Arabesque III
6 Kasr El Nil Street
Tel. 759 896
First-class Egyptian cuisine – especially molokhia soup and bamia lamb – but also European dishes.

Arafa I
Midan Dowaran
Shoubra
Popular local dishes, notably koushari macaroni, rice and lentils.

Arouss El Nil II
Cairo Sheraton
Galaa Square
Giza
Tel. 348 8700
Copious buffet of international and Egyptian dishes.

Asia House III
Shepheard's Hotel
Corniche El Nil
Tel. 355 3800
Good Chinese and Indian cuisine, served with great courtesy.

Ba'albek III
Sonesta Hotel
4 El Tayaran Street
Heliopolis
Tel. 262 8111
Lebanese cuisine, good mezze.

Balmoral Chinese Restaurant II
157 July 26th Street
Zamalek
Tel. 340 6761
Easy-going atmosphere for Cantonese cuisine.

Bawadi II
10 Hussein Wassef Street
Dokki
Tel. 348 4878
Varied first-rate Lebanese and Middle Eastern cooking, good salads, fassuliyah, sautéed green beans, great desserts.

Bukhara II
43 Misr Helwan Road
Maadi
Tel. 375 5999
Classical Indian fare, friendly service.

Chandani II
5 Wissa Wassef
Riyadh Tower
Giza
Tel. 737 592
Both Indian and Chinese dishes served in Oman restaurant complex. No alcohol.

Christo ‖
10 Pyramid Street
Giza
Tel. 383 3582
Within view of the Pyramids, seafood specialities, plainly grilled or more elaborately Egyptian-style.

Ciao Italia ‖
Gezirah Sheraton
Gezirah Island
Tel. 341 1333
Romantic riverfront Italian restaurant, dinner only.

Citadel Grill ‖‖
Ramses Hilton
1115 Corniche El Nil Street
Tel. 744 400
Smart supper-club atmosphere for steaks, grilled beef and seafood. Formal.

Club Med Restaurant ‖
Manial Palace Hotel
Kasr Mohammed Ali
El Manial
Tel. 844 524
In delightful garden setting, serves the club's classic gargantuan buffet of Egyptian and French dishes.

Dahan ‖
Meshhet Al Hussein
Khan El Khalili
Celebrated Middle Eastern grill popular with political and showbiz celebrities – lamb kofta *and kebabs.*

Darna ‖
Pullman Maadi Towers
29 Corniche El Nil Street
Maadi
Tel. 350 6092
Buffet-service for Egyptian country cooking.

Dragon ‖‖
Gezirah Sheraton
Gezirah Island
Tel. 341 1333
Elegant riverfront dining-room for classical Chinese cuisine, dinner only.

El Arze ‖‖
Nile Hilton
Tahrir Square
Tel. 767 444
Lebanese cuisine, grills a speciality, served in hotel garden.

El Nasr ‖
Bab El Louk Square
Hearty spicy liver dishes for the adventurous, in clean tiled décor.

El Nil Rôtisserie ‖‖
Nile Hilton
Tahrir Square
Tel. 767 444
International and Egyptian cuisine in elegant atmosphere, with classical music. Formal.

El Omda ‖
6 El Gazzar Street
Mohandessin
Tel. 347 8652
Authentic traditional Egyptian peasant dishes. No alcohol.

Falafel ‖‖
Ramses Hilton
1115 Corniche El Nil Street
Tel. 744 400
Refined Middle Eastern cuisine with spectacular music and dance show. Dinner only.

Felfela Garden ‖
15 Hoda Sharawi Street
Tel. 392 2833
Charming oasis-like décor for simple Egyptian cuisine. (There are four other Felfela outlets around the city.)

Ferahat ‖
Sharia El Azhar
Hussein
Great bargain for pigeon-fanciers – as soup, stuffed or grilled – in modest surroundings.

Flying Fish ‖
166 El Nil Street
Agouza
Tel. 349 3234
Egyptian-style seafood and traditional dishes.

Golden Gondola ‖
23 Ahmed Orabi Street
Mohandessin
Tel. 345 6554
Modest but good quality Lebanese and other Middle Eastern cuisine.

Justine's ‖‖
4 Hassan Sabry Street
Zamalek
Tel. 341 2961
French cuisine for the Cairo élite. Good place to observe serious jewellery. Understandably formal.

Kandahar ‖
3 Gamaet El Dowal El Arabia Street
Mohandessin
Tel. 344 3773
First-class Indian restaurant run by same management as the Oberoi's Moghul.

Kebabgy ‖
Gezirah Sheraton
Gezirah Island
Tel. 341 1333
Very good grilled Egyptian cuisine. Arab music in evening.

Khan El Khalili ‖
5 El Badistan Lane
Khan El Khalili
Tel. 903 788
Air-conditioned haven for footsore tourists in the bazaar, serving Egyptian meals and snacks.

Kowloon ‖‖
Cleopatra Hotel
2 Abdel Salam Araf Street
Tel. 759 831
Wide variety of Chinese, Korean and Japanese dishes.

La Charmerie ‖‖
157 July 26th Street
Zamalek
Tel. 340 9640.
Inventive European cuisine, seafood specialities.

La Gondola ‖
Sonesta Hotel
4 El Tayaran Street
Heliopolis
Tel. 262 8111
Cheerful family restaurant for Italian classics, good pizza.

La Mamma ‖
Cairo Sheraton
Giza
Tel. 348 8700
Hearty Italian pasta and pizza dishes, good desserts.

La Paëlla ‖
20 Riyadh Street
Mohandessin
Tel. 347 5135
Besides traditional Spanish paëlla, good fresh seafood.

Le Champollion ‖‖
Le Méridien
Corniche El Nil Street
Garden City
Tel. 362 1717
Méridien flagship hotel's flagship French restaurant. Haute cuisine, classical music. Formal.

Le Château ‖‖
El Nasr Building
Corniche El Nil, Giza
Tel. 362 1717
Swissair's French and Swiss restaurant.

Le Grill Gezira ▮▮▮
Cairo Marriott
Saraya El Gezira Street
Zamalek
Tel. 340 8888
French cuisine in the grand style.
Classical music.

Madura ▮▮▮
Cairo Sheraton
Galaa Square
Giza
Tel. 348 8700
Savoury Indonesian cuisine,
including nasi *and* bakmi goreng.
Dinner only.

Maha ▮
Jasmin Hotel
Gezirat El Arab Street
Mohandessin
Tel. 347 2278
Good Indian curries served round
the clock.

Marco Polo ▮▮▮
Méridien Heliopolis
51 Oruba Street
Heliopolis
Tel. 290 5055
Italian cuisine in elegant
atmosphere.

Mashrabia ▮▮▮
4 Ahmed Nassim Street
Orman Garden
Giza
Tel. 348 2801
Interesting menu of high-class
Middle Eastern cooking.

Moghul ▮▮▮
Mena House Oberoi
Pyramids Road
Giza
Tel. 383 3222
Best Indian restaurant in town,
serving refined moghul cuisine and
accompanied by authentic Indian
musical entertainment. Formal.

Naniwa ▮▮▮
Ramses Hilton
1115 Corniche El Nil Street
Tel. 744 400
Japanese cuisine much appreciated
by local Cairo gourmets.

Nubian Village ▮▮
Le Méridien
Corniche El Nil Street
Garden City
Tel. 362 1717
Offering excellent Egyptian dishes
served in delightful open-air river-
side setting.

Oasis ▮▮▮
Mena House Oberoi
Pyramids Road
Giza
Tel. 383 3222
Outdoor dining: Egyptian and inter-
national cuisine served in a pleasant
poolside garden.

Paprika ▮▮
1129 Corniche El Nil Street
Tel. 749 447
Riverfront restaurant, offering good
value European or Egyptian cuisine,
especially the mezze. *Paprika is es-*
pecially popular with showbiz stars
from neighbouring radio and TV
centre.

Peking ▮
14 Saraya El Ezbekiya Street
Tel. 912 381
Solid Chinese fare in central down-
town location.

Prestige ▮▮
43 Gezirat El Arab Street
Mohandessin
Tel. 347 0383
Italian cuisine, renowned for its
veal dishes as well as the pizza and
pasta.

Roy's ▮▮
Cairo Marriott
Saraya El Gezira Street
Zamalek
Tel. 340 8888
One of the city's rare Tex-Mex
establishments offering the usual
variety and quality.

Sakura ▮▮▮
5 Wissa Wassef
Riyadh Tower
Giza
Tel. 737 592
Japanese grills and other speciali-
ties served in style.

Sapporo ▮▮▮
Cairo Sheraton
Galaa Square
Giza
Tel. 348 8700
In modern Japanese décor, deli-
cious teppanyaki *grills of beef and*
seafood.

Sea Horse ▮▮
Corniche El Nil
Maadi
Tel. 363 8830
Offering seafood Egyptian-style,
plus tasty traditional grilled kebabs
and chicken.

Silver Fish ▮▮
39 Mohy El Din Abul Ezz Street
Dokki
Tel. 349 2272
Seafood prepared in the savoury
Egyptian manner.

Taj Mahal ▮▮
15 Ibn Affan Street
Dokki
Tel. 348 3881
Good solid, no-holds-barred Indian
curries. Live Indian music at week-
ends.

Tandoori ▮▮
11 Shehab Street
Mohandessin
Tel. 348 6301
Good north Indian fare, tandoori
'barbecue' and vegetarian, in clean,
simple décor. No alcohol.

Tarboush ▮▮▮
Heliopolis Sheraton
Oruba Street
Heliopolis
Tel. 290 2027
Superb Egyptian-style lamb, quail
and duck specialities.

The Grill ▮▮▮
Semiramis Intercontinental
Corniche El Nil Street
Garden City
Tel. 355 7171
Nicely served French cuisine,
steaks, lamb, excellent seafood, with
not too obtrusive piano accompani-
ment. Dinner only.

Tia Maria ▮
32 Jeddah Street
Mohandessin
Tel. 713 273
Simple Italian pasta and pizza at a
bargain price.

Zahle ▮▮▮
Siag Pyramids Hotel
Sakkara Road
Ahram
Tel. 385 6022
Convenient après-pyramides *dining,*
good Lebanese cuisine in nightclub
setting.

Zanouba ▮▮
Atlas Zamalek Hotel
20 Gamaet El Dowal El Arabia
Street
Mohandessin
Tel. 346 4175
Serving a wide variety of robust
Egyptian and Middle East cooking
in simple style.

Cairo's Riverboat Restaurants

Varying according to season, the boats serve Egyptian and European cuisine, lunch and dinner, many with music and dance shows, at least in the evening. Unless described as 'cruising restaurants', the boats remain in their moorings.

Alf Laila Cruising Restaurant ‖
Corniche El Nil
Garden City (near Le Méridien)
Tel. 354 0417

El Safina ‖
9 El Saray El Gezira Street
Zamalek
Tel. 341 0430

Farah Boat ‖
40 Corniche El Nil
Giza
Tel. 620 783

Golden Pharaoh Cruising Restaurant ‖‖
31 Corniche El Nil
Giza
Tel. 570 1000

Nile Pharaoh ‖‖
31 Corniche El Nil
Giza
Tel. 570 1000

Saladin ‖
El Nil Street
Giza (in front of Foreign Ministry)
Tel. 731 370

Scarabee Cruising Restaurant ‖‖
Corniche El Nil (in front of Shepheard's Hotel)
Tel. 355 4481

Sultana ‖
Corniche El Nil
Maadi
Tel. 351 2521

Sunset ‖‖
33 El Nil Street
Giza (behind the French Embassy)
Tel. 729 261

Luxor

BBQ Around the Pool ‖‖
Luxor Sheraton
El Awameya Road
Tel. 374 544
Poolside European and Egyptian barbecue dinners only, with live entertainment.

Class Restaurant ‖
Class Shopping Centre
Khaled Ibn Walid Street
Tel. 376 327
Pleasant clean family restaurant for both good Egyptian and European cuisine.

Club Med ‖‖
Club Méditerranée
Khaled Ibn El Walid Street
Tel. 580 850
Copious European buffet at lunch, à la carte for dinner.

Dakka ‖‖
ETAP Luxor Hotel
Corniche El Nil Street
Tel. 374 944
Outdoor dining: European cuisine and barbecue buffet served by the poolside, dinner only, with live entertainment.

El Dawar ‖
Isis Hotel
Khaled Ibn El Walid Street
Tel. 373 3366
Good rustic Egyptian fare served in country guest-house décor.

El Karnak ‖‖
Luxor Sheraton
El Awameya Road
Tel. 374 544
All-day international cuisine à la carte, buffet of speciality dinners changing daily – Russian, Egyptian, seafood, etc.

El Sakkia ‖‖
ETAP Luxor Hotel
Corniche El Nil Street
Tel. 374 944
Good Middle Eastern cuisine, dinner only.

Gorna ‖
ETAP Luxor Hotel
Corniche El Nil Street
Tel. 374 944
All-day international buffet.

Jolie Ville ‖‖
Mövenpick Jolie Ville
Crocodile Island
Tel. 374 855
First-class European buffet with daily specialities.

Khan El Khalili ‖
Isis Hotel
Khaled Ibn El Walid Street
Tel. 373 3366
Good range of Egyptian and other Middle Eastern dishes.

La Mamma ‖
Luxor Sheraton
El Awameya Road
Tel. 374 544
Italian cuisine with live accordion entertainment.

La Terrazza ‖
Isis Hotel
Khaled Ibn El Walid Street
Tel. 373 3366
Hearty home-made pasta and pizza.

Le Belvedere ‖‖
Novotel Evasion
Khaled Ibn El Walid Street
Tel. 580 925
Serving all-day French and Egyptian cuisine.

Mövenpick ‖‖
Mövenpick Jolie Ville
Crocodile Island
Tel. 374 855
Swiss cooking in genteel atmosphere, dinner only.

Palm Restaurant ‖‖
Luxor Hilton
New Karnak
Tel. 374 933
Egyptian and European cuisine, both buffet and à la carte.

Shadoof Terrace ‖
Luxor Hilton
New Karnak
Tel. 374 933
Open air barbecue and Italian pasta and pizza.

Sheherazade Terrace ‖‖
Mövenpick Jolie Ville
Crocodile Island
Tel. 374 855
Barbecue and buffet with international specialities changing daily – Caribbean, Egyptian, Italian, seafood, etc.

White Corner ‖
Isis Hotel
Khaled Ibn El Walid Street
Tel. 373 3366
Excellent seafood restaurant with superb view across river to Valley of Kings.

Luxor's Riverboat Restaurants

Some riverside hotels have cruiseboats serving dinner while you sail past the sights of Luxor and Karnak, or lunch for a daytime cruise north to the temple of Denderah.

Le Lotus ▮▮▮
Novotel Evasion
Khaled Ibn El Walid Street
Tel. 580 925
*International cuisine for dinner
cruises round Luxor and Karnak,
and daytime cruises to Denderah.*

M.S. Africa ▮▮▮
Mövenpick Jolie Ville
Crocodile Island
Tel. 374 855
*Barbecue lunches served on sight-
seeing cruise to Denderah.*

Meri Ra ▮▮▮
Luxor Sheraton
El Awameya Road
Tel. 374 544
*Luncheon buffet for sightseeing
cruise to Denderah;
Luxor–Karnak dinner cruise.*

Aswan
Darna ▮▮▮
New Cataract Hotel
Abtal El Tahrir Street
Tel. 323 434
*Southern Egyptian cuisine in
Nubian décor, dinner only.*

El Nashwa ▮▮▮
Aswan Oberoi
Elephantine Island
Tel. 323 455
*Egyptian and European cuisine with
nightclub entertainment.*

La Palmeraie ▮▮
Kalabsha Hotel
Abtal El Tahrir Street
Tel. 322 999
*Egyptian cuisine served in the ter-
race garden.*

La Trattoria ▮▮
Isis Aswan Hotel
Corniche El Nil Street
Tel. 315 200
Home-made Italian pasta and pizza.

Le Club 1902 ▮▮▮
Pullman Cataract Hotel
Abtal El Tahrir Street
Tel. 316 002
*European and Egyptian cuisine in
grand Moorish dining room.*

Nefertari ▮▮▮
Isis Island Hotel
Isis Island
Tel. 317 400
*Elegant décor for à la carte French
and Egyptian cuisine.*

Nefertiti ▮▮
Kalabsha Hotel
Abtal El Tahrir Street
Tel. 322 999
Egyptian and international dishes.

Orangerie ▮▮▮
Aswan Oberoi
Elephantine Island
Tel. 323 455
*Poolside service for European and
Egyptian dishes.*

Osiris ▮▮
Isis Aswan Hotel
Corniche El Nil
Tel. 315 200
All-day international buffet.

Ramses ▮▮
Isis Island Hotel
Isis Island
Tel. 317 400
*European and Middle Eastern
buffet.*

Hurghada
Arlene's ▮▮
Dr Saïd Korayem Street
*American-run Tex-Mex, steaks and
seafood.*

Dolphin ▮▮
Magawish Tourist Village
Hurghada
Tel. 442 620
Waterfront seafood restaurant.

Sheraton Seafood Restaurant ▮▮▮
Sheraton Hurghada
Tel. 442 000
*Spiny lobster and other Red Sea
delicacies.*

Alexandria
Abou Ashraf ▮▮
28 Safar Bash Elgomrak
Tel. 816 597
Seafood Egyptian-style. No alcohol.

Al Khan ▮▮
Lord's Inn Centre
17A Syria Street
Roushdy
Tel. 546 2016
*Varied Egyptian and other Middle
Eastern dishes.*

Alexander's Terrace ▮▮▮
Ramada Renaissance Hotel
544 El Gueish Street
Tel. 866 111
French cuisine. Dinner only.

Andrea ▮
Agami Beach
El Asal Street
Tel. 433 3227
*Grilled chicken popular speciality,
plus Greek and Egyptian dishes.*

Atheneos ▮
21 Saad Zaghloul Square
Tel. 482 0421
*Seafood, with nightclub entertain-
ment at dinner.*

Calithea ▮
180 July 26th Street
Tel. 489 7764
*Greek seafood and Middle Eastern
cuisine.*

Chez Gaby ▮
Foad Street (next to Royal Cinema)
Tel. 484 4300
*Italian pasta and pizza and Greek
specialities.*

Chicken Tikka ▮
Montazah Gardens
Tel. 547 5438
*Indian tandoori and Egyptian
cuisine.*

Dynasty ▮▮
Ramada Renaissance Hotel
544 El Gueish Street
Tel. 866 111
Chinese cuisine, dinner only.

El Ikhlass ▮▮
49 Safeya Zaghloul Street
Tel. 482 3571
*Genteel first-floor restaurant for
Middle Eastern and European
cuisine.*

El Mashrabia ▮▮
El Mamoura Beach
Tel. 567 2603
Middle Eastern cooking.

El Saraya ▮▮▮
El Gerish Street
Stanley Bay
Tel. 546 773
First-class Egyptian cuisine.

Farag Fish ▮▮
7 Souq Tabbakhien Street
Tel. 811 047
*Fresh Mediterranean seafood. No
alcohol.*

Fish Market ▮▮
26 Corniche El Nil
Tel. 805 119
*Seafood in the French or Egyptian
manner.*

Fleur
Lord's Inn Centre
17A Syria Street
Roushdy
Tel. 546 2016
Good Italian pizza and pasta.

Hossny
30 Safar Basha Street
Tel. 812 350
Egyptian and Middle Eastern dishes, no alcohol.

Kadoura
74 July 26th Street
Tel. 800 967
Seafood Egyptian style.

Kasr El Agami
Agami
Tel. 433 0383
Egyptian and Lebanese cooking.

La Mamma
Montazah Sheraton
Corniche Road
Tel. 548 0550
Fine pizzas and other Italian dishes.

Le Plat d'Or
Pullman Cecil
16 Saad Zaghloul Square
El Ramleh
Tel. 807 055
French and Italian cuisine in old-fashioned décor.

Lord's Inn
12 Mohammed Ahmed El Alili Street
Tel. 586 5664
High-class German cooking.

Nassar
146 El Gueish Street
Tel. 809 724
Seafood specialities with Egyptian and other Middle Eastern dishes.

Omar El Khayam
200 July 26th Street
Tel. 483 3665
Good, simple Egyptian cuisine.

Petro
El Asal Street
Agami
Pizza and pasta.

Rang Mahal
Pullman Cecil
16 Saad Zaghloul Square
El Ramleh
Tel. 807 055
Reputed to serve the best Indian food in Alexandria.

Samakmak
42 Kasr Ras El Tin
Anfushi
Tel. 811 560
Very good seafood, especially grilled.

San Giovanni
San Giovanni Hotel
El Gueish Street
Stanley
Tel. 546 7773
Landmark French restaurant overlooking Mediterranean, amiable service.

Santa Lucia
40 Safia Zaghloul
Tel. 482 0332
Elegantly served European cuisine in pleasant surroundings .

Sea Gull
El Max
Tel. 445 8777
High-class seafood restaurant.

Taverna El Ramel
1 Saad Zaghloul Square
Tel. 482 8189
Greek cuisine and a few Egyptian dishes.

Taverna Beach
Montazah Gardens
Tel. 547 5438
Outdoor dining: seafood and Greek cuisine served in pleasant garden surroundings.

Zephyrion
Aboukir
Tel. 546 2016
Seafront restaurant renowned for serving the best and freshest seafood in Egypt, including superb giant prawns.

Sinai
Sharm El Sheikh
Fairouz Fish Restaurant
Hilton Fairouz Village
Na'ama Bay
Tel. 770 501
Beachfront seafood restaurant.

Nuweiba
El Sharkawi
Nuweiba village square
Simple but good barbecued seafood, wall-menu in English, Arabic and Hebrew.

Taba
Casa Taba
Taba Hilton
Taba Beach
Tel. 763 544
Elegant décor for refined Italian cuisine.

Marhaba
Taba Hilton
Taba Beach
Tel. 763 544
High-class Middle Eastern cuisine.

Palm Court
Taba Hilton
Taba Beach
Tel. 763 544
All-day family-style international buffet.

Salah El Deen
Salah El Deen Hotel
Taba
Tel. 771 345
Excellent beachfront seafood restaurant.

Suez Canal
Port Said
Hati El Madina
Tel. 229 986
Egyptian cuisine, seafood specialities.

Ismailiya
Ashur
Makne Street
Tel. 228 718
Traditional Egyptian cuisine in cheerful setting, good lamb dishes.

Georges
Sultan Hussein Street
Tel. 228 368
Popular for European and Egyptian cuisine.

King Edward
Sultan Hussein Street.
International cuisine.

Le Grill d'Eugénie
ETAP Forsan Island
Tel. 222 292
European cuisine, good steaks.

El Gandoul
El Geish Street
Tel. 328 251
Traditional Egyptian cooking, good mezze.

Index

References to illustrations are in *italic*; those in **bold** refer to main entries; those with an asterisk refer to maps.

INDEX

315

Discover the world

with BERLITZ®

Australia
Britain
Brittany
California
Egypt
Europe
Florida
France
Germany
Greece
Ireland
Israel
Italy
Kenya
Loire Valley
New England
Normandy
Portugal
Prague
Pyrenees
Rome
Singapore
Spain
Switzerland
Thailand
Tuscany

IN PREPARATION
Canada
Scandinavia
Turkey

BERLITZ DISCOVER GUIDES do more than just map out the sights – they entice you to travel with lush full-colour photography, vivid descriptions and intelligent advice on how to plan and enjoy your holiday or travel experience. Covering the world's most popular destinations, these full-colour travel guides reveal the spirit and flavour of each country or region. Use *DISCOVER* as a travel planner or as a practical reference guide. You'll find sightseeing information and suggested leisure routes, extensive full-colour maps and town plans, local hotel and restaurant listings plus special essays highlighting interesting local features. Colourful historical and cultural background is complemented by practical details such as what to visit and where to stay, where to eat and how much you should expect to pay.

No matter where you're going, make the most of your trip:

DISCOVER the world with BERLITZ.